MEXICO IN CRISIS

Lost Borders and the Struggle for Regional Status

STRATFOR
700 Lavaca Street, Suite 900
Austin, Texas 78701

Copyright © 2009 by STRATFOR
All rights reserved, including the right of reproduction
in whole or in part

Printed in the United States of America

The contents of this book originally appeared as analyses
on STRATFOR's *subscription Web site.*

ISBN: 1449905714
EAN-13: 9781449905712

Publisher: Walter H. Howerton Jr.
Editor: Michael McCullar
Copy Editor/Project Coordinator: Tim French
Designer: TJ Lensing

CONTENTS

ILLUSTRATIONS

INTRODUCTION

Mexico in Crisis: Lost Borders and the Struggle for Regional Status is a compilation of STRATFOR's coverage of current events in Mexico from Jan. 15, 2004, to Nov. 17, 2009. As one of the few U.S.-based media outlets doing in-depth work on Mexico, our coverage has been mainly of internal tactical issues — the drug war, cartel composition, some politics and economics — and occasionally of broader geopolitical issues. STRATFOR has touched on the country's relevant history and followed the grinding, day-to-day struggle of Mexico as it transitioned from single-party to multiparty rule, dealt with geographic handicaps and tried to prosecute an all-out war against powerful drug cartels.

In this volume, the reader will find an extensive look at the major geopolitical, tactical and security challenges confronting Mexico. These include what distinguishes Mexican immigrants from others who settle in the United States, how close Mexico has actually come to being a failed state, government corruption in Mexico and the need for reform, and the impact of the global recession on Mexico. Special attention is paid to the drug war in Mexico, including the organizational composition of the drug cartels, the government's drug war strategy and the role of the Mexican military, cartel tactics and the foot soldiers who employ them, the spreading violence across the U.S. border and the emerging role of Central America in the drug trade.

In his book, *The Next 100 Years: A Forecast for the 21st Century,* STRATFOR founder Dr. George Friedman paints a provocative picture of North America in the latter part of this century and how Mexico might fit into that picture.

Friedman believes that by the end of the century, U.S. dominance of the continent will no longer be a foregone conclusion. A declining population and shortage of labor will have invited an influx of new workers from around the world, including more immigrants from Mexico, long a primary source of labor for the U.S. workforce. He writes that by mid-century, the territory the United States obtained from Mexico in the 1840s will be predominately inhabited by Mexicans. These immigrant Mexican workers will contribute to an economic boom in the United States, helping develop the technologies necessary to address alternative energy and manufacturing needs, but eventually these technologies will displace labor and U.S. unemployment will rise. Managing the resulting population surplus, the economic imbalance and the changing demographic reality (the so-called Mexican Cession) will be a debilitating burden for the United States, which could see the rise of a challenger to its dominance of North America.

That challenger, Friedman writes, would be Mexico (perhaps allied loosely with Brazil). Already the 15th largest economy in the world, Mexico by mid-century will be benefiting from rising oil prices, demographic shifts in the United States, and remittances from legal and illegal Mexican immigrants. Friedman sees a possible economic benefit in organized crime and the drug trade. With so much money being made by the cartels, it has to be invested and laundered somewhere, and an increasingly productive Mexico could see more of that money invested at home. But the road Mexico is traveling is likely to be long and hard. The country is currently passing through what Friedman describes as "an inevitable period of turbulence and growth on the way to order and stability" as the drug wars play out and as economic and population patterns adjust to the shifting North American playing field.

The scenario described above is an extended forecast, which is beyond this book's perspective. Given Mexico's dire internal straits over the past few decades, it is hard to imagine the country ever assuming a dominant stance in North America. But stranger things have happened. As Friedman points out in *The Next 100 Years*, the world order can be rearranged dramatically in a couple of decades — just look at a time line of world events from 1900 to the present. For now, however, we will consider a Mexico with promise at a decidedly low point, whatever its future may hold.

Perhaps Friedman's glimpse far into the future is a good way to introduce STRATFOR's coverage of Mexico's struggle over the past six years. Indeed, both perspectives are essential in putting Mexico's challenges in context and plotting its journey as a modern nation-state. To what end could or should the current struggle be devoted? How can progress be measured? And what national ills must be remedied if Mexico is to rise as a regional power?

Much of the intelligence we have received, analyzed and reported in recent years has been almost as raw and violent as the mayhem in Iraq in 2006-2007. And we have often wondered why the extreme level of violence on the southern doorstep of the U.S. has not received more attention by the mainstream U.S. media. In any case, as we hope the collected work in this book shows, STRATFOR has tried to do its part.

STRATFOR
Austin, Texas
Nov. 19, 2009

PART 1: GEOPOLITICS

1: The Geopolitics of Immigration
Jan. 15, 2004

The United States came into being through mass movements of populations. The movements came in waves from all over the world and, depending upon the historical moment, they served differing purposes, but there were two constants. First, each wave served an indispensable economic, political, military or social function. The United States — as a nation and regime — would not have evolved as it did without them. Second, each wave of immigrants was viewed ambiguously by those who were already in-country. Depending upon the time or place, some saw the new immigrants as an indispensable boon; others saw them as a catastrophe. The debate currently under way in the United States is probably the oldest in the United States: Are new immigrants a blessing or catastrophe? So much for the obvious.

What is interesting about the discussion of immigration is the extent to which it is dominated by confusion, particularly about the nature of immigrants. When the term "immigrant" is used, it is frequently intended to mean one of two things: Sometimes it means non-U.S. citizens who have come to reside in the United States legally. Alternatively, it can mean a socially or linguistically distinct group that lives in the United States regardless of legal status. When you put these together in their various permutations, the discourse on immigration can become chaotic. It is necessary to simplify and clarify the concept of "immigrant."

Initial U.S. immigration took two basic forms. There were the voluntary migrants, ranging from the Europeans in the 17th century to Asians today. There were the involuntary migrants — primarily Africans — who were forced to come to the continent against their will. This is one of the critical fault lines running through U.S. history. An immigrant who came from China in 1995 has much more in common with the Puritans who arrived in New England more than 300 years ago than either has with the Africans. The former came by choice, seeking solutions to their personal or political problems. The latter came by force, brought here to solve the personal or political problems of others. This is one fault line.

The second fault line is between those who came to the United States and those to whom the United States came. The Native American tribes, for example, were conquered and subjugated by the immigrants who came to the United States before and after its founding. It should be noted that this is a process that has taken place many times in human history. Indeed, many Native American tribes that occupied the United States prior to the foreign invasion had supplanted other tribes — many of which were obliterated in the process. Nevertheless, in a strictly social sense, Native American tribes were militarily defeated and subjugated, their legal status in the United States was sometimes ambiguous and their social status was frequently that of outsiders. They became immigrants because the occupants of the new United States moved and dislocated them.

There was a second group of people in this class: Mexicans. A substantial portion of the United States, running from California to Texas, was conquered territory, taken from Mexico in the first half of the 19th century. Mexico existed on terrain that Spain had seized from the Aztecs, who conquered it from prior inhabitants. Again, this should not be framed in moral terms. It should be framed in geopolitical terms.

When the United States conquered the southwest, the Mexican population that continued to inhabit the region was not an immigrant population, but a conquered one. As with the Native Americans, this was less a case of them moving to the United States than the United States moving to them.

The response of the Mexicans varied, as is always the case, and they developed a complex identity. Over time, they accepted the political dominance of the United States and became, for a host of reasons, U.S. citizens. Many assimilated into the dominant culture. Others accepted the legal status of U.S. citizens while maintaining a distinct cultural identity. Still others accepted legal status while maintaining intense cultural and economic relations across the border with Mexico. Others continued to regard themselves primarily as Mexican.

The U.S.-Mexican border is in some fundamental ways arbitrary. The line of demarcation defines political and military relationships but does not define economic or cultural relationships. The borderlands — and they run hundreds of miles deep into the United States at some points — have extremely close cultural and economic links with Mexico. Where there are economic links there always are movements of population. It is inherent.

The persistence of cross-border relations is inevitable in borderlands that have been politically and militarily subjugated but in which the prior population has been neither annihilated nor expelled. Where the group on the conquered side of the border is sufficiently large, self-contained and self-aware, this condition can exist for generations. A glance at the Balkans offers an extreme example. In the case of the United States and its Mexican population, it also has continued to exist.

This never has developed into a secessionist movement for a number of reasons. First, the preponderance of U.S. power when compared to Mexico made this a meaningless goal. Second, the strength of the U.S. economy compared to the Mexican economy did not make rejoining Mexico attractive. Finally, the culture in the occupied territories evolved over the past 150 years, yielding a complex culture that ranged from wholly assimilated to complex hybrids to predominantly Mexican. Secessionism has not been a viable consideration since the end of the U.S. Civil War. Nor will it become an issue unless a remarkable change in the balance between the United States and Mexico takes place.

It would be a mistake, however, to think of the cross-border movements along the Mexican-U.S. border in the same way we think of the migration of people to the United States from other places such as India or China; these movements are an entirely different phenomenon — part of the long process of migration to the United States that has taken place since before its founding. In these, individuals made decisions — even if they were part of a mass movement from their countries — to move to the United States and, in moving to the United States, to adopt the dominant American culture to facilitate assimilation. The Mexican migrations are the result of movements in a borderland that has been created through military conquest and the resulting political process.

The movement from Mexico is, from a legal standpoint, a cross-border migration. In reality, it is simply an internal migration within a territory whose boundaries were superimposed by history. Put differently, if the United States had lost the Mexican-American war, these migrations would be no more noteworthy than the mass migration to California from the rest of the United States in the middle of the 20th century. But the United States did not lose the war — and the migration is across international borders.

It should be noted that this also distinguishes Mexican population movements from immigration from other Hispanic countries. The closest you can come to an equivalent is in Puerto Rico, whose inhabitants are U.S. citizens due to prior conquest. They neither pose the legal problems of Mexicans nor can they simply slip across the border.

The Mexican case is one-of-a-kind, and the difficulty of sealing the border is indicative of the real issue. There are those who call for sealing the border and, technically, it could be done although the cost would be formidable. More important, turning the politico-military frontier into an effective barrier to movement would generate social havoc. It would be a barrier running down the middle of an integrated social and economic reality. The costs for the region would be enormous, piled on top of the cost of walling off the frontier from the Gulf of Mexico to the Pacific.

If the U.S. goal is to create an orderly migration process from Mexico that fits into a broader immigration policy that includes the rest of the world, the goal probably cannot be achieved. Controlling immigration in general is difficult, but controlling the movement of an indigenous population in a borderland whose frontiers do not cohere to social or economic reality is impossible.

This is not intended to be a guide to social policy. Our general view is that social policies dealing with complex issues usually have such wildly unexpected consequences that they are more like rolling the dice than crafting strategy. We nevertheless understand that there will be a social policy, hotly debated by all sides, that will wind up not doing what anyone expects, but actually will do something very different.

The point we are trying to make is simpler. First, the question of Mexican population movements has to be treated completely separately from other immigrations. These are apples and oranges. Second, placing controls along the U.S.-Mexican frontier is probably impossible. Unless we are prepared to hermetically seal the frontier, populations will flow endlessly around barriers, driven by economic and social factors. Mexico simply does not end at the Mexican border, and it hasn't since the United States defeated Mexico. Neither the United States nor Mexico can do anything about the situation.

The issue, from our point of view, cuts to the heart of geopolitics as a theory. Geopolitics argues that geographic reality creates political, social, economic and military realities. These can be shaped by policies and perhaps even controlled to some extent, but the driving realities of geopolitics can never simply be obliterated except by overwhelming effort and difficulty. The United States is not prepared to do any of these things and, therefore, the things the United States is prepared to do are doomed to ineffectiveness.

2: Borderlands
April 4, 2006

The United States has returned to its recurring debate over immigration. This edition of the debate, focused intensely on the question of illegal immigration from Mexico, is phrased in a very traditional way. One side argues that illegal migration from Mexico threatens both American economic interests and security. The other side argues that the United States historically has thrived on immigration, and that this wave of migration is no different.

As is frequently the case, the policy debate fails to take fundamental geopolitical realities into account.

To begin with, it is absolutely true that the United States has always been an immigrant society. Even the first settlers in the United States — the American Indian tribes — were migrants. Certainly, since the first settlements were established, successive waves of immigration have both driven the American economy and terrified those who were already living in the country. When the Scots-Irish began arriving in the late 1700s, the English settlers of all social classes thought that their arrival would place enormous pressure on existing economic processes, as well as bring crime and immorality to the United States.

The Scots-Irish were dramatically different culturally, and their arrival certainly generated stress. However, they proved crucial for populating the continent west of the Alleghenies. The Scots-Irish solved a demographic problem that was at the core of the United States: Given its population at that time, there simply were not enough Americans to expand settlements west of the mountains — and this posed a security threat. If the U.S. population remained clustered in a long, thin line along the Atlantic sea board, with poor lines of communication running north-south, the country would be vulnerable to European, and especially British, attack. The United States had to expand westward, and it lacked the population to do so. The Americans needed the Scots-Irish.

Successive waves of immigrants came to the United States over the next 200 years. In each case, they came looking for economic opportunity. In each case, there was massive anxiety that the arrival of these migrants would crowd the job market, driving down wages, and that the heterogeneous cultures would create massive social stress. The Irish immigration of the 1840s, the migrations from Eastern and Southern Europe in the 1880s — all triggered the same concerns. Nevertheless, without those waves of immigration, the United States would not have been able to populate the continent, to industrialize or to field the mass armies of the 20th century that established the nation as a global power.

Population Density and Economic Returns

Logic would have it that immigration should undermine the economic well-being of those who already live in the United States. But this logic assumes that there is a zero-sum game. That may be true in Europe or Asia. It has not been true in the United States. The key is population density: The density of the United States, excluding Alaska, is 34 people per square kilometer. By comparison, the population density in the United Kingdom is 247 per square kilometer, 231 in Germany and 337 in Japan. The European Union, taken as a whole, has a population density of 115. If the United States were to equal the United Kingdom in terms of density, it would have a population of about 2 billion people.

Even accepting the premise that some parts of the United States are uninhabitable and that the United Kingdom is over-inhabited, the point is that the United States' population is still small relative to available land. That means that it has not come even close to diminishing economic returns. To the extent to which the population-to-land ratio determines productivity — and this, in our view, is the critical variable — the United States still can utilize population increases. At a time when population growth from native births is quite low, this means that the United States still can metabolize immigrants. It is, therefore, no accident that over the past 40 years, the United States has absorbed a massive influx of Asian immigrants who have been net producers over time. It's a big country, and much of it is barely inhabited.

On this level, the immigration issue poses no significant questions. It is a replay of a debate that has been ongoing since the founding of the country. Those who have predicted social and economic disaster as a result of immigration have been consistently wrong. Those who have predicted growing prosperity have been right. Those who have said that the national character of the United States would change dramatically have been somewhat right; core values have remained in place, but the Anglo-Protestant ethnicity represented at the founding has certainly been transformed. How one feels about this transformation depends on ideology and taste. But the simple fact is this: The United States not only would not have become a transcontinental power without immigration; it would not have industrialized. Masses of immigrants formed the armies of workers that drove industrialism and made the United States into a significant world power. No immigration, no United States.

Geography: The Difference With Mexico

Now, it would seem at first glance that the current surge of Mexican migration should be understood in this context and, as such, simply welcomed. If immigration is good, then why wouldn't immigration from Mexico be good? Certainly, there is no cultural argument against it; if the United States could assimilate Ukrainian Jews, Sicilians and Pakistanis, there is no self-evident reason why it could not absorb Mexicans. The argument against the Mexican migration would seem on its face to be simply a repeat of old, failed arguments against past migrations.

But Mexican migration should not be viewed in the same way as other migrations. When a Ukrainian Jew or a Sicilian or an Indian came to the United States, their arrival represented a sharp geographical event; whatever memories they might have of their birthplace, whatever cultural values they might bring with them, the geographical milieu was being abandoned. And with that, so were the geopolitical consequences of their migration. Sicilians might remember Sicily, they might harbor a cultural commitment to its values and they might even have a sense of residual loyalty to Sicily or to Italy — but Italy was thousands of miles away. The Italian government could neither control nor exploit the migrant's presence in the United States. Simply put, these immigrants did not represent a geopolitical threat; even if they did not assimilate to American culture — remaining huddled together in their "little Italys" — they did not threaten the United States in any way. Their strength was in the country they had left, and that country was far away. That is why, in the end, these immigrants assimilated, or their children did. Without assimilation, they were adrift.

The Mexican situation is different. When a Mexican comes to the United States, there is frequently no geographical split. There is geographical continuity. His roots are just across the land border. Therefore, the entire immigration dynamic shifts. An Italian, a Jew, an Indian can return to his home country, but only with great effort and disruption. A Mexican can and does return with considerable ease. He can, if he chooses, live his life in a perpetual ambiguity.

The Borderland Battleground

This has nothing to do with Mexicans as a people, but rather with a geographical concept called "borderlands." Traveling through Europe, one will find many borderlands. Alsace-Lorraine is a borderland between Germany and France; the inhabitants are both French and German, and in some ways neither. It also is possible to find Hungarians — living Hungarian lives — deep inside Slovakia and Romania.

Borderlands can be found throughout the world. They are the places where the borders have shifted, leaving members of one nation stranded on the other side of the frontier. In many cases, these people now hold the citizenship of the countries in which they reside (according to recognized borders), but they think and speak in the language on the other side of the border. The border moved, but their homes didn't. There has been no decisive geographical event; they have not left their homeland. Only the legal abstraction of a border, and the non-abstract presence of a conquering army, has changed their reality.

Borderlands sometimes are political flash points, when the relative power of the two countries is shifting and one is reclaiming its old territory, as Germany did in 1940, or France in 1918. Sometimes the regions are quiet; the borders that have been imposed remain inviolable, due to the continued power of the conqueror. Sometimes, populations move back and forth in the borderland, as politics and economics shift. Borderlands are everywhere. They are the archaeological remains of history, except that these remains have a tendency to come back to life.

The U.S.-Mexican frontier is a borderland. The United States, to all intents and purposes, conquered the region in the period between the Texan Revolution (1835-1836) and the Mexican-American War (1846-1848). As a result of the war, the border moved and areas that had been Mexican territory became part of the United States. There was little ethnic cleansing. American citizens settled into the territory in increasing numbers over time, but the extant Mexican culture remained in place. The border was a political dividing line but was never a physical division; the area north of the border retained a certain Mexican presence, while the area south of the border became heavily influenced by American culture. The economic patterns that tied the area north of the Rio Grande to the area south of it did not disappear. At times they atrophied; at times they intensified; but the links were always there, and neither Washington nor Mexico City objected. It was the natural characteristic of the borderland.

It was not inevitable that the borderland would be held by the United States. Anyone looking at North America in 1800 might have bet that Mexico, not the United States, would be the dominant power of the continent. Why that didn't turn out to be the case is a long story, but by 1846, the Mexicans had lost direct control of the borderland. They have not regained it since. But that does not mean that the borderland is unambiguously American — and it does not mean that, over the next couple of hundred years, should Washington's power weaken and Mexico City's increase, the borders might not shift once again. How many times, after all, have the Franco-German borders shifted? For the moment, however, Washington is enormously more powerful than Mexico City, so the borders will stay where they are.

The Heart of the Matter

We are in a period, as happens with borderlands, when major population shifts are under way. This should not be understood as immigration. Or more precisely, these shifts should not be understood as immigration in the same sense that we talk about immigration from, say, Brazil, where the geographical relationship between migrant and home country is ruptured. The immigration from Mexico to the United States is a regional migration within a borderland between two powers — powers that have drawn a border based on military and political history, and in which two very different populations intermingle. Right now, the United States is economically dynamic relative to Mexico. Therefore, Mexicans tend to migrate northward, across the political border, within the geographical definition of the borderland. The map declares a border. Culture and history, however, take a different view.

The immigration debate in the U.S. Congress, which conflates Asian immigrations with Mexican immigrations, is mixing apples and oranges. Chinese immigration is part of the process of populating the United States — a process that has been occurring since the founding of the Republic. Mexican immigration is, to borrow a term from physics, the Brownian motion of the borderland. This process is nearly as old as the Republic, but there is a crucial difference: It is not about populating the continent nearly as much as it is about the dynamics of the borderland.

One way to lose control of a borderland is by losing control of its population. In general, most Mexicans cross the border for strictly economic reasons. Some wish to settle in the United States, some

11

wish to assimilate. Others intend to be here temporarily. Some intend to cross the border for economic reasons — to work — and remain Mexicans in the full sense of the word. Now, so long as this migration remains economic and cultural, there is little concern for the United States. But when this last class of migrants crosses the border with political aspirations, such as the recovery of lost Mexican territories from the United States, that is the danger point.

Americans went to Texas in the 1820s. They entered the borderland. They then decided to make a political claim against Mexico, demanding a redefinition of the formal borders between Mexico and the United States. In other words, they came to make money and stayed to make a revolution. There is little evidence — flag-waving notwithstanding — that there is any practical move afoot now to reverse the American conquest of Mexican territories. Nevertheless, that is the danger with all borderlands: that those on the "wrong" side of the border will take action to move the border back.

For the United States, this makes the question of Mexican immigration within the borderland different from that of Mexican immigration to places well removed from it. In fact, it makes the issue of Mexican migration different from all other immigrations to the United States. The current congressional debate is about "immigration" as a whole, but that makes little sense. It needs to be about three different questions:

1. Immigration from other parts of the world to the United States.

2. Immigration from Mexico to areas well removed from the southern border region.

3. Immigration from Mexico to areas within the borderlands that were created by the U.S. conquests.

Treating these three issues as if they were the same thing confuses matters. The issue is not immigration in general, nor even Mexican immigration. It is about the borderland and its future. The question of legal and illegal immigration and various solutions to the problems must be addressed in this context.

3: The Geopolitics of Dope
Jan. 29, 2008

Over recent months, the level of violence along the U.S.-Mexican border has begun to rise substantially, with some of it spilling into the United States. Last week, the Mexican government began military operations on its side of the border against Mexican gangs engaged in smuggling drugs into the United States. The action apparently pushed some of the gang members north into the United States in a bid for sanctuary. Low-level violence is endemic to the border region. But while not without precedent, movement of organized, armed cadres into the United States on this scale goes beyond what has become accepted practice. The dynamics in the borderland are shifting and must be understood in a broader, geopolitical context.

The U.S. border with Mexico has been intermittently turbulent since the U.S. occupation of northern Mexico. The annexation of Texas following its anti-Mexican revolution and the Mexican-American War created a borderland, an area in which the political border is clearly delineated but the cultural and economic borders are less clear and more dynamic. This is the case with many borders, including the U.S.-Canadian one, but the Mexican border has gone through periods of turbulence in the past and is going through one right now.

There always have been uncontrolled economic transactions and movements along the border. Both sides understood that the cost of controlling and monitoring these transactions outstripped the benefit. Long before NAFTA came into existence, social and economic movement in both directions — but particularly from Mexico to the United States — were fairly uncontrolled. Borderland transactions in particular, local transactions in proximity to the border region (retail shopping, agricultural transfers and so on), were uncontrolled. So was smuggling. Trade in stolen U.S. cars and parts shipped into Mexico, labor from Mexico shipped into the United States, etc., were seen as tolerable costs for an open border.

A low-friction border, one that easily could be traversed at low cost — without extended waits — was important to both sides. In 2006, the United States imported $198 billion in goods from Mexico and exported $134 billion to Mexico. This makes Mexico the third-largest trading partner of the United States and also makes it one of the more balanced major trade relationships the United States has. Loss of Mexican markets would hurt the U.S. economy substantially. The U.S. advantage in selling to Mexico is low-cost transport. Lose that through time delays at the border and the Mexican market becomes competitive for other countries. About 13 percent of all U.S. exports are bought by Mexico.

Not disrupting this trade and not raising its cost has been a fundamental principle of U.S.-Mexican relations, one long predating NAFTA. Leaving aside the contentious issue of whether illegal immigration hurts or helps the United States, the steps required to control that immigration would impede bilateral trade. The United States therefore has been loath to impose effective measures, since any measures that would be effective against population movement also would impose friction on trade.

The United States has been willing to tolerate levels of criminality along the border. The only time when the United States shifted its position was when organized groups in Mexico both established themselves north of the political border and engaged in significant violence. Thus, in 1916, when the Mexican revolutionary Pancho Villa began operations north of the border, the U.S. Army moved into Mexico to try to destroy his base of operations. This has been the line that, when crossed, motivated the United States to take action, regardless of the economic cost. The current upsurge in violence is now pushing that line.

The United States has built-in demand for a range of illegal drugs, including heroin, cocaine, methamphetamines and marijuana. Regardless of decades of efforts, the United States has not been able to eradicate or even qualitatively reduce this demand. As an advanced industrial country, the United States has a great deal of money available to satisfy the demand for illegal drugs. This makes the supply of narcotics to a large market attractive. In fact, it almost doesn't matter how large demand is. Regardless of how it varies, the economics are such that even a fraction of the current market will attract sellers.

Even after processing, the cost of the product is quite low. What makes it an attractive product is the differential between the cost of production and the price it commands. In less-developed countries, supplying the American narcotics market creates huge income differentials. From the standpoint of a poor peasant, the differential between growing a product illegal in the United States compared with a legal product is enormous. From the standpoint of the processor, shippers and distributors, every step in the value chain creates tremendous incentives to engage in this activity over others.

There are several factors governing price. The addictive nature of the product creates an inelastic demand curve in a market with high discretionary income. People will buy whatever the price and somehow will find the money for the purchase. Illegality suppresses competition and drives cartelization. Processing, smuggling and distributing the drugs requires a complex supply chain. Businesses not prepared to engage in high-risk illegal activities are frozen out of the market. The cost of market entry is high, since the end-to-end system (from the fields to the users) both is a relationship business (strangers are not welcome) and requires substantial expertise, particularly in covert logistics. Finally, there is a built-in cost for protecting the supply chain once created.

Because they are involved in an illegal business, drug dealers do not have recourse to the courts or police to protect their assets. Protecting the supply chain and excluding competition are opposite sides of the same coin. Protecting assets is major cost of running a drug ring. It suppresses competition, both by killing it and by raising the cost of entry into the market. The illegality of the business requires that it be large enough to manage the supply chain and absorb the cost of protecting it. It gives high incentives to eliminate potential competitors and new entrants into the market. In the end, it creates a monopoly or small oligopoly in the business, where the comparative advantage ultimately devolves into the effectiveness of the supply chain and the efficiency of the private police force protecting it.

That means that drug organizations evolve in several predictable ways. They have huge amounts of money flowing in from the U.S. market by selling relatively low-cost products at monopolistic prices into markets with inelastic demand curves. Second, they have unique expertise in covert logistics, expertise that can be transferred to the movement of other goods. Third, they develop substantial security capabilities, which can grow over time into full-blown paramilitary forces to protect the supply chain. Fourth, they are huge capital pools, investing in the domestic economy and manipulating the political system.

Cartels can challenge — and supplant — governments. Between huge amounts of money available to bribe officials, and covert armies better equipped, trained and motivated than national police and military forces, the cartels can become the government — if in fact they didn't originate in the government. Getting the government to deploy armed forces against the cartel can become a contradiction in terms. In their most extreme form, cartels are the government.

Drug cartels have two weaknesses. First, they can be shattered in conflicts with challengers within the oligopoly or by splits within the cartels. Second, their supply chains can be broken from the outside. U.S. policy has historically been to attack the supply chains from the fields to the street distributors. Drug cartels have proved to be extremely robust and resilient in modifying the supply chains under pressure. However, when conflict occurs within and among cartels and systematic attacks against the supply chain take place, specific cartels can be broken — although the long-term result is the emergence of a new cartel system.

In the 1980s, the United States manipulated various Colombian cartels into internal conflict. More important, the United States attacked the Colombian supply chain in the Caribbean as it moved from Colombia through Panama along various air and sea routes to the United States. The weakness of the Colombian cartel was its exposed supply chain from South America to the United States. U.S. military operations raised the cost so high that the route became uneconomic.

The main route to American markets shifted from the Caribbean to the U.S.-Mexican border. It began as an alliance between sophisticated Colombian cartels and still-primitive Mexican gangs, but the balance of power inevitably shifted over time. Owning the supply link into the United States, the Mexicans increased their wealth and power until they absorbed more and more of the entire supply chain. Eventually, the Colombians were minimized and the Mexicans became the decisive power.

The Americans fought the battle against the Colombians primarily in the Caribbean and southern Florida. The battle against the Mexican drug lords must be fought in the U.S.-Mexican borderland. And while the fight against the Colombians did not involve major disruptions to other economic patterns, the fight against the Mexican cartels involves potentially huge disruptions. In addition, the battle is going to be fought in a region that is already tense because of the immigration issue, and at least partly on U.S. soil.

The cartel's supply chain is embedded in the huge legal bilateral trade between the United States and Mexico. Remember that Mexico exports $198 billion to the United States and — according to the Mexican Economy Ministry — $1.6 billion to Japan and $1.7 billion to China, its next biggest markets. Mexico is just behind Canada as a U.S. trading partner and is a huge market running both ways. Disrupting the drug trade cannot be done without disrupting this other trade. With that much trade going on, you are not going to find the drugs. It isn't going to happen.

Police action, or action within each country's legal procedures and protections, will not succeed. The cartels' ability to evade, corrupt and

17

absorb the losses is simply too great. Another solution is to allow easy access to the drug market for other producers, flooding the market, reducing the cost and eliminating the economic incentive and technical advantage of the cartel. That would mean legalizing drugs. That is simply not going to happen in the United States. It is a political impossibility.

This leaves the option of treating the issue as a military action rather than a police action. That would mean attacking the cartels as if they were a military force rather than a criminal group. It would mean that procedural rules would not be in place, and that the cartels would be treated as an enemy army. Leaving aside the complexities of U.S.-Mexican relations, cartels flourish by being hard to distinguish from the general population. This strategy not only would turn the cartels into a guerrilla force, it would treat northern Mexico as hostile occupied territory. Don't even think of that possibility, absent a draft under which college-age Americans from upper-middle-class families would be sent to patrol Mexico — and be killed and wounded. The United States does not need a Gaza Strip on its southern border, so this won't happen.

The current efforts by the Mexican government might impede the various gangs, but they won't break the cartel system. The supply chain along the border is simply too diffuse and too plastic. It shifts too easily under pressure. The border can't be sealed, and the level of economic activity shields smuggling too well. Farmers in Mexico can't be persuaded to stop growing illegal drugs for the same reason that Bolivians and Afghans can't. Market demand is too high and alternatives too bleak. The Mexican supply chain is too robust — and too profitable — to break easily.

The likely course is a multigenerational pattern of instability along the border. More important, there will be a substantial transfer of wealth from the United States to Mexico in return for an intrinsically low-cost consumable product — drugs. This will be one of the sources of capital that will build the Mexican economy, which today is 14th largest in the world. The accumulation of drug money is and will continue finding its way into the Mexican economy, creating a pool of investment capital. The children and grandchildren of the Zetas will be running banks, running for president, building art museums and telling amusing anecdotes about how grandpa made his money running blow into Nuevo Laredo.

It will also destabilize the U.S. Southwest while grandpa makes his pile. As is frequently the case, it is a problem for which there are no good solutions, or for which the solution is one without real support.

4: On the Road to a Failed State?
May 13, 2008

Edgar Millan Gomez was shot dead in his own home in Mexico City on May 8. Millan Gomez was the highest-ranking law enforcement officer in Mexico, responsible for overseeing most of Mexico's counternarcotics efforts. He orchestrated the January arrest of one of the leaders of the Sinaloa cartel, Alfredo Beltran Leyva. (Several Sinaloa members have been arrested in Mexico City since the beginning of the year.) The week before, Roberto Velasco Bravo died when he was shot in the head at close range by two armed men near his home in Mexico City. He was the director of organized criminal investigations in a tactical analysis unit of the federal police. The Mexican government believes the Sinaloa drug cartel ordered the assassinations of Velasco Bravo and Millan Gomez. Combined with the assassination of other federal police officials in Mexico City, we now see a pattern of intensifying warfare in Mexico City.

The fighting also extended to the killing of the son of the Sinaloa cartel leader, Joaquin "El Chapo" Guzman Loera, who was killed outside a shopping center in Culiacan, the capital of Sinaloa state. Also killed was the son of reputed top Sinaloa money launderer Blanca Margarita Cazares Salazar in an attack carried out by 40 gunmen. According to sources, Los Zetas, the enforcement arm of the rival Gulf cartel, carried out the attack. Reports also indicate a split between Sinaloa and a resurgent Juarez cartel, which also could have been behind the Millan Gomez killing.

Spiraling Violence

Violence along the U.S.-Mexican border has been intensifying for several years, and there have been attacks in Mexico City. But last week was noteworthy not so much for the body count, but for the type of people being killed. Very senior government police officials in Mexico City were killed along with senior Sinaloa cartel operatives in Sinaloa state. In other words, the killings are extending from low-level operatives to higher-ranking ones, and the attacks are reaching into enemy territory, so to speak. Mexican government officials are being killed in Mexico City, Sinaloan operatives in Sinaloa. The conflict is becoming more intense and placing senior officials at risk.

The killings pose a strategic problem for the Mexican government. The bulk of its effective troops are deployed along the U.S. border, attempting to suppress violence and smuggling. The attacks in Mexico raise the question of whether forces should be shifted from these assignments to Mexico City to protect officials and break up the infrastructure of the Sinaloa and other cartels there. The government also faces the secondary task of suppressing violence between cartels. The Sinaloa cartel struck in Mexico City not only to kill troublesome officials and intimidate others but also to pose a problem for the Mexican government by increasing areas requiring forces, thereby requiring the government to consider splitting its forces — thus reducing the government presence along the border. It was a strategically smart move by Sinaloa, but no one has accused the cartels of being stupid.

Mexico now faces a classic problem. Multiple well-armed and organized groups have emerged. They are fighting among themselves while simultaneously fighting the government. The groups are fueled by vast amounts of money earned via drug smuggling to the United States. The amount of money involved — estimated at some $40 billion a year — is sufficient to increase tension between these criminal groups and give them the resources to conduct wars against each other. It also provides them with resources to bribe and intimidate government officials. The resources they deploy in some ways are superior to the resources the government employs.

Given the amount of money they have, the organized criminal groups can be very effective in bribing government officials at all levels, from squad leaders patrolling the border to high-ranking state and federal officials. Given the resources they have, they can reach out and kill government officials at all levels as well. Government officials are human; and faced with the carrot of bribes and the stick of death, even the most incorruptible are going to be cautious in executing operations against the cartels.

Toward a Failed State?

There comes a moment when the imbalance in resources reverses the relationship between government and cartels. Government officials, seeing the futility of resistance, effectively become tools of the cartels. Since there are multiple cartels, the area of competition ceases to be solely the border towns, shifting to the corridors of power in Mexico City. Government officials begin giving their primary loyalty not to the government but to one of the cartels. The government thus becomes both an arena for competition among the cartels and an instrument used by one cartel against another. That is the prescription for what is called a "failed state" — a state that no longer can function as a state. Lebanon in the 1980s is one such example.

There are examples in American history as well. Chicago in the 1920s was overwhelmed by a similar process. Smuggling alcohol created huge pools of money on the U.S. side of the border, controlled by criminals both by definition (bootlegging was illegal) and by inclination (people who engage in one sort of illegality are prepared to be criminals, more broadly understood). The smuggling laws gave these criminals huge amounts of power, which they used to intimidate and effectively absorb the city government. Facing a choice between being killed or being enriched, city officials chose the latter. City

21

government shifted from controlling the criminals to being an arm of criminal power. In the meantime, various criminal gangs competed with each other for power.

Chicago had a failed city government. The resources available to the Chicago gangs were limited, however, and it was not possible for them to carry out the same function in Washington. Ultimately, Washington deployed resources in Chicago and destroyed one of the main gangs. But if Al Capone had been able to carry out the same operation in Washington as he did in Chicago, the United States could have become a failed state.

It is important to point out that we are not speaking here of corruption, which exists in all governments everywhere. Instead, we are talking about a systematic breakdown of the state, in which government is not simply influenced by criminals but becomes an instrument of criminals — either an arena for battling among groups or under the control of a particular group. The state no longer can carry out its primary function of imposing peace, and it becomes helpless or itself a direct perpetrator of crime. Corruption has been seen in Washington — some of it triggered by organized crime — but never state failure.

The Mexican state has not yet failed. If the activities of the last week have become a pattern, however, we must begin thinking about the potential for state failure. The killing of Millan Gomez transmitted a critical message: No one is safe, no matter how high his rank or how well protected, if he works against cartel interests. The killing of El Chapo's son transmitted the message that no one in the leading cartel is safe from competing gangs, no matter how high his rank or how well protected.

The killing of senior state police officials causes other officials to recalculate their attitudes. The state is no longer seen as a competent protector, and being a state official is seen as a liability — potentially a fatal liability — unless protection is sought from a cartel, a protection that can be very lucrative indeed for the protector. The killing of senior cartel members intensifies conflict among cartels, making it even more difficult for the government to control the situation and intensifying the movement toward failure.

It is important to remember that Mexico has a tradition of failed governments, particularly in the 19th and early 20th centuries. In those periods, Mexico City became an arena for struggle among army officers and regional groups straddling the line between criminal and political. The Mexican army became an instrument in this struggle and its control a prize. The one thing missing was the vast amounts of money at stake. So there is a tradition of state failure in Mexico, and there are higher stakes today than before.

The Drug Trade's High Stakes

To benchmark the amount at stake, assume that the total amount of drug trafficking is $40 billion, a frequently used figure, but hardly an exact one by any means. In 2007, Mexico exported about $210 billion worth of goods to the United States and imported about $136 billion from the United States. If the drug trade is $40 billion, it represents almost 20 percent of all exports to the United States. That in itself is huge, but what makes it more important is that while the $210 billion is divided among many businesses and individuals, the $40 billion is concentrated in the hands of a few, fairly tightly controlled cartels. Sinaloa and Gulf, currently the strongest, have vast resources at their disposal; a substantial part of the economy can be controlled through this money. This creates tremendous instability as other cartels vie for the top spot, with the state lacking the resources to control the situation and having its officials seduced and intimidated by the cartels.

We have seen failed states elsewhere. Colombia in the 1980s failed over the same issue — drug money. Lebanon failed in the 1970s and 1980s. The Democratic Republic of the Congo was a failed state.

Mexico's potential failure is important for three reasons. First, Mexico is a huge country, with a population of more than 100 million. Second, it has a large economy — the 14th-largest in the world. And third, it shares an extended border with the world's only global power, one that has assumed for most of the 20th century that its domination of North America and control of its borders is a foregone conclusion. If Mexico fails, there are serious geopolitical repercussions. This is not simply a criminal matter.

The amount of money accumulated in Mexico derives from smuggling operations in the United States. Drugs go one way, money another. But all the money doesn't have to return to Mexico or to third-party countries. If Mexico fails, the leading cartels will compete in the United States, and that competition will extend to the source of the money as well. We have already seen cartel violence in the border areas of the United States, but this risk is not limited to that. The same process that we see under way in Mexico could extend to the United States; logic dictates that it would.

The current issue is control of the source of drugs and of the supply chain that delivers drugs to retail customers in the United States. The struggle for control of the source and the supply chain also will involve a struggle for control of markets. The process of intimidation of government and police officials, as well as bribing them, can take place in market towns such as Los Angeles or Chicago, as well as production centers or transshipment points.

Cartel Incentives for U.S. Expansion

That means there are economic incentives for the cartels to extend their operations into the United States. With those incentives comes inter-cartel competition, and with that competition comes pressure on U.S. local, state and, ultimately, federal government and police functions. Were that to happen, the global implications obviously would be stunning. Imagine an extreme case in which the Mexican scenario is acted out in the United States. The effect on the global system economically and politically would be astounding, since U.S. failure would see the world reshaping itself in startling ways.

Failure for the United States is much harder than for Mexico, however. The United States has a gross domestic product of about $14 trillion, while Mexico's economy is about $900 billion. The impact of the cartels' money is vastly greater in Mexico than in the United States, where it would be dwarfed by other pools of money with a powerful interest in maintaining U.S. stability. The idea of a failed American state is therefore far-fetched.

Less far-fetched is the extension of a Mexican failure into the borderlands of the United States. Street-level violence already has crossed the border. But a deeper, more-systemic corruption — particularly on the local level — could easily extend into the United States, along with paramilitary operations between cartels and between the Mexican government and cartels.

U.S. Secretary of Defense Robert Gates recently visited Mexico, and there are potential plans for U.S. aid in support of Mexican government operations. But if the Mexican government became paralyzed and couldn't carry out these operations, the U.S. government would face a stark and unpleasant choice. It could attempt to protect the United States from the violence defensively by sealing off Mexico or controlling the area north of the border more effectively. Or, as it did in the early 20th century, the United States could adopt a forward defense by sending U.S. troops south of the border to fight the battle in Mexico.

There have been suggestions that the border be sealed. But Mexico is the United States' third-largest customer, and the United States is Mexico's largest customer. This was the case well before NAFTA, and has nothing to do with treaties and everything to do with economics and geography. Cutting that trade would have catastrophic effects on both sides of the border, and would guarantee the failure of the Mexican state. It isn't going to happen.

The Impossibility of Sealing the Border

So long as vast quantities of goods flow across the border, the border cannot be sealed. Immigration might be limited by a wall, but the goods that cross the border do so at roads and bridges, and the sheer amount of goods crossing the border makes careful inspection impossible. The drugs will come across the border embedded in this trade as well as by other routes. So will gunmen from the cartel and anything else needed to take control of Los Angeles' drug market.

A purely passive defense won't work unless the economic cost of blockade is absorbed. The choices are a defensive posture to deal with the battle on American soil if it spills over, or an offensive posture to suppress the battle on the other side of the border. Bearing in mind that Mexico is not a small country and that counterinsurgency is not the United States' strong suit, the latter is a dangerous game. But the first option isn't likely to work either.

One way to deal with the problem would be ending the artificial price of drugs by legalizing them. This would rapidly lower the price of drugs and vastly reduce the money to be made in smuggling them. Nothing hurt the American cartels more than the repeal of Prohibition, and nothing helped them more than Prohibition itself. Nevertheless, from an objective point of view, drug legalization isn't going to happen. There is no visible political coalition of substantial size advocating this solution. Therefore, U.S. drug policy will continue to raise the price of drugs artificially, effective interdiction will be impossible, and the Mexican cartels will prosper and make war on each other and on the Mexican state.

We are not yet at the worst-case scenario, and we may never get there. Mexican President Felipe Calderon, perhaps with assistance from the United States, may devise a strategy to immunize his government from intimidation and corruption and take the war home to the cartels. This is a serious possibility that should not be ruled out. Nevertheless, the events of last week raise the serious possibility of a failed state in Mexico. That should not be taken lightly, as it could change far more than Mexico.

5: The Geopolitics of Mexico: A Mountain Fortress Besieged
Nov. 17, 2009

A Difficult Hand

"Poor Mexico, so far from God, so close to the United States!"
— Attributed to Mexican leader Porfirio Diaz (1830-1915)

As the southernmost portion of North America, Mexico was dealt a difficult geographic hand. It has a small and limited core territory surrounded by mountains, deserts and jungles that are inherently hard to control and nearly impossible to defend against threats from within or without.

The country is funnel-shaped, its high plateau anchored in the mountains and jungles of Central America to the south. The funnel fans and expands northwest toward a 2,000-mile-long desert border with the United States. Bordering the plateau to the east and west are Mexico's two mountain ranges, the Sierra Madre Oriental and the Sierra Madre Occidental. With peaks as high as 18,000 feet, these mountain ranges are extensive and formidable — indeed, the country can be thought of as a kind of mountain fortress that must secure outlying territories that serve as approaches to its core.

On Mexico's western flank, the slopes of the Sierra Madre Occidental drop precipitously toward the Pacific Ocean. Blanketed alternately with dense deciduous tropical forests and so-called "spine forests," the vegetation of Mexico's western slopes is as inhospitable as it sounds. Though patches of savanna in Sinaloa and Sonora states serve as adequate grazing land for cattle and other livestock, western Mexico requires significant infrastructure to divert water from the region's relatively sparse river system for agricultural use.

On the eastern slopes of the Sierra Madre Oriental, the land drops away to wider flatlands compared to the narrow littoral strip on the western coast, flatlands characterized by dense tropical forests. Despite the relative richness of the land, with its face to the Gulf of

Mexico and the vast majority of the world's great powers to its east, Mexico's eastern shores have also proved to be a military vulnerability for the Mexican heartland.

No less challenging to the Mexican state are the country's deserts, which characterize the northern border and boast some of the most desolate territory in all of North America. This no-man's-land forms an impressive buffer between Mexico and its powerful northern neighbor, but it is also the historical seat of insurrection for any force (most often domestic) seeking to challenge Mexico's core.

The Heartland

The heart of Mexico is roughly the region also known as ancient Mesoamerica, which lies between the Tropic of Cancer and the 18th parallel. This region is the native home of the Olmec, Toltec, Aztec and many other North American tribes. Within this region is the true core of Mexico, which STRATFOR views as a double core, with two geographically distinct yet vital centers: the region around the Valley of Mexico and the region of Veracruz.

Situated at the crux of the sierras in the Valley of Mexico, Mexico City is the unquestionable political core of Mexico. This high plateau was home to the Aztecs and was the origin of one of the world's most important grains: corn. Though this region lies at tropical latitudes, the high altitude of the plateau mitigates the tropical influence, providing for a mild, temperate climate suitable for agriculture and sustaining relatively large populations. The sheer heights of the mountains to the east and west of the city also afford the high plateau a certain amount of fortification from outside threats.

Established in the middle of a lake that filled the Valley of Mexico, Mexico City was originally the Aztec capital of Tenochtitlan. Hardly the choicest land in the area, the location was originally selected for settlement at a time when the Aztecs were one of the weakest tribes in the region. The Aztecs ingeniously built the city literally right out of the water, using stone and lime to build temples and growing crops on platforms in the middle of the lake, called chinampas. In the 16th century, the Spaniards built a canal linking the Valley of Mexico to the Tula river system. The project effectively drained the lake but left the city with numerous problems, including severe foundational instability and vulnerability to earthquakes (recent years have ironically been characterized by severe water shortages).

Despite its questionable location, Mexico City is a critical component of national control: Whoever controls the capital can control the highlands. That said, Mexico's rough terrain makes it difficult to secure control of the rest of the country, and Mexico City often finds itself fending off threats from all sides.

The greatest threats, historically, have come from the city of Veracruz, which forms the second pole of Mexico's double core, on the eastern shore of Southern Mexico. This lowland tropical region was home to the Olmecs, one of Mesoamerica's earliest tribes. The lush tropical climate in Veracruz has historically permitted the growth of a wide variety of plants to sustain the Olmec diet, including squash and beans. However, the humid climate makes it difficult to grow grains, thus the coastline is unsuitable for sustaining large populations.

The city of Veracruz has also been the point from which foreign (and domestic) powers have been able to successfully launch invasions of Mexico City. As one of Mexico's main Gulf ports, with direct access to Mexico City, Veracruz is a key jumping-off point from the coast to Mexico City. Veracruz was originally established by Spanish explorer Hernan Cortez, who used his time there to form alliances with local tribes that had been subjugated by the Aztecs and were only too happy to support a new regional strongman. In the company of thousands of native warriors, Cortez successfully laid siege to and captured Tenochtitlan from the Aztecs in 1521.

In time, following the collapse of the Spanish empire, the chaos of Mexico's wars of independence was exploited by France, which crowned Ferdinand Maximilian Joseph Hapsburg Emperor of Mexico in Mexico City in 1864. After battling inland from their landing point in Veracruz, the French occupied Mexico City for three years. They soon discovered that taking Mexico City was one thing. Taking Mexico was quite another. The problem for the French was the sheer time and manpower required to conquer Mexico's far-flung deserts, mountains and plateaus — and even solidifying control over areas as close to Mexico City as the state of Oaxaca, where rebel forces were able to find sanctuary. The French were unable to solidify their control over Mexico's territory, and in 1867 French Emperor Napoleon III withdrew troops, leaving the hapless Maximilian to be executed by irate Mexicans.

It is of the highest priority for Mexico to control the highland region around Mexico City as well as the lowland region on the Gulf coast around Veracruz in order to guarantee the existence of the state. As the French example shows, however, there are nearby areas that must also be controlled. We refer to these regions as the outer core, which consists of the states within the boundaries of ancient Mesoamerica but outside the immediate vicinity of Mexico City or Veracruz. These states include the mountainous, rugged states of Chiapas, Oaxaca, Michoacan and Guerrero. Because of their mountainous terrain, these states can be difficult to control and can serve as jumping-off points for rebellious forces. For Mexico City, it is critical — at a minimum — to contain and mitigate unrest in these areas in order to guarantee the physical security of the core.

Political Boundaries

Mexico's core territories are critically important to the survival of the state. Less critical — but still important — are Mexico's current political boundaries, which encompass a much larger territory that has repeatedly defied subjugation.

The Spanish viceroyalty established Mexico's southern borders with Guatemala and Belize (which were solidified by treaty in 1882). Upon independence, there was no impetus to push farther south, primarily because the land in Central America is mountainous, difficult to defend or control and not suited for agriculture. The next patch of useful territory is well over 1,000 miles south — in the highlands of Colombia — and everything in between is far more trouble than it is worth. For Mexico, there was nothing to be gained in challenging the southern borderline (indeed, it might actually behoove Mexico to cede more of the mountainous, half-wild territory of Chiapas to its southern neighbor).

The northern borders are a different story altogether. Two seminal events defined the northern border: the Texas War for Independence and the U.S.-Mexican War (known in Mexico as the War of Northern Aggression). The war with Texas effectively released the vast majority of Texas to independence, but it also set the stage for a war between the United States and Mexico by leaving the actual border hotly disputed. Once Texas joined the United States, this dispute erupted into all-out war between the two North American neighbors. The conquering of Mexico City in 1847 by the United States ended the war, with the United States taking about half of Mexico's total original territory — all of Texas along with the land that would become the modern U.S. states of Arizona, California and New Mexico. In one crushing blow, the United States satisfied critical strategic needs (namely an undisputed path to the Pacific Ocean and a strategic buffer for the Greater Mississippi Valley) by relieving Mexico of some of its most promising territory, leaving the country in a state of turmoil.

To put it simply, Mexico's northern border is neither a product of inevitable geographic dictation nor a border of Mexico's choosing. Stretching across vast expanses of the Sonora, Chihuahua and Baja deserts, the U.S.-Mexico border bisects a section of Mexico that is at most points only barely habitable. To make things more complicated, the mountains that stretch up into this region allow for pockets of unrest to simmer, and eventually boil over. The physical isolation of northern Mexico and the difficulty Mexico City had in projecting power into the area was one of the most important reasons it lost Texas and what is now the American Southwest, and one of the key causes of the Mexican Revolution of 1910-1920.

The mountains, deserts and isolation of northern Mexico provide fertile ground for civil dissent and lawless activity. Thus, while northern Mexico provides a substantial strategic buffer between Mexico City and its northern neighbor, it is also a severe vulnerability. Add to that the fact that Mexico City remains highly vulnerable on its eastern flank, and the benefits of the buffer zone seem negligible.

In addition to its northern expanse, Mexico has two other territories that fall outside the core and are noteworthy. Neither of these territories is particularly useful, but both are strategically important to hold. The first is the Baja California Peninsula, which Mexico managed to retain after the U.S.-Mexican War, despite the U.S. desire to hold the mouth of the Colorado River. Baja stretches nearly 800 miles down the western coast of Mexico, and while it provides little in the way of economic opportunities (outside of tourism), if it were in the hands of a foreign country, Mexico's entire northern Pacific coast would be very vulnerable to external attack.

The second territory in this category is the Yucatan Peninsula. The Yucatan is essentially a large, flat limestone shelf with very few fresh water resources. So while the outcropping has verdant vegetation, it has none of the necessary elements of economically viable terrain. Yucatan does, however, give Mexico a strategic position in the Caribbean. It also allows Mexico to control one of the avenues of approach into the Gulf of Mexico and, of course, Veracruz.

In the cases of both the Baja California and Yucatan peninsulas, Mexico is the owner of seriously inhospitable territory. But the important point is that not having that territory would expose Mexico to even greater territorial vulnerabilities, particularly regarding naval threats.

Even with the relative advantages of having strategic possessions like the Yucatan and Baja California peninsulas, the national borders of Mexico do not make for a politically coherent and manageable state. The mountainous core makes it difficult to solidify control over the southern highlands, and the southeastern coast is devastatingly vulnerable to outside interference. Add to that the hard-to-control northern border zone — a fertile breeding ground for autonomous or rebellious groups — and Mexico has a geography that presents extreme challenges to any central government.

Ideal Boundaries

So, then, what would Mexico's ideal territorial boundaries be, taking into account the geopolitical necessities of a state that has proved so vulnerable to external influence? First and foremost, Mexico must establish control over the main routes of attack on its territory, and only after that will it have the capability to look farther afield for prosperous lands.

It is not easy to invade Mexico via land routes, since the northern Mexican frontier historically has made invasion from the north difficult (though defending this territory is also a challenge), and the highlands of Central America are a barrier to the south. It is far easier to invade Mexico from the sea. This means that if Mexico is to achieve any semblance of true security it must be able to guard the sea approaches to its core. Not only does Europe lie across the Atlantic, but the vast majority of the United States' populated coastline also lies just to the northeast. In the future, rising Brazilian naval capacity could pose yet another possible challenge to Mexico in the Caribbean. In order to protect the core from these potential threats, Mexico must exert influence over the mouth of the Caribbean. And to effectively do this, Mexico needs Florida and Cuba. This puts Mexico in direct competition with the United States for its key strategic needs.

Just as the United States needs to control Florida and at least neutralize any threat posed by Cuba in order to protect its export facilities at the mouth of the Mississippi River, Mexico needs to control transit through the Gulf. Without the ability to project naval force into the most historically proven and geographically sound path of invasion, Mexico will never be a truly independent and secure nation-state.

The implication, of course, is that there is only room for one great power in North America, and as long as the United States dominates the naval approaches to the southern portion of the continent, Mexico must maintain a non-hostile relationship with the United States in order to secure its own territory.

However, if Mexico were able to control those territories itself, it would assure its physical security, and the next likely strategic goal would be to regain territory lost to the United States. Assuming it had the military capacity to secure and hold them, having the fertile valleys of California and the expansive range land of Texas would be a great boon to the income-strapped Mexican government. But security must come first, or Mexico would never be able to hold those territories.

Geopolitical Imperatives

To secure its core:

- Mexico must first control and consolidate what can be labeled as the inner core, which includes both the highlands of Mexico City and the Veracruz coastal region. If these two regions cannot be wielded as a single zone, what we currently think of as Mexico will suffer from insufficient agricultural land and trade opportunities and will degenerate into an assortment of small, impoverished, sub-regional entities.

- Mexico must then control all pockets of potential dissent within the outer core territories that directly interact with the inner core, including Oaxaca, Chiapas, Guerrero and Michoacan. To do so, Mexico has two options: It can provide economic growth and employment opportunities to its citizens or it can rely on the rule of strongmen or a single strong party.

- Mexico must push north to control the wild northern territories from which threats might originate. The exact placement of the border is relatively academic, given the lack of clear geographic barriers. However, there is a cost-benefit ratio to take into account: The farther Mexico pushes north, the farther it must project power from its core, and the wider and less useful the plateau becomes.

- Mexico must control the sea approaches to its core as well as the chokepoints of the Caribbean in order to achieve absolute security. There are two phases to this. The first is the easiest, which is to control the Baja California and Yucatan peninsulas (modern Mexico has achieved this). The second is more difficult and requires gaining command of Cuba and Florida. Without these territories, Mexico has no choice but to engage in a subordinate relationship with the United States.

- Finally, with physical security ensured, Mexico can afford to reach past its buffer zones to richer territories and more useful coastlines — including the U.S. states of California, Texas and Louisiana.

Clearly, Mexico has not achieved all of its geopolitical imperatives. However, it has achieved just about all of the imperatives that it can without challenging the territorial integrity of the United States. There are also recurrent challenges to its economic stability and physical security, and Mexico still struggles to maintain the status quo on its second and third imperatives.

Economic Fundamentals

Sustained economic development has been a relentless challenge for Mexico. The root of Mexico's slow development (compared to its northern neighbor) lies in its geographic challenges. Whereas the United States has a massive agricultural heartland divided by a highly navigable river, Mexico lacks both a concentrated breadbasket as well as a navigable river network. The geographic advantages of the United States have been rooted in the ease of transport. With the Mississippi River bisecting the U.S. agricultural heartland, access to international markets was incredible simple — and cost only as much as it took to build a boat. Mexico, by contrast, must invest a great deal of capital for every mile of road and rail network. During 300 years of ruling Mexico, the Spanish failed to develop any substantial transport networks, leaving the newly independent Mexico to start from scratch.

With insufficient transportation infrastructure in place, Mexico's first decades of development were difficult. The cost of transporting goods from producing areas to consumer markets was prohibitive and reduced the profitability of private investment. Developing efficient transportation networks requires a massive amount of capital, right up front, which means that Mexico started out its independent statehood with no choice but to go deep into debt. Once Mexico is able to secure an influx of capital, however, it has generally been able to kick start growth sufficiently to sustain a substantial long-term expansion. But without its own domestic capital reserves (or particularly easy ways of developing them), Mexico's development has been cyclical in nature, with great highs followed by crashes as resources deplete.

Since independence, there have been two major boom and bust cycles, starting with the rule of Mexican President Porfirio Diaz, who took power in 1880, at the end of the wars of independence, and remained in power until 1911 (a period referred to as the "Porfiriato"). In addition to seizing power and maintaining stability, Diaz was able to make substantial improvements to the country's transportation network. With the help of a great deal of foreign investment, Diaz led a 30-year modernization push, including building Mexico's railway system from scratch. The country's rail network not only cut transportation costs drastically and made access to external markets easier, it also facilitated the extension of military power to the outer reaches of the country.

Unfortunately for Mexico, this period of growth and development slowed and was unable to translate foreign investment into overall welfare gains; capital collected in the hands of only a small segment of society. Political maneuvering by the elite, coupled with rising public discontent, eventually ousted Diaz from power in what evolved into the decade-long Mexican Revolution. But the railway infrastructure laid down during the Porfiriato became the foundation for postrevolutionary (and post-Great Depression) growth and development, once Mexico was able to access capital again.

In the wake of the Great Depression and with the onset of World War II, Mexico experienced its second major influx of foreign capital. The government's increased access to foreign lending was made possible by the renegotiation of outstanding debt (which, with the intervention of the United States on behalf of Mexico, was reduced by 90 percent) and the settlement of outstanding disputes with oil companies whose property had been seized in the oil nationalization project of 1938. Mexico was also aided by a boom in global demand for Mexican goods, particularly textile exports, as its northern neighbor went to war.

Renewed access to international capital markets and a surge in demand for exports catapulted Mexico into a five-year period of growth that averaged well over 6 percent per year. When the war ended, the export sector became less important for growth, but the five-year boost gave Mexico the industrial and developmental momentum it needed to continue growing through the 1950s and 1960s, albeit at a slower pace.

The 1970s told a slightly different story. With the oil price spike of the 1970s, European banks became flush with cash deposited by Middle Eastern countries. The resulting fall in interest rates encouraged developing countries around the world, and particularly in Latin America, to take out loans to finance industrialization projects. Mexico was no exception — the country was quick to take up debt in this period. Mexico's discovery of major oil deposits in the late 1970s led to a sharp uptick in exports of oil — which jumped from a net worth of $500 million in 1976 to more than $13 billion in 1980. This led, in turn, to the optimistic belief that capital would always be cheap and oil prices always high. At this point it looked like Mexico would have a chance to complement a period of sustained growth with a brand new, and substantial, tranche of capital. This was not the case.

The collapse of oil prices in 1981 triggered a major devaluation of the Mexican peso, making it impossible for Mexico to make its debt payments on time. The resulting debt crisis of 1982 triggered a period of economic turmoil for Mexico — and the rest of the region — that is known simply as "the lost decade." The International Monetary Fund (IMF) came to Mexico's rescue with financing, preventing a debt default. However, Mexico struggled mightily to regain lost ground while at the same time meeting the IMF's structural adjustment demands. Although stabilization was achieved for a few years, the policies enacted were insufficient. A severe overvaluation of the peso triggered a second financial hiccup in 1994 — the so-called "Tequila crisis."

Since the revaluation of the peso in the wake of the Tequila crisis, Mexico has experienced moderate growth, averaging just over 3.5 percent between 1996 and 2008. Mexico's modest growth rates have surprised observers, particularly given the fact that exports grew by an average of 11.1 percent per year between 1993 and 2003, which was facilitated by the enactment of the North American Free Trade Agreement.

Despite this impressive performance in the export sector, Mexico's growth has once again been impeded by a lack of capital. Low investment levels have not resulted from a lack of international investment interest, as foreign direct investment has increased dramatically, from less than $5 billion in 1993 to a high of nearly $30 billion in 2001. The capital shortage has instead come from the public sector, where spending has held steady at a relatively low level in the wake of the 1982 debt crisis. Furthermore, in the wake of the crisis and the privatization of the banking sector, lending to non-financial businesses fell by half from 1995 to 2007.

Mexico's lack of capital investments has translated into an inability to sufficiently develop its own human capital resources. This lack of development is the main driver behind the constant flow of migration from Mexico to the United States, with Mexico's labor market fortifying the U.S. labor pool and helping to underwrite the United States' low-inflation growth. While workers in the United States do send back over $20 billion worth of remittances every year to Mexico — contributing to the overall growth of Mexico's gross domestic product — it is difficult to determine if this money is being reinvested into Mexico in a way that contributes to growth in Mexican productivity.

This situation is being exacerbated by the decline of the energy industry. Income from Mexican state-owned energy company Petroleos Mexicanos (Pemex) accounts for 30 to 40 percent of the federal budget in any given year. With profits absorbed by the government for operating expenses, Pemex has very little spare cash to invest in its own industry, and the industry is facing serious declines in production. With prospective income headed downhill, Mexico is facing a grave fiscal problem — and the question will be whether to take the political risk of raising taxes or the financial risk of assuming greater amounts of debt. These energy woes are the most recent manifestation of Mexico's boom-and-bust cycle of capital shortage.

Shifting Politics

Mexico is unique among countries in Latin America in that the seat of national power has been occupied for most of Mexico's modern history by a single party: the Institutional Revolutionary Party (PRI), or its historical antecedents. But despite the rule of a single entity, Mexico's modern history has been relatively peaceful, avoiding (with some exceptions) the bloody political tangles that characterized many South American countries in the latter half of the 20th century.

This was in part possible because of the post-WWII prosperity that buoyed Mexico through the middle of the 20th century. In the context of sustained growth and sufficient capital, Mexican politicians didn't need to do very much in order to keep the country on an even keel. The key to maintaining stability in a complex system characterized by a proliferation of interests — from business to farmers to unions — was a very strong party that used political inclusion to soothe all comers. This meant that, for the PRI, it made more sense to entice political opponents into inclusive political cooperation than it did to threaten them with force. The rule of the PRI was still authoritarian, but it was very gentle compared to the brutal dictatorships of the 1960s and 1970s in other Latin American countries.

The strength of the party, at least in large part, is a result of Mexico's single-term limit for politicians. An idea that has been a rallying cry since the 19th century and was cemented by the Mexican Revolution, the edict that no politician should seek re-election is designed to avoid rulers who overstay their welcome.

The policy has had a number of consequences. It has made it difficult for individuals to build up their own power centers, or hold on to any single office for very long. The president can serve for only one six-year term — and for decades finding a successor was as simple as selecting an obvious heir. Theoretically designed to prevent despotism, the one-term limit also has made it very difficult to achieve standard goals of statehood — like economic or political reform. The primary problem is that Mexican politicians are not actually answerable to democratic processes. This creates an incentive structure that has very little to do with accountability to voters, and provides little to no incentive for politicians to achieve campaign promises.

Indeed, Mexican legislators often begin searching for their next job soon after entering office. And without the need to hold on to voter approval, Mexican politicians are much more free to engage in cronyism (something that helps with the job search). Indeed, in the politics of inclusion, this is actually quite beneficial. When the business of governance is dealt with through deal-making and favor distribution, having a system that leaves its legislators free to make such deals is conducive to the party's strategy for power consolidation.

This structure is not, however, beneficial for setting a political trajectory, or enacting policy over the long term. Without any continuity in personnel, there is little to no institutional memory of legislative efforts. This allows Mexico to move forward only in short bursts of legislative action, if at all.

While these dynamics and PRI rule have shaped the foundation of modern Mexico's political system, important shifts have occurred in the past decade. In 2000 the first elected president from the National Action Party — Vicente Fox — came into office. The transition of Mexico from a one-party system to a multiparty system pushed the country into relatively uncharted territory.

The dynamics of a multiparty system are different, with parties now able to openly oppose the will of the president in the legislature as a way of positioning themselves to propose candidates for the presidency. Though the system under the PRI was never particularly unified (nor in any way polite), all political maneuvering happened within the rubric of the PRI party machine, and dissent was relatively easy to control. Now such maneuvering occurs beyond that machine.

This dynamic is new, so it is too early to say how it will evolve, but the system appears to encourage political polarization in part because each party seeks to distinguish itself from the others. Additionally, as the inclusive framework used by the PRI to manage the country's myriad interests breaks down, it will expose sharp regional and factional differences. The multiparty system has likely made Mexico a much more difficult country to rule, since the president now represents a swath of voters and doesn't simply sit at the apex of a power balance held steady by a broad and inclusive effort.

Opportunities for divisiveness have flourished, and a willingness to break with past political arrangements has become clear. This is nowhere more evident than in the current administration's decision to use the military to fight the power structures built and maintained for years by Mexico's powerful criminal organizations.

Modern Challenges

Drugs

Like most of Mexico's problems, the drug wars are also a result of the country's geography. The flow of drugs is an ever-shifting river that follows the path of least resistance on its way from producer to consumer. When the United States and its international partners started shutting down direct air and sea traffic from Colombia to the United States in the 1990s, drug smugglers began to bring cocaine through the land corridor of Central America and Mexico. Mexico's border with the United States became ground zero for drug smugglers, and Mexican organized crime found itself with a much larger portion of the drug money at its fingertips.

Both Mexico's southern and northern borders are rugged and as populated as they are guarded (which is to say not much). This is the perfect combination for robust smuggling, particularly of goods that are in great demand in the United States. Since these border regions have few economic opportunities (the costs of development are simply too high and the state's resources too few), this smuggling is met with the de facto participation, if not outright approval, of local authorities. Mexico's fragmented geography also allowed plenty of room for different organizations to gain power in their local areas by controlling particular transport corridors or critical cities — even to the point of operating like a local government. These gangs jostled for control of territory and the state turned a blind eye.

But infighting and violence among drug smugglers did not go unnoticed, and as the political system shifted, so too did the rules of the drug game.

Under previous PRI governments, the need to keep local governments and power structures under the party umbrella meant that Mexico City ignored smuggling. That was the price of inclusion. Now that the government has shifted to an untested model, however, inclusion is not the only goal — and the model has become less predictable. The result has been the decision by Mexican President Felipe Calderon to deploy federal military forces to fight the influence and activities of the drug cartels throughout the country's periphery. This war between the states and the smugglers has put Mexico at war with itself at many levels. In some ways, the drug war is simply a repeat of the Mexican Revolution of 1910-1920.

The end game for the cartel wars is unclear. As the violence continues, the government will have to choose between continuing a confrontational strategy against the cartels or returning to the old system of inclusive acquiescence, and any decision on the matter could very likely be forced by public opinion turning against the anti-cartel effort. As the military is exposed to the cartels, it will become increasingly vulnerable to corruption, reducing its effectiveness. The bottom line is that, as long as drugs are produced in South America and consumed in North America and Mexico's borders remains porous (for the geographic reasons described above, this would be very difficult to change), the drug challenge will not go away. The challenge for Mexico is to decide when fighting the war on drugs is no longer concordant with its domestic political stability.

Energy

A direct result of Mexico's more inclusive political system is that it is very difficult to make sharp changes in policy, which is a primary reason behind the country's suffering energy sector. Because of the high costs of development, the state has never managed to implement policies that would promote growth — they would have too damaging an impact on the regional power balance. Oil proved to be a way around the distribution imbroglio.

Early costs were borne by foreign investors, assets were nationalized and the industry was seen as a free income stream for the state. But now those assets have been squeezed for everything they can produce, and Mexico requires a new wave of capital and technology — capital and technology it does not have — if it is to maintain its energy revenues.

The only option is to open up the industry to foreigners once again, but the 1917 constitution makes this illegal, and any attempt to change it would greatly upset powerful entrenched interests. Attempts at reform have so far fallen flat, and there is little to suggest that the country has the wherewithal to substantially change its energy policy.

Conclusion

Mexico is fundamentally challenged, first and foremost, by its physical geography. With mountain ranges for dissidents to hide in, expansive deserts that are difficult to control or defend and serious vulnerabilities to naval incursions, Mexico is inherently susceptible to serious security challenges. Throughout its history these threats have ranged from foreign invaders to leftist militants to upper-class rebels. Today's drug-trafficking organizations are only the latest manifestation of this challenge.

The country's rugged terrain lacks natural river transport networks, which makes it exceedingly difficult for Mexico to generate and accumulate capital. This leaves the country dependent on external capital and at the mercy of international market dynamics. Mexico shares an underdefended 2,000-mile-long border with the United States, the world's largest consumer market. This leaves Mexico's economy, which relies on the United States to import from Mexico everything from computers to drugs as well as to export to Mexico critical foodstuffs, highly dependent on the vagaries of the U.S. market. Mexico is also militarily reliant on the United States to defend Mexico's vulnerable eastern flank, and thus is highly vulnerable to U.S. political influence.

In the face of all of these challenges, it is no surprise that Mexico has remained embattled and underdeveloped compared its northern neighbor. Even before addressing issues arising at a political and policy level, Mexico must overcome the challenges of its physical geography.

PART 2: STRATEGIES AND TACTICS

6: Kaibiles: A New and Lethal Force
May 25, 2006

The investigation into the April beheadings of two Mexican police officers in the Pacific resort city of Acapulco has led to the Kaibiles, Guatemalan special forces deserters who have taken on the role of hired guns for Mexico's Gulf cartel, one of the most powerful drug cartels operating in the country.

Acapulco is fast becoming a battleground for cartels vying for control of drug-trafficking supply routes. The Zetas, the Mexican version of the Kaibiles, already are fighting on the Gulf cartel's side against skinhead gangs hired by the Beltran Leyva brothers, leaders of the rival Sinaloa cartel. With Mexican anti-drug authorities bearing down on the cartel, however, Kaibiles — as many as 40, according to Mexico's attorney general — were brought in to assist the Zetas in dealing with that front. With the Kaibiles now in the mix, fighting is likely to increase in the near future.

The Kaibiles, who are particularly brutal fighters trained in unconventional tactics, are infamous for forcing recruits to bite the heads off live chickens during training. In February 1999, the U.N. Commission for Historical Clarification (CEH), a body established after Guatemala's civil war to investigate human rights abuses that occurred during the conflict, harshly criticized the Kaibiles, citing human rights abuses. Kaibil actions during fighting in the 1980s made the group one of the most feared special forces units in Latin America. According to the CEH, for instance, Kaibil units responding to guerrilla attacks near the Guatemalan town of Las Dos Erres in December 1982 entered a village believed to be sympathetic to rebel groups. Although the Kaibiles reportedly found no weapons caches or guerrillas, they proceeded to conduct a two-day purge, killing everyone in the village, including women and children.

As part of a national reconciliation process following Guatemala's civil war, the Guatemalan army has been restructuring and transforming its units, and has since dropped the name "Kaibil" from its special forces units, referring to them only as the Special Forces Brigade. The units have participated in U.N. peacekeeping operations in Africa.

On Sept. 10, 2005, Mexican authorities arrested seven Guatemalan nationals in the southern Chiapas town of Comitan for smuggling weapons into Mexico. Guatemalan authorities later confirmed that at least four of the seven were former Kaibiles who had deserted their special operations unit at different times, the most recent one in 2004. Unlike the Zetas, the majority of whom deserted at the same time, Kaibiles apparently have been deserting in small numbers for several years now.

A former high-ranking Mexican military official, Gen. Ramon Mota Sanchez, said in an October 2005 interview that former Mexican soldiers who deserted to join the Zetas possibly were trained by Kaibiles. Between 1994 and 1999, he said, Kaibiles trained several dozen Mexican special operations soldiers.

After the end of wars in Central America, bands of militants, mercenaries and death squads suddenly found themselves without a war to fight. Like many of these groups, the Kaibiles looked abroad for work as hired guns, some of them entering the Mexican drug scene through contacts with the Zetas. Special forces units in one region often will share training or establish partnerships with neighboring units.

The presence of Kaibiles in Mexico has introduced an additional foreign element into the Mexican drug wars, along with Mara Salvatrucha from El Salvador and Calle 18 gangs from Guatemala. With the well-trained and brutal Kaibiles and Zetas now in the mix, however, Mexico's drug wars are likely to get even uglier. Moreover, it is only a question of time before their level of violence reaches fronts in the drug war on the U.S. border, such as Tijuana and Nuevo Laredo.

7: A Small Stone in a Big River
Dec. 14, 2006

Mexican President Felipe Calderon sent 6,500 federal police and troops to his home state of Michoacan on Dec. 12 in a bid to restore government control over an area that has witnessed some of the most brutal acts of violence at the hands of drug cartels. The deployment of such a large federal force specifically for combating the cartels is unprecedented in Mexico — though at best it will serve only to temporarily disrupt criminal activity in Michoacan, or divert it to other parts of Mexico.

Several cartels, chiefly the powerful Gulf and Sinaloa cartels, are vying for control of Michoacan, which now leads the country in the number of beheadings. The state is valuable to the cartels because its coastline offers many coves and inlets that can be used to receive shipments of drugs from South America for transshipment to U.S. markets. However, while the federal forces are disrupting cartel operations in Michoacan, the drug lords currently there could shift their activities to other coastal states, such as Guerrero or Jalisco. In that case, other ports of entry not solidly under the control of a single cartel, such as the popular tourist resorts of Acapulco and Puerto Vallarta, could witness more bloodshed.

In smaller-scale operations in the past, the military has failed to firmly establish long-term control in areas run by cartels. Calderon's predecessor, Vicente Fox, sent the army into Nuevo Laredo in Tamaulipas state in June 2005 and to Acapulco in Guerrero state in early 2006 to restore order. In Nuevo Laredo, the army completely took over the city's corrupt police department, though the cartels were able to effectively resume their operations after a short time — and the violence resumed. The military could yet experience some success in its Michoacan deployment, though the first day of operations — which focused on burning crops at more than 100 marijuana and heroin plantations and searching cars at roadblocks — netted just 13 arrests.

The military's ineffectiveness can be attributed not only to the sheer size of the problem, but to a great extent to corruption within the military and the government itself. The cartels are able to pay off military commanders or local officials to tip them off about impending raids or other operations. If the drug cartels have influence at the higher levels of Mexico's government and security forces, it is likely that the Michoacan operation will see federal troops taking aggressive action against some criminal groups, while others are left alone.

Calderon campaigned on a promise of controlling government corruption in Mexico, and followed up on that a week after taking office Dec. 1 by ordering federal police to raid the attorney general's office in Oaxaca state. This operation is his first major attempt to address the ongoing cycle of violence at the hands of the cartels.

Narcotics flow through Mexico like a river and, like rushing water, they will follow the path of least resistance. Placing a stone in one place will only make the flow divert around it — if not wash right over it. In order to make a serious dent in organized crime, Calderon would have to conduct a wide-scale operation throughout the whole country, not just send troops to one state. By using a large force, by Mexican standards, Calderon could be trying to ensure that his effort in Michoacan succeeds. Considering the strength of the cartels and the corruption at all levels of Mexican government, however, the operation likely will suffer the same fate as earlier ones.

8: The Vital Role of 'Gatekeepers' in the Smuggling Business
Dec. 23, 2006

In mid-2005, then-Mexican President Vicente Fox sent some 1,500 soldiers and federal police to the U.S.-Mexican border city of Nuevo Laredo in an effort to bring escalating drug-related violence under control. The effort failed, and by May 2006 the homicide rate had more than doubled compared with the same five-month period a year earlier. One possible reason for the violence in Nuevo Laredo is the continuing war between two rival cartels over whose "gatekeeper" will control the transshipment of drugs and other contraband through the city on their way north into the United States.

Until now, little has been revealed about the all-important role of gatekeepers in the flow of narcotics from Mexico into the United States, and the flow of money back into the hands of Mexico's drug lords. Sources familiar with this aspect of the drug trade, however, say the gatekeeper is one of the highest and most powerful people in a cartel's hierarchy, perhaps second only to the kingpin.

In drug-trade lingo, the "gatekeeper" controls the "plaza," the transshipment point off of one of the main highways on the Mexican side of the border where drugs and other contraband are channeled. In Spanish, the word "plaza" means a town square, though it also can mean a military stronghold or position. In this case, it means a cartel stronghold. A gatekeeper oversees the plaza, making sure each operation runs smoothly and that the plaza bosses are collecting "taxes" on any contraband that passes through. The going rate on a kilo of cocaine is approximately $500, while the tax on $1 million in cash heading south is about $10,000.

Gatekeepers also ensure that fees are collected on the movement of stolen cargo and illegal immigrants — including any militants who might be trying to enter the United States through Mexico. Regardless of a person's country of origin, money buys access into the United States through these plazas, though the fees charged for smuggling Middle Eastern and South Asian males into the United States are higher than for Mexicans or Central Americans. The gate-keepers' primary concern is ensuring that appropriate fees are collected and sent to cartel coffers — and they operate in whatever manner best suits a given circumstance: intimidation, extortion or violence. Of course, one of their main jobs is to ensure that corrupt Mexican police and military personnel are paid off so plaza operations can proceed undisturbed.

The main plazas in Mexico along the Texas border are in Matamoros, south of Brownsville; Reynosa, across the border from McAllen; Nuevo Laredo, across from Laredo; and Juarez, south of El Paso. These locations provide easy access to the U.S. interstate highway system, which the cartels use to deliver their drugs to the markets they control in major U.S. cities. Plazas also are operated in Piedras Negras opposite Eagle Pass and in Ojinaga opposite Presidio.

The plaza between Matamoros and Brownsville is controlled by Ezequiel Cardenas Guillen, or "Tony Tormenta," the brother of Gulf cartel leader Osiel Cardenas Guillen, who reportedly is running his cartel from a Mexican prison. Other gatekeepers operating in the area are Juan Gabriel Montes-Senano and Alfonso Lam-Lui.

Control of the Reynosa-McAllen plaza, which belongs to the Gulf cartel, reportedly is in flux. There are two prominent commanders from Los Zetas in the area: Gregorio "El Goyo" Sauceda-Gamboa and Jaime "El Humme" Gonzalez Duran. Some reports suggest that El Goyo recently was removed from his position as gatekeeper on the orders of Gulf chief Guillen, possibly because he was losing effectiveness due to alcoholism, drug addiction and cancer complications. El Humme, believed to be second-in-command of Los Zetas, might have been brought in to take over.

Edgar Valdez Villareal "La Barbie" and Miguel Trevino Morales operate in the contested plaza of Nuevo Laredo. La Barbie is a highly placed leader in the Sinaloa federation of cartels and chief of its enforcement arm, Los Pelones — the Sinaloa equivalent of Los Zetas. He previously operated out of Acapulco, where he reportedly oversaw the capture, videotaped torture and execution of a team of

Zeta operatives. Another gatekeeper in this area is Miguel Trevino Morales, who is believed to be affiliated with the rival Gulf cartel. The war between the two cartels over this important plaza is one of the reasons for the skyrocketing violence in the city.

Martin Romo-Lopez controls the plaza in Piedras Negras, while Sergio Abranda, Crispin Borinda-Cardenas and Benjamin Cuchtas-Valisrano operate in the plaza in Ojinaga.

The area around Juarez is firmly under Sinaloa federation control, and more cartel members appear to be moving into the area. The plaza in Juarez reportedly is controlled by the Escajeda family, through cousins Oscar Alonso Candelaria Escajeda and Jose Rodolfo Escajeda. Other alleged smugglers operating in the Juarez area are Jose Luis Portillo, Gonzalo Garcia and Pedro Sanchez. These men and the Escajeda cousins reportedly were associated with the Juarez cartel, which has been heavily damaged by the inter-cartel wars and the arrests of leaders. Many of the cartel members have since aligned themselves with the Sinaloa federation.

Because some provisions of the U.S. Patriot Act have made wiring money out of the United States more complicated than before — forcing the cartels to physically transfer money between operatives along the border — the gatekeepers also must ensure that these operations run smoothly. To facilitate this, the gatekeepers also operate the cartels' money-laundering operations, using small businesses along the border. U.S. law enforcement sources say there has been a fivefold increase in bulk currency seizures along the border in 2006 alone.

Although there are multiple smuggling routes through Mexico for drugs and other contraband, the plazas are the cartels' critical chokepoints. Therefore, efforts to shut down the flow of drugs or illegal immigrants cannot be effective until the gatekeepers are dealt with effectively. The gatekeepers' ability to heavily influence Mexican law enforcement and government officials through cash payouts and intimidation, however, suggests this will be no easy feat.

Even if Mexican law enforcement officers were to begin focusing their efforts on the gatekeepers, any success would be short-lived unless a sweeping, nationwide effort were made. When Fox sent the Mexican army into Nuevo Laredo in 2005, the impact on the cartels was minimal. A large, overwhelming law enforcement effort on both sides of the entire border would be required to shut down the plazas and bring down the gatekeepers, something Mexico is ill-equipped to do.

The Mexican government's recent efforts against the cartels in Michoacan state could prove to be effective against local organizations in the short term, but as long as the plazas are controlled by powerful gatekeepers, and the other routes through Mexico to the U.S. border are not impeded, the narcotics and drug money will continue to flow north and south.

9: The Price of Peace
May 2, 2007

So far, 2007 has been a bad year for one of Mexico's two most powerful drug-trafficking enterprises: the Gulf cartel. In January, the organization suffered a major hit when Mexico extradited its captured leader, Osiel Cardenas, to the United States. Then, on April 17, authorities arrested five Gulf members just south of the Texas border in Reynosa. Among those taken into custody was Juan Oscar Garza, purportedly an important Gulf cartel leader in the city. Less than a week later, authorities in Nuevo Laredo captured Gulf cartel leader Eleazar Medina Rojas. The Mexican Attorney General's office described Medina as "a major killer."

During his 2006 election campaign, Mexican President Felipe Calderon pledged to take measures to quell the brutal cartel war that has been raging in his country since 2003 — a war that has escalated dramatically over the past two years. Calderon, in attempting to fulfill his campaign promise, is responsible for the angst currently being felt by the Gulf cartel. Sources familiar with the operation say the Gulf cartel is the government's primary target now, and that Calderon hopes to have it dismantled within a year. Should this operation succeed, it will have public security ramifications on both sides of the U.S.-Mexico border.

The immediate benefit, of course, would go to Mexico's other main cartel, the Sinaloa organization, which would assume control of the Gulf cartel's operations in many areas. However, with the long-running turf war between these two organizations concluded, the brutal violence that has spread across the country could subside, at least for a time. On the other hand, members of the cartel's infamous Los Zetas enforcement arm would be left without a master — or the protection that comes with being part of a powerful cartel. At least some of the Zetas would flee into the United States, spreading their particularly brutal style of violence north of the border.

The Cartels

Given its geographic location, Mexico has long been used as a staging and transshipment point for narcotics, illegal aliens and other contraband destined for U.S. markets from Mexico, South America and elsewhere. The smuggling routes into the United States are controlled by the cartels, which operate major transshipment points, or plazas, run by a top figure within each cartel known as the "gatekeeper."

Currently, the majority of Mexico's smuggling routes are controlled by three key cartels: Gulf, Sinaloa and Tijuana — though Tijuana is the least powerful. This has not always been the case. As recently as November 2005, the Juarez cartel was the dominant player in the center of the country, controlling a large percentage of the cocaine traffic from Mexico into the United States. The death of Amado Carrillo Fuentes in 1997, however, was the beginning of the end of the Juarez cartel. After the organization collapsed, some elements of it were absorbed into the Sinaloa cartel — a relatively young and aggressive organization that has gobbled up much of the Juarez cartel's former territory.

Over time, the balance of power between the various cartels shifts as new ones emerge and older ones weaken and collapse. The interplay between cartels is, in fact, very much like that between some nations: The chances for peace are highest when a kind of stable coexistence is maintained and profits flow freely. However, a disruption in the system — such as the arrests or deaths of cartel leaders — generates tensions and, frequently, bloodshed as rivals move in to exploit the power vacuum.

Leadership vacuums sometimes are created by law enforcement successes against a particular cartel — thus, cartels often will attempt to use law enforcement against one another, either by bribing Mexican officials to take action against a rival or by leaking intelligence about a rival's operations to the Mexican government or the U.S. Drug Enforcement Administration.

The Current Cartel War

The collapse of the Juarez cartel, the February 2002 death of Tijuana cartel leader and chief enforcer Ramon Arellano Felix, who was killed in a shootout with police in Mazatlan, and the March 14, 2003, capture of Gulf cartel kingpin Cardenas in Matamoros combined to spark the current period of brutal warfare among what were then the three main cartels. The aggressive Sinaloa cartel saw those developments as an opportunity to expand its territory — and profits — and made its move.

Sinaloa's expansion efforts forced the Tijuana cartel to cede the plaza in the northwestern border city of Mexicali, while Sinaloa's move into Gulf territory in Nuevo Laredo made that town a war zone. The Gulf and Tijuana organizations did unite briefly against the powerful Sinaloa cartel through a deal their leaders struck in prison in 2004. The alliance crumbled, however, as Cardenas and Benjamin Arellano Felix fell to squabbling in 2005. At that point, the Gulf cartel began launching violent incursions into the Tijuana cartel territories of Mexicali and Tijuana, and the three-way war was on again, though the heaviest fighting has been between Gulf and Sinaloa.

The Tijuana cartel was further weakened in August 2006 when its chief, Javier Arellano Felix, was arrested by the U.S. Coast Guard on a boat off the coast of Southern California. Mexican army troops also were sent to Tijuana in January in an operation to restore order to the border city and root out corrupt police officers, who mostly were cooperating with the Tijuana cartel. As a result of these efforts, the Tijuana cartel is unable to project much power outside of its base in Tijuana.

This current cartel war is being waged not only for control of the smuggling plazas into the United States, such as Nuevo Laredo, Mexicali and Tijuana, but also for the locations used for Mexico's incoming drug shipments, in places such as Acapulco, Cancun and Michoacan, and for control of critical points on transshipment routes through the center of the country, such as Hermosillo.

While there has always been some level of violence between the Mexican cartels, the current war has resulted in a notable escalation in the level of brutality. One significant cause of this uptick is the change in the composition of the cartels' enforcement arms. Historically, cartel leaders performed much of their own dirty work, and figures such as Cardenas and Ramon Arellano Felix were recognized for the number of rivals they killed on their rise to the top of their respective organizations. In the recent past, however, the cartels have begun to contract out the enforcement functions to highly trained outsiders. For example, when cartels such as the Tijuana organization began to use active or retired police officers against their enemies, their rivals were forced to find enforcers capable of countering this strength. As a result, the Gulf cartel hired Los Zetas, a group of elite anti-drug paratroopers and intelligence operatives who deserted their federal Special Air Mobile Force Group in 1991. The Sinaloa cartel, meanwhile, formed a similar armed force called Los Pelones, literally meaning "the bald ones" but typically understood to mean "new soldiers" for the shaved heads normally sported by military recruits. Although the cartels had long outgunned Mexican police, these highly trained and aggressive enforcers upped the ante even further, introducing military-style tactics and even more advanced weapons.

The life of a Mexican drug cartel enforcer can be exciting, brutal — and short. Los Zetas and Los Pelones are constantly attacking one another, and some members of the groups even have posted videos on the Internet of them torturing and executing their rivals. Beheading rival enforcers also has become common. The current cartel war has proved to be a long and arduous struggle, and there has been heavy attrition among both organizations. Because of this attrition, the cartels have recently begun to bring fresh muscle to the fight. Los Zetas have formed relationships with former members of the Guatemalan special forces known as Kaibiles, and with members of the Mara Salvatrucha (MS-13) street gang.

It is this environment of extreme and often gratuitous violence — killings, beheadings and rocket-propelled grenade attacks — that has sparked Calderon's actions against the Gulf cartel. Why he is focusing specifically on the Gulf cartel is unclear, though it is possible the government has better intelligence on it than on the others. Or perhaps it is because the Gulf cartel has a more centralized command structure than does Sinaloa, which is a federation of several smaller cartels. Of course, the Gulf cartel itself has argued that the Calderon administration is on the Sinaloa payroll and is being used by Sinaloa to destroy its rival. Another possible reason is that taking out Los Zetas — who have become emblematic of extreme cartel violence — would be a major accomplishment for the new president.

The Organizational Structure

The cartels are large, intricate crime syndicates often made up of supporting alliances of smaller cartels, such as the Sinaloa federation. Thus, even if the arrest of a leader or other figure damages one part of the organization, another part of the group can assume the damaged part's role. Additionally, the cartels often are compartmentalized so that one section's removal does not compromise the group as a whole. Further hardening them against law enforcement efforts are the cartels' robust organizational structures. They are distributed horizontally, and are based on family relationships and personal alliances.

Because of this, multiple figures can fill leadership vacuums when high-ranking members are arrested or killed.

That said, however, the Gulf cartel has borne the brunt of Calderon's anti-cartel offensive to date — and even a robust organization with redundant structures will begin to crack when it is hit repeatedly and in different locations, as the Gulf cartel has been. This pressure has resulted in retaliatory attacks against law enforcement and the Sinaloa cartel, which is being blamed for the government's targeting of the Gulf cartel. In the short term, then, the violence will continue, perhaps even escalating as the Gulf cartel fights to survive and maintain its territories and profit stream.

Once there is blood in the water, so to speak, other cartels are likely to swarm over the share of the market the weakened Gulf organization no longer can defend. Sinaloa already is attempting to wrest Nuevo Laredo from Gulf control, and there are indications that Sinaloa also has begun to make a grab for Matamoros. Should the Sinaloa cartel succeed in taking these vital (and lucrative) plazas from the Gulf cartel, it would significantly reduce Gulf's revenues and power. If that happens, and the government action against the Gulf cartel continues, the once-powerful organization could go the way of the Juarez cartel.

On the public security front, however, if Sinaloa is able to make a powerful move and quickly consolidate control over Gulf territory, the result could be the end of the current cartel war and a period of relative calm. The drugs and other contraband will continue to flow, but the violence that has placed so much pressure on the Mexican government will be over — at least for a season.

Although the ferocious shootouts have been the most pressing issue in the press and public opinion — and one that can be resolved by taking out one of the main cartels involved — not all the violence is connected to inter-cartel warfare. Mexico also has a long history of attacks against journalists, as well as honest police officers and others who oppose the cartels and their criminal activities. Thus, even if the inter-cartel warfare is dampened by establishing Sinaloa as the new dominant entity, journalists, police and pro-justice crusaders still will have to live in fear of their area warlords. Ordinary civilians, however, will be less likely to be killed in the crossfire between the cartels.

Consequences

Implosion of the Gulf cartel, though, would leave Los Zetas and their Kaibile and MS-13 allies exposed. Certainly, considering the number of government officials and Sinaloa and Tijuana cartel members Los Zetas and their confederates have killed and terrorized, there will be many who would seek to hunt them down. A collapse of the Gulf cartel infrastructure and the organization and revenues required to maintain safety for the group could result in open hunting season on Los Zetas.

Facing that situation, the remaining Zetas could attempt to form an alliance with another cartel, form their own cartel or perhaps even be forced to flee from Mexico. Should they run, their links with the Kaibiles and MS-13 could prove to be mutually beneficial. MS-13 could help shelter Los Zetas in Central America or even the United States. Los Zetas, on the other hand, possess a level of training, discipline and experience that would be quite useful to MS-13. One thing is certain: the Zetas are brutal thugs and, wherever they land, they will continue to commit crimes.

Years of operating in towns along the U.S.-Mexico border has allowed the Zetas to form close relationships with a number of criminals and organized crime organizations in the United States. Some, in fact, already have been associated with killings as far north as Dallas. There also is far more money to be made in the United States than in Central America. Although that opportunity brings with it the risk of having to evade U.S. law enforcement, it is highly likely that a number of Zetas will find their way to U.S. cities.

Their history suggests they would be most comfortable living in cities along or near the border, where they could quickly flee back to Mexico should U.S. law enforcement close in. Being part of the Gulf cartel, Los Zetas would have better connections in places adjacent to the cartel's plazas, such as the Texas border cities of Laredo and

Brownsville, or in cities along the smuggling route, like San Antonio or Houston. However, the Gulf cartel's distribution network stretches to places such as New Orleans, Atlanta and Washington — meaning Zetas also could turn up in those cities as well.

10: The Dynamics of the Gun Trade
Oct. 24, 2007

The number of drug-related killings in Mexico in 2007 already has surpassed 2,000, an increase of 300 over the same period last year, according to statistics reported by Mexican media outlets. Moreover, sources familiar with the issue say police officials in some jurisdictions have been purposely underreporting drug-related homicides, which suggests that the real body count is even higher.

In addition to the Mexican drug cartels that engage in torture and killings (and at times beheadings), armed criminal gangs are notorious kidnappers — prompting some to call Mexico the "kidnapping capital of the world." This has resulted in a boom for armored car manufacturers and security companies, given that most wealthy people living in the country own armored vehicles, and many employ executive protection teams to provide security for themselves, their families and their homes. Additionally, heavily armed criminal gangs regularly commit armed robberies, muggings and express kidnappings.

The one constant in these violent crimes is guns. Mexico's robust gun culture stretches back to revolutions, counterrevolutions and revolutionary bandits such as Pancho Villa. Because of this culture, guns are common in Mexico — despite strict gun-control laws and licensing procedures. This demand for guns has created an illicit market that not only is intimately related to the U.S. market for illegal narcotics but also, in many ways, mirrors the dynamics of that market. Drugs flow north and guns flow south — resulting in handsome profits for those willing to run the risks.

Mexican Laws

Similar to the U.S. Constitution, the 1917 Mexican Constitution guarantees Mexico's inhabitants the right to have "arms of any kind in their possession for their protection and legitimate defense." However, the constitution includes many caveats on private citizens' ownership of guns, prohibiting those "expressly forbidden by law" and those "the nation may reserve for the exclusive use of the army, navy or national guard." Furthermore, Mexican law calls for long prison terms for violators.

Mexico, then, has some of the world's strictest gun-control laws — making guns difficult to obtain legally. Average citizens who want to purchase guns for self-defense or recreational purposes must first get approval from the government. Then, because there are no private-sector gun stores in the country, they must buy weapons through the Defense Department's Arms and Ammunition Marketing Division (UCAM). In accordance with Mexican law, the UCAM carefully limits the calibers of guns it sells. For example, it does not sell handguns larger than a .380 or .38 Special. Also, under Mexican law, popular handguns such as .357 magnum revolvers and 9mm pistols are exclusively reserved for the armed forces.

Regardless of these efforts, the illicit arms market has been thriving for decades — not only because firearm laws are not evenly enforced but also because criminals have found a way to circumvent efforts to stem the flow of guns. Moreover, not all illegal guns are in the hands of cartel members and street criminals. A healthy percentage of them are purchased by affluent Mexicans who are not satisfied with the selection of calibers available through the UCAM. Sources say it is not at all unusual to find Mexicans who own prohibited .357 magnum revolvers or .45-caliber pistols for self-defense against kidnappers and armed robbers. In addition to ballistic considerations, Latin machismo is also a factor — some Mexican men want to own and carry powerful, large-caliber pistols.

The Mechanics of the Gun Trade

This mixture of the historical Mexican gun culture, machismo, strong desire for guns, lax enforcement of gun laws, official corruption and a raging cartel war has created a high demand for illegal guns. Guns sold on the black market in Mexico can fetch as much as 300 percent of their normal market value — a profit margin similar to that of the cocaine trafficked by the cartels. The laws of economics dictate that where there is a strong demand — and a considerable profit margin — entrepreneurs will devise ways to meet that demand. Of course, the illicit markets are no different from the legitimate economy in this respect, and a number of players have emerged to help supply Mexico's appetite for illicit weaponry.

Millions of Mexicans reside (legally and otherwise) in the United States, and the two countries conduct a staggering amount of commerce (legal and otherwise) across the border. In this context, then, when one considers that there are more gun stores in a typical small town in Texas than there are in all of Mexico City, it should come as no surprise that a large number of the weapons found on the illicit arms market in Mexico originated in the United States. In fact, Mexican officials say that as much as 90 percent of the illegal weapons they seize are of U.S. origin.

The most obvious players in the gun trade are the cartels themselves, which not only have the financial resources to buy guns in the United States but also are in a position to receive guns in trade for narcotics from their distribution contacts north of the border. The traditional pattern for cartel operations over the past few decades has been to smuggle drugs north over the border and return with money and guns — many times over the same routes and by the same conveyances. In addition to the problem of the notoriously corrupt Mexican customs officials, efforts to stem the flow of guns into Mexico also have been hampered by technological limitations. For example, until recently, Mexican authorities lacked X-ray equipment to inspect vehicles entering the country, and this inspection capacity still remains limited.

The cartels also obtain weapons from contacts along their supply networks in South and Central America, where substantial quantities of military ordnance have been shipped over decades to supply insurgencies and counterinsurgencies. Explosives from domestic Mexican sources also are widely available and are generally less expensive than guns.

Aside from the cartels, other criminal syndicates are dedicated to the arms trade. These groups can range from small mom-and-pop operations involving a few individuals who obtain weapons from family members residing in the United States or Central America to large organizations with complex networks that buy dozens or hundreds of weapons at a time.

As in other criminal enterprises in Mexico, such as drug smuggling or kidnapping, it is not unusual to find police officers and military personnel involved in the illegal arms trade. On Sept. 12, three high-ranking police commanders from Baja California and Baja California Sur states were arrested by U.S. Bureau of Alcohol, Tobacco and Firearms (ATF) agents in Phoenix for illegally purchasing weapons at a gun show. (U.S. law prohibits foreigners from buying weapons.) Over the past few years, several Mexican government officials have been arrested on both sides of the border for participating in the arms trade.

Although it is illegal for Mexican nationals to buy guns in the United States and for Americans to haul guns to Mexico, entrepreneurs have found a variety of ways to skirt such laws. Perhaps one of the least recognized ploys is plain old document fraud. Fake documents — which are easily obtained along the border — range in quality (and price) from poorly rendered counterfeits to genuine documents obtained with the assistance of corrupt government officials. Using such documents, a Mexican citizen can pose as a U.S. citizen and pass the required background checks to buy guns — unless, that is, the prospective gun buyer was foolish enough to assume the identity of an American with a criminal record.

Perhaps the most common way to purchase guns is by using a "straw-man" buyer (sometimes in combination with document fraud).

That is, paying a person with a clean record who has legal standing to buy the gun. This also is a tried-and-true tactic used by criminals in the United States who are ineligible to purchase guns due to prior convictions. The "straw man" in these cases often is a girlfriend or other associate who is paid to buy a gun for them. Also, with so many family relations spanning the border, it is easy for a Mexican citizen to ask an American relative to purchase a gun or guns on their behalf.

While document fraud and straw-man purchases can be used to bypass the law and fool respectable gun dealers, not all gun dealers are respectable. Some will falsify their sales records in order to sell guns to people they know are not legally permitted to have them — especially if the guns are being sold at a premium price. ATF does conduct audits of gun dealers, but even after a steep decline in the number of federal firearms dealers over the past decade, there still are not enough inspectors to regularly audit the records of the more than 50,000 federal firearms license holders. This lack of oversight and the temptation of easy money cause some dealers to break the law knowingly.

Guns also can be obtained for the Mexican black market through theft. The cartels traditionally have tasked groups of young street thugs in the United States with stealing items (such as pickup trucks and sport utility vehicles) for the cartels to use or resell in Mexico. Now, intelligence reports suggest that these thugs have begun to rob gun stores in towns along the border. One such group is the Gulf cartel-related "Zetitas" (little Zetas), which is active in the Texas cities of Houston, Laredo and San Antonio, as well as other places.

A cartel connection is suspected when the weapons and ammunition stolen are popular with the cartels, such as assault rifles and FN Five-Seven pistols. The FN Five-Seven and the FN P-90 personal defense weapon shoot a 5.7 x 28mm round that has been shown to penetrate body armor, as well as vehicle doors and windows. Because of this, they recently have become very popular with cartel enforcers, who have begun to call the weapons matapolicias — police killers. Several police officials have been killed with these guns this year — though officers also have been killed with .357 magnum revolvers,

.45-caliber pistols and AK-47- or M16-style assault rifles. Still, due to the rising popularity of the 5.7 x 28mm weapons among cartel gunmen, many of these somewhat esoteric (and excellently manufactured) weapons are acquired in the United States and end up south of the border. Any time one of these weapons is connected to a crime on either side of the border, a cartel link should be considered.

The gun problem in Mexico is similar to the drug problem in the United States in that it is extremely difficult to reduce the supply of the illicit items without first reducing the demand. Any small reduction in the supply leads to an increase in price, which further stimulates efforts to provide a supply. Therefore, as long as the demand for such weapons persists, people will continue to find creative ways to meet that demand and make a profit. With that demand being fed, at least in part, by drug cartels that are warring for control of drug-trafficking routes into the United States, the two problems of drugs and guns will continue to be deeply intertwined.

11: The Big Business of Organized Crime
Feb. 13, 2008

Mexican President Felipe Calderon told a U.N. representative in Mexico City recently that the deployment of the Mexican military in counternarcotics operations is only a temporary solution, and that he plans to phase out the military's role in these efforts. In recent weeks, the military launched a large-scale security operation in select cities along the U.S.-Mexico border, disarming local police forces and conducting sweeps and raids in an effort to strike back at the increasingly violent Mexican drug cartels.

Calderon's comments address a standing question on both sides of the border: What is the best way to deal with cartel activity? Germane to that question is defining just what it is that the security forces are up against.

The violence taking place in northern Mexico — and leaking across the border into the southern United States — is viewed by some as the result of the actions of narco-terrorists, while others call it an insurgency. But for the most part, those charged with countering the problem refer to it as criminality — more specifically, as organized crime. Defining the problem this way shapes the decisions regarding the tools and policies that are best suited to fighting it.

On both sides of the border, the primary forces tasked with dealing with the drug cartels and the spillover effects are law enforcement elements. In a law enforcement operation, as opposed to a counterinsurgency or counterterrorism operation, the ultimate goal is not only to stop the criminal behavior but also to detain the criminals and amass sufficient evidence to try them in court. The need for such evidence is not always as pressing in counterterrorism cases, in which the intelligence case can be made without having to reach the stricter threshold prosecution would require. Since taking office, Calderon has involved the military more than his predecessors in what traditionally has been the realm of law enforcement. This has had positive results against drug traffickers, at the expense of occasional higher tensions between federal and local authorities.

Meanwhile, on the U.S. side of the border, the Bush administration's war on terrorism appears much more pressing and therefore receives many more resources than the fight against illegal drug activity and border violence. This does not mean the United States has not devoted modern technological resources to battle drug traffickers along the border. In fact, it has devoted significant intelligence assets to assist in tracking and cracking down on the drug cartels, from collecting signals and electronic intelligence to offering training and assistance to Mexican forces.

In viewing this as mainly a law enforcement issue, rather than a military one, several additional problems are being encountered on both sides of the border — not the least of which is a significant lack of coordination. On the Mexican side, local law enforcement often is infiltrated by the cartels and does not cooperate fully with essential government agencies — a phenomenon not unheard of north of the border as well. On the U.S. side, the various counties along the border like to run their own programs, and there are issues of federal American Indian land and private land to consider as well. A similar split between federal and local regulations and enforcement occurs on the Mexico side, where drug laws are all federal, so local officials can make arrests but must hand over suspects to the federal police. Further, while there is some level of coordination between the Mexican and the U.S. sides, frequently there is a lack of communication or significant miscommunication (for example, an operation on one side of the border may not be communicated to the other side).

These problems exist in many places, but they are particularly sensitive on the U.S.-Mexico border. A miscommunication between the United States and, say, the Colombian government does not have the immediate impact as a similar miscommunication along the U.S. border. Moves are under way to increase the coordination of overall counterdrug efforts along the border, but the contentious issue of immigration adds a second layer to the problem. For the United States, while there apparently are similarities between what is happening in Mexico and previous counterdrug fights in Colombia — or even in Thailand and Afghanistan — the contiguous border consistently adds a layer of complexity to the problem.

The United States has experience shutting down major drug-trafficking routes. It significantly disrupted the Caribbean drug routes using naval interdiction (though this shifted many of these routes to Mexico, accelerating the rise of the Mexican cartels). And there is plenty of global experience sealing borders. The Germans were quite effective at sealing the border after World War II, as were many of the Soviet bloc states. The problem, of course, with completely sealing a border is that it stops trade, something the United States is not willing to do. Therefore, if the United States cannot effectively seal the border without risking trade, it instead can channel the flow of traffic and migration across the border. But even by channeling the flow, it is extremely difficult to separate the illegal trade from the legal.

As we have mentioned before, there is a significant economic component to this trade, both legal and illegal. By some estimates, some $24 billion a year is transferred to Mexico as a result of the drug trade. This is essentially free money and needs to go somewhere, making it a substantial portion of the Mexican economy. While the Mexican government is keen to stop the violence along the border and among the cartels, in some ways it is less interested in stopping the flow of money. History has shown that countries with large-scale criminal enterprises — such as the United States in the 1920s and 1930s — get rich, given the tremendous pool of capital available for investment. This illicit money eventually works it way into the system through legal channels.

This is a fundamental aspect of the phenomenon we are seeing now in Mexico. It is a classic case of organized crime. The Mexican drug cartels are, for the most part, organized crime groups. What distinguishes Mexican organized crime groups and others from revolutionaries, terrorists and hybrid organizations such as the Revolutionary Armed Forces of Colombia (FARC) is the underlying principle of making money.

In the global system, there is an economy of crime. It currently is built around drugs, but any item that is illegal in one place and legal in other and has an artificially inflated price quickly can become the center of the system. Human trafficking, smuggling and counterfeiting are cases in point, as was alcohol during Prohibition. Products move from where they are legal (or at least not well controlled) to where they are in demand but illegal. The money, of course, moves in the opposite direction and eventually ends up in the normal banking system. Organized crime wants to make money and it might want to manipulate the system, but it does not seek to overthrow the system or transform society. Insurgencies and revolutions seek to transform.

In the end, organized crime is about making money. Endemic organized crime leads to corruption and collusion, and in the long term often burns itself out as the money earned through its activities eventually moves into the legal economic system. When organized crime groups become rich enough, they move their money into legitimate businesses in order to launder it or a least use it, eventually turning it into established money that has entered the realm of business.

This can get more complicated when organized crime and insurgents/ guerrillas overlap, as is the case with FARC.

The problems we are seeing in Mexico are similar to those we have seen in past cases, in which criminal elements become faction-alized. In Mexico, these factions are fighting over control of drug routes and domain. The battles that are taking place are largely the result of fighting among the organized crime groups, rather than cartels fighting the Mexican government. In some ways, the Mexican military and security forces are a third party in this — not the focus. Ultimately, the cartels — not the government — control the level of violence and security in the country.

As new groups emerge and evolve, they frequently can be quite violent and in some sense anarchic. When a new group of drug dealers moves into a neighborhood, it might be flamboyant and excessively violent. It is the same on a much larger scale with organized crime cartels. However, although cartel infighting is tolerated to some extent, the government is forced to react when the level of violence starts to get out of hand. This is what we are seeing in Mexico.

However, given that organized crime tends to become more conservative as it grows and becomes more established, the situation in Mexico could be reaching a tipping point. For example, during the summer of 2007, the Gulf and Sinaloa cartels declared a temporary truce as their rivalry began to impact their business operations. As the competition among the cartels settles, they could begin to draw back their forces and deal with those members who are excessively violent or out of control. This is simply a way of ensuring the existence of their operations. The American Mafia followed a similar pattern, evolving into an organism with strong discipline and control.

There is a question now as to whether the Mexican cartels are following the American model or imitating the Colombian model, which is a hybrid of organized crime and an insurgency. In fact, they might be following both. Mexico, in some sense, is two countries. The North has a much higher standard of living than the rest of the country, especially the area south of Mexico City. In the North, we could ultimately see a move in the direction of the American Mafia, whereas in the South — the home of the domestic guerrilla groups Zapatista National Liberation Army and Popular Revolutionary Army — it could shift more toward the Colombian model.

While the situation is evolving, the main battle in Mexico continues to be waged among various cartel factions, rather than among the cartels and the Mexican government or security forces. The goal of organized crime, and the goal of many of these cartels, is to get rich within the system, with minor variations on how that is achieved. A revolutionary group, on the other hand, wants to overthrow and change the system. The cartels obviously are working outside the legal framework, but they are not putting forward an alternative — nor do they seem to want to. Rather, they can achieve their goals simply through payoffs and other forms of corruption. The most likely outcome is not a merger between the cartels and the guerrilla groups, or even a shift in the cartels' priorities to include government overthrow. As the government turns up the pressure, the real concern is that the cartels will adopt insurgent-style tactics.

Organized crime is not street crime; it is systemic geopolitical crime. It is a significant social force, bringing huge amounts of capital into a system. This flow of money can reshape the society. But this criminal supply chain runs parallel to, and in many cases intersects, the legitimate global supply chain. Whether through smuggling and money laundering or increased investment capital and higher consumption rates, the underground and aboveground economies intersect.

U.S. and Mexican counternarcotics operations have an instant impact on the supply chain. Such operations shift traffic patterns across the border, affect the level of stability in the border areas — where there is a significant amount of manufacturing and trade — and impact sensitive social and political issues between the two countries, particularly immigration. In this light, then, violence is only one small part of the total impact that cartel activities and government counternarcotics efforts are having on the border.

12: Mexico Security Memo
Feb. 18, 2008

IEDs in the Arsenal

The daily routine of drug cartel violence in Mexico was punctuated this past week by an improvised explosive device (IED) that exploded Feb. 15 in Mexico City. The bomb detonated in front of an empty lot about two blocks from a Mexico City police building and one block from a subway entrance. An unidentified man died and one woman was wounded in the explosion. The homemade device appears to have been composed of a small amount of explosives and ball bearings and rigged to be detonated by a cellular telephone. Police said the small size of the device suggests that it was intended to grab attention, not to cause mass casualties. However, the presence of the ball bearings clearly suggests otherwise.

It is still unclear exactly what happened, though the most likely scenario is that the device detonated prematurely while the bomber was carrying it; he likely intended to place it in the vicinity of the police building. The woman wounded in the blast, who is thought to be the bomber's accomplice, is believed to have links to Sinaloa drug traffickers, which suggests the bombing was carried out on behalf of one of the country's most powerful cartels.

If the bombing was in fact carried out by a drug cartel, the significance of the incident cannot be overstated. This effectively would mean that the country's heavily armed and capable drug cartels have added IEDs to their already powerful arsenals of assault rifles, rocket-propelled grenades and light anti-tank rockets. Up to this point, the use of IEDs was noticeably — and somewhat surprisingly — absent from the country's drug war, despite the fact that suitable explosives are readily available and quite inexpensive on the black market. In other countries with strong cartel presences, such as Colombia, car bombs and IEDs have become part of daily life. The use of IEDs in Mexico would fit with part of an emerging trend STRATFOR has observed: Mexican drug cartels' adoption of insurgent-style tactics in their battle against security forces.

At this point, it is difficult to determine whether the Sinaloa cartel or any other cartel intends to continue with an escalating IED campaign against the government. However, there appear to be few disincentives, especially since this incident was carried out without detection. In addition, the premature detonation will be an important part of this bombmaker's learning curve in constructing future devices (provided, of course, that it was not the bombmaker who died). While the high number of killings so far has been a nightmare for President Felipe Calderon's administration, it pales in comparison to the prospect of large IEDs causing mass casualties — including innocent civilians.

Intimidating Tipsters

Beyond the guns and bombs, one of the most effective weapons used by Mexico's drug cartels is intimidation. This has taken many forms over the years, most of it aimed at corrupt or uncooperative police and government officials. A twist in this practice emerged this past week in Tijuana, Baja California state, when bodies began to appear with signs of torture and notes warning residents not to use the army's telephone or Internet tip line, which was established for citizens to report suspicious drug activity. Some of the victims were found with severed fingers, an apparent reference to dialing a telephone, while others were found with notes listing the army's tip line telephone number or e-mail address, or more explicit notes warning others not to cooperate with authorities.

While intimidation is nothing new in the Mexican drug trade, these incidents underscore the brutality of the business — and the lengths to which cartel members will go to continue their operations.

13: Organized Crime in Mexico
March 11, 2008

Organized crime in Mexico is centered on the transit of illegal drugs into the United States. In essence, Mexican organized crime groups are supply chain entities, competing for suppliers in Central and South America, rapid and low-friction transit routes in Mexico and across borders and consumers in the United States. Competition among the major Mexican cartels is about geography — access to and control of the most lucrative trade paths. This competition leads to wars between cartels, which can spill over into the civilian population. The cartels generally try to avoid confrontations with law enforcement and the military in Mexico and instead seek to mitigate their security risks through bribery, extortion, threats and incentives. The trafficking of illegal drugs through Mexico generates billions of dollars a year, and the Mexican cartels launder this money through construction and real estate companies, small businesses and restaurants and hotels and money exchanges. In many ways the cartels are personality-dependent — controlled by family groups and subject to rapid disintegration or disruption when the leadership is killed or imprisoned. However, leadership vacuums are filled quickly as the cartels continue working to take over lucrative drug routes.

History

Organized crime in Mexico has a long history. Outlaw gangs with limited power in northern Mexico existed as far back as the 19th century. Through the 1960s, the main organized criminal element along the U.S.-Mexico border involved small smuggling operations. These groups had limited reach and resources.

As the popularity of cocaine grew in the United States in the 1970s, criminal organizations began to gain much more power and influence on a national level. This rise in power accelerated in the 1980s as the United States government moved to shut down the Caribbean smuggling corridor, primarily run by Colombian drug traffickers, which had served as the primary route of drugs into the United States through the 1970s. In response to this move, drug traffickers began using Mexico as a transshipment point for U.S.-bound cocaine, as the country represented the path of least resistance to the movement of contraband. It was during this time that Mexican cartels evolved into the powerful organizations they are today.

Changes in the cartels' standing and composition can be described most accurately as a system of shifting and adjusting alliances inside Mexico, though outside factors such as the death or arrest of a leader have also played a role in shaping the fate of individual groups.

Geography

Organized crime exists in nearly every corner of Mexico. Small local street gangs involved in a variety of crimes, including robbery, theft, extortion and kidnapping, can be found in every city. However, it is the country's drug cartels — extended criminal organizations with a monopoly on the drug trade — that hold the real power, and these criminal organizations tend to be concentrated in specific geographic locations. Several cartels have also begun to establish logistics and criminal networks in the United States in order to facilitate the movement of contraband into and out of Mexico. Mexican cartels have not yet established a significant presence in Central or South America — the former being of only minimal value to the drug supply chain, the latter (i.e., Colombia) already under the sway of South American organized crime — relying instead on criminal groups in those areas to transport drugs to be moved through Mexico.

Mexico's location between the world's largest producer and the world's largest consumer of cocaine makes it a natural transshipment point for narcotics. Mexico's location became even more important for drug traffickers due to the U.S. government's increased efforts to shut down air and maritime routes in the Caribbean smuggling corridor.

Within Mexico, the areas under cartel control generally correspond to routes used to ship drugs from South America to the United

States and shipment channels for precursor chemicals and pirated goods from China. Whether or not a region is of strategic importance to the movement of drugs is the primary factor determining the likelihood that it will come under the control of a major cartel. Areas of cartel concentration are the area along the U.S. border; coastal port cities on the Pacific Ocean, Gulf of Mexico and Caribbean Sea; and cities and towns located on federal highways between these points. Mexico's large cartels are not as concentrated in the remainder of the country, including Mexico City and much of the country's central and southern interior.

While some South American drugs come into Mexico on land at the Guatemalan border, most are shipped via air or boat along two main routes. The first route enters the Yucatan Peninsula by either remote airstrips or the port of Cancun and then goes across the border into Texas by land, air or sea along the Gulf of Mexico. The second route enters the country via port cities in Guerrero and Michoacan states and then goes either inland or along the Pacific coast toward the U.S. border.

Historically, the largest and most powerful drug cartels in Mexico have been based in northern Mexico, and most important, they have all established control over entry points into the United States (which is to say they have established predominance and have bribed police, immigration/customs officials and government officials in towns at these entry points). These groups have based their operations out of large to medium-sized Mexican cities located along the U.S. border: the Arellano Felix Organization in Tijuana, the Juarez cartel in Ciudad Juarez, the Gulf cartel in Reynosa. The one exception has been the Sinaloa federation, which is based out of Sinaloa state, approximately 500 miles south of the Arizona border. Drug cartels that have developed in southwestern Mexico have never achieved the same amount of power as their northern counterparts, which control the final step in the supply chain of drugs moving north.

One way to describe the territorial control of these groups is to divide Mexico into cartel "states." With its capital city in Reynosa, the Gulf cartel's territory includes Tamaulipas state, the eastern portion

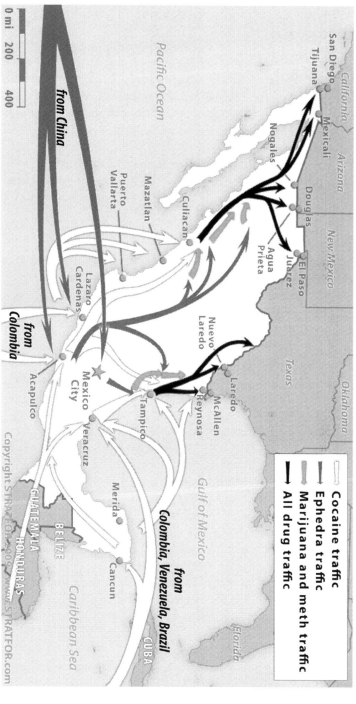

DRUG TRAFFICKING THROUGH MEXICO

Legend:
- Cocaine traffic
- Ephedra traffic
- Marijuana and meth traffic
- All drug traffic

from China

from Colombia

from Colombia, Venezuela, Brazil

Pacific Ocean

Gulf of Mexico

Caribbean Sea

California

Arizona

New Mexico

Texas

Oklahoma

Florida

San Diego
Tijuana
Mexicali
Nogales
Douglas
Agua Prieta
Juárez
El Paso
Nuevo Laredo
Laredo
McAllen
Reynosa
Puerto Vallarta
Mazatlan
Culiacan
Lazaro Cardenas
Acapulco
Mexico City
Tampico
Veracruz
Merida
Cancun

GUATEMALA
BELIZE
HONDURAS
CUBA

0 mi   200   400

of Nuevo Leon state and much of Veracruz state. It controls two main port cities — Veracruz and Tampico — and shares a land border with the United States. The Sinaloa federation's capital city is Culiacan, while its territory includes Sinaloa and Sonora states and eastern Jalisco state. It also shares a land border with the United States and controls the port cities of Mazatlan, Manzanillo and Puerto Vallarta. Both states also have relationships with other cartel states that are important for their supply chain, including the Guerrero-Michoacan "state" and the Yucatan region.

Political Structure

One or two cartels with the most power tend to control Mexican organized crime at any given time. Currently the Gulf cartel and the Sinaloa federation control the bulk of the drug trade, though this has not always been the case. The Juarez cartel and the Arellano Felix Organization have each occupied the top spot in the past. Both of these organizations lost power after their leaders were captured or killed fighting with each other or the government, and other groups moved in to take over territory. Occasionally a top-ranking cartel will reach out to its rival to form a truce or an alliance. These agreements are generally motivated by business concerns and are usually short-lived. The Mexican drug trade simply involves too much money and too many volatile personalities for such agreements to be honored for very long.

There is a better track record for mergers and partnerships between small and medium-sized criminal organizations as a way to expand territory. The mergers with the greatest success involve combining organizations with distinct geographic areas of responsibility (such agreements were important in the Sinaloa federation's formation and rise to power). On a smaller scale, large cartels often establish partnerships with local gangs to assist in the cartel's mission. These gangs are tasked with a range of duties, including kidnapping, drug distribution, security, intimidation and assassinations.

Drug cartels in Mexico have a hierarchical leadership structure, with some of the largest cartels controlled by members of a family. The leadership structure in most Mexican organized crime groups shows sophistication and efficiency. Many criminal activities are compartmentalized, with particular groups focusing on specific duties. Top cartel management is based primarily on geography. High-ranking and mid-level members known as gatekeepers take responsibility for cartel activities in a specific city or state. There appears to be little oversight as to how gatekeepers choose to manage their territories, as long as they succeed with the overall business plan. The top-down approach makes the cartels vulnerable, however, as the death or arrest of a key leader can collapse the entire chain of relationships.

Mexican cartels interact differently with their suppliers and their distributors. One person or a handful of individuals in the cartel with the appropriate contacts handle South American suppliers; the same appears to be true for coordinating ephedra shipments from China. On the other hand, distribution networks involve a relatively larger number of people, though a small number of Mexican organized crime members hand off the shipments to distribution teams in the United States, which have a better understanding of the lay of the land north of the border.

The movement of drugs over long distances requires not only a great deal of coordination but also official complicity. An important part of cartel management, then, involves bribes and intimidation of police officers, military personnel and government officials. In fact, many cartel members are former police officers or army deserters.

Economics

Drug trafficking is the most profitable organized criminal business in Mexico. It is estimated that from $25 billion to $30 billion worth of illegal drugs comes through Mexico into the United States each year. A wide range of illegal substances enter the United States from Mexico, though the primary ones are cocaine, heroin, marijuana and methamphetamines (meth). Most cocaine and heroin shipments originate in other countries and pass through Mexico on the way to the United States, meaning that the proceeds must be shared between Mexican traffickers and foreign producers. Marijuana and meth, however, are produced in large quantities inside Mexico, which means that Mexican cartels receive a higher portion of the sales profits. Marijuana crops are cultivated in rural areas throughout western Mexico, while meth is mass produced in large production laboratories, whose operation has been facilitated by bulk shipments from China of ephedra, a precursor chemical in the production of the drug.

Other organized criminal activities are widespread but do not generate nearly as much money as drug trafficking. These activities include kidnapping, extortion, human trafficking, and weapons trafficking. In general, the major drug cartels do not rely on these activities as a major source of income, but rather use them in a limited way in order to supplement drug profits or as a way to support the overall organization. Smaller organized crime groups often rely on these activities as primary income sources, but their income pales in comparison to that of the large drug-trafficking organizations. The Arellano Felix Organization, for example, has begun to diversify its criminal activities and rely more heavily on kidnapping for ransom in order to fund itself. After it lost access to Colombian cocaine sources, the cartel continued to move marijuana and meth and expanded its activities outside of the drug trade.

Drug cartels go to great lengths to conceal the movement of drug money. As drug money makes its way back to the source of supply it passes through a network of money laundering operations that often use front companies on both sides of the border to provide for the transfer of large sums of money. Popular front businesses include real estate companies, hotels, currency exchange houses, automotive sales companies, restaurants and other small businesses. In some cases drug traffickers have kept large amounts of money in bank accounts in the United States or Caribbean or European countries.

Security

The largest criminal organizations in Mexico employ between 500 and 1,000 well-armed security "enforcers" who work exclusively for the cartel that hired them. Enforcers are generally well-disciplined fighters with law enforcement or military backgrounds. Many elite enforcer units are capable of deploying anywhere in Mexico within 24 hours. Cartels also hire small local gangs to perform specific tasks in a particular area of responsibility. These contract gangs may carry out tasks of lesser importance, while the enforcers will be tasked with higher priority assignments. Among the most notorious groups of enforcers are the Gulf cartel's Zetas and the Sinaloa federation's Gente Nueva and Los Pelones.

Cartel enforcers perform several duties, including protective security of high-ranking members, escorting valuable shipments of contraband and carrying out assassinations of rivals or government officials. They are armed primarily with small arms, including handguns, assault rifles, grenades, rocket-propelled grenades and lightweight anti-tank rockets. The majority of weapons for enforcers are smuggled into Mexico from the United States. It is believed that properly outfitting a single enforcer costs between $500 and $1,000 annually.

Some enforcers are loyal to an individual cartel leader, but most are loyal to their operational commanders. As long as the enforcers are paid well, they will continue working for their cartel; however, there have been cases (though rare) of entire enforcer groups switching sides in the middle of a cartel war if the other side offers more money.

Currently, the Gulf cartel and the Sinaloa federation are engaged in a war to conquer territory and weaken each other. The two cartels are fairly equally matched, and the fighting has taken place both in disputed areas and in territories firmly under cartel control. There is little that is unique about this situation, as conflict is the nature of the drug business in Mexico.

At the same time, the cartels are battling a crackdown by government security forces. This government operation is unique; never before has the Mexican government deployed so many military and federal law enforcement forces on a counternarcotics mission for such an extended period of time. The operation has so far had both positive and negative results, including a decreased flow of cocaine into the United States and a record number of killings.

Cartels generally engage in warfare by conducting targeted assassinations, both of rivals and of security forces. Most targeted killings are preceded by surveillance of the target and often involve a kidnapping before execution so that the enforcers have a chance to interrogate the victim. Occasionally a group of cartel enforcers ambush police or army patrols or buildings. Most attacks on buildings have a specific purpose, such as to free a cartel member that has been detained.

Social Aspects/Culture

Mexican organized crime enjoys no small degree of prestige within certain portions of the population. Local music groups occasionally compose songs — popular on a local level in rural areas of northern Mexico — singing the praises of one drug cartel over another. Beyond this, organized crime invokes a combination of fear and respect in the community, making it difficult for law enforcement to locate witnesses willing to cooperate in investigations.

In general, criminal organizations in Mexico are not known for providing large-scale humanitarian services or making it a priority to win over the local population. Some cartel leaders, however, do occasionally try to buy loyalty from local residents by providing money for a child's education or basic necessities, for example. Family connections are an important aspect of Mexican organized crime. Relatives of cartel members are often used to launder drug money, and cartel leaders have been known to provide financial support to the families of members who were captured or killed while performing services for the cartel.

Prison life is another important aspect of cartel culture. Many lasting criminal relationships are formed in prison, and having done prison time in the United States is also an important rite of passage for many organized criminal elements in Mexico.

Dependence on the Drug Trade

There are two important conditions for Mexican organized crime to survive in its current form. The first is the survival of the drug trade — specifically a high demand for illegal drugs in the United States. The second is Mexico's use as a transshipment point for U.S.-bound drugs. There is currently no indication that either of these conditions will change anytime soon, though this second one is likely to change before the first one.

Any change in the supply route of drugs toward the United States would have a profound impact on the future of Mexican organized crime. If, for example, the Caribbean smuggling corridor reopened, Mexican drug cartels would no longer be competing just for control of territory within Mexico; they would be competing against drug traffickers operating alternative routes. Consequently, Mexican cartels would no longer have a corner on the drug market and would end up losing a great deal of the power that they currently hold.

Even in this scenario, organized crime in Mexico would by no means disappear. Other profitable criminal activities such as kidnapping and human trafficking will be around for the foreseeable future. Regardless of how developed these criminal enterprises might become, however, they would not come close to providing the money and power Mexico's drug cartels currently enjoy.

14: The Cartel Turf War Intensifies
May 9, 2008

Mexican media report that Edgar Guzman Beltran, the son of Sinaloa cartel leader Joaquin "El Chapo" Guzman, was killed at 8:50 p.m. on May 8 in Culiacan, Sinaloa state. According to STRATFOR sources, 20 members of Los Zetas, the Gulf cartel's security arm, approached Guzman in five vehicles and fired on him with AK-47s and a rocket-propelled grenade launcher. His murder coincides with the murders of Mexican federal police chief Edgar Millan Gomez and anti-kidnapping director Esteban Robles in Mexico City, suspected to be the work of the Sinaloa cartel.

Edgar Guzman's death is the latest in a string of high-profile murders in Mexico, but his connection to the Sinaloa cartel means that the ongoing turf war between the Gulf and Sinaloa cartels will become very violent as the Sinaloa cartel is sure to take revenge for the killing.

The Mexican government has limited options for responding to the attacks in Mexico City and for containing the violence in Sinaloa state. The government said yesterday it will send reinforcements to Sinaloa, but it would take several thousand soldiers to have any real impact, and the government cannot spare that many without affecting security operations elsewhere.

Government officials claim that the spate of high-level killings is evidence that the drug cartels are suffering from the government clampdown on drug violence that has been in effect since 2006 and that they are desperately lashing out. However, another possible explanation is that the Sinaloa cartel, by redirecting attention to Mexico City, is forcing the military to make a decision between continuing its efforts on the border and redeploying elsewhere.

Given the severity of the situation in Mexico City and the certainty of reprisal violence between the Sinaloa and Gulf cartels, government crackdowns will certainly be needed in other parts of Mexico. But diverting forces from the border region will likely result in an increase in drug trafficking from Mexico into the United States.

15: Examining Cartel War Violence through a Protective Lens
May 14, 2008

Mexico's long and violent drug cartel war has recently intensified. The past week witnessed the killings of no fewer than six senior police officials. One of those killed was Edgar Millan Gomez, acting head of the Mexican federal police and the highest-ranking federal cop in Mexico. Millan Gomez was shot to death May 8 just after entering his home in Mexico City.

Within the past few days, six suspects have been arrested in connection with his murder. One of the ringleaders is said to be a former federal highway police officer. The suspects appear to have ties to the Sinaloa cartel. In fact, Millan Gomez was responsible for a police operation in January that led to the arrest of Alfredo Beltran Leyva, the cartel's second-in-command. Mexican police believe Beltran Leyva's brother Arturo (who is also a significant player in the Sinaloa cartel structure) commissioned the hit.

During the same time period, violence from the cartel war has visited the family of Joaquin "El Chapo" Guzman Loera, the Sinaloa cartel leader who has the distinction of being Mexico's most-wanted drug kingpin. On May 8, Guzman Loera's son Edgar Guzman Beltran and two companions were killed by a large-scale ambush as they left a shopping mall in Culiacan, Sinaloa.

In addition to discussing the geopolitical implications of this escalation in the violence (which STRATFOR has done elsewhere), we thought it would be instructive to look at the recent wave of violence through the lens of protective intelligence. Such an effort can allow us not only to see what lessons can be learned from the attacks but also gain insight into how similar attacks can be avoided in the future, which is the real aim of protective intelligence.

Tactical Details of the Recent Attacks

On the evening of May 1, Roberto Velasco Bravo, director of investigations against organized crime for Mexico's state public security police (SSP), was gunned down as he returned to his Mexico City home. Two assailants reportedly approached Velasco Bravo as he parked his sport utility vehicle and shot him in the head at close range before fleeing the scene. Although the incident initially was believed to have been a robbery attempt gone bad, the discovery of a .380 caliber handgun fitted with a suppressor near the crime scene suggests the shooting was actually a professionally targeted assassination. Local press also reported that Velasco Bravo died on his day off and that his bodyguard had been ordered to stand down because he was planning to travel outside the city.

On May 2, less than 24 hours after the Velasco Bravo shooting, inspector Jose Aristeo Gomez Martinez, the administrative director of the Federal Preventative Police (PFP), was gunned down in front of his home in the wealthy Coyoacan neighborhood of Mexico City. Gomez Martinez and a woman were talking in front of the house around midnight when two armed men surprised them and reportedly attempted to force Gomez Martinez into the back seat of his own car. Gomez Martinez struggled with the men and was shot in the arm and chest. Mexican authorities say the motive for the Gomez Martinez killing remains murky. However, the circumstances surrounding the case — he was shot with a suppressed .380 pistol outside of his residence — are certainly very similar to the Velasco Bravo and Millan Gomez killings.

In the Millan Gomez attack, alleged members of a murder-for-hire gang shot and killed the federal police chief as he returned to his home in the early hours of the morning. Millan Gomez was reportedly shot eight times at close range by a gunman armed with two handguns — one of which was a .380 with a suppressor. The gunman was reportedly waiting inside Millan Gomez's apartment building. The victim apparently struggled with his assailant and attempted to grab the suppressed weapon from the gunman. During the struggle, the gunman reportedly shot Millan Gomez in the hand once with the suppressed weapon and then several times in the torso with his back-up weapon, which was not suppressed. Millan Gomez's two-man protection team, who had just dropped him off at the door, heard the unsuppressed shots and returned to the apartment building to investigate. One member of the protection team was wounded in the chest by the fleeing gunman, but the team was able to wound and apprehend him alive. The interrogation of the gunman and the investigation of the equipment and other items found in his possession led to the recent arrest of the five other suspects allegedly tied to the assassination gang.

Also on May 8, Edgar Guzman Beltran, the son of Sinaloa cartel leader Joaquin "El Chapo" Guzman Loera, was killed at 8:50 p.m. local time in Culiacan, Sinaloa state. Guzman Beltran was leaving a local shopping mall with two friends — one of whom was Arturo Meza Cazares, the son of Blanca Margarita Cazares Salazar, reputed to be the cartel's top money launderer — when the three were caught in a heavy hail of gunfire. Reports from the scene indicate that the team that attacked Guzman Beltran may have involved as many as 40 gunmen from a rival cartel who opened up on the three men with AK-47 rifles and a rocket-propelled grenade launcher. Other reports put the number of ambushers at around 20. In any event, even 20 men armed with AKs and a rocket-propelled grenade launcher is a significant force, and something one would expect to see in a war zone such as Iraq or Afghanistan rather than in Mexico.

On May 9, Esteban Robles Espinosa, commander of Mexico City's investigative police force, was attacked by a group of armed men shortly after he left his house at about 8:30 a.m. Four gunmen traveling in a truck and another in a compact car opened fire on him at an intersection near his home. The attack appears to be a classic vehicular ambush involving a blocking vehicle and an assault team. Robles Espinosa apparently attempted to avoid the attacks and flee the site, but his escape attempt ended when his vehicle struck a tree. Robles Espinosa was shot seven times — four times in the throat, once in the neck, and twice in the head. He died shortly after arriving at a hospital. Authorities reportedly found 20 casings from 9mm and .40-caliber cartridges at the scene of the attack. The placement of the shots in this case appears to be uncharacteristically controlled for Mexico, where victims are normally wounded in various parts of their bodies. The concentration of wounds in the head and neck would appear to indicate that at least one of the shooters was an accomplished marksman. The shot placement might also indicate that Robles Espinosa was wearing a protective vest, and the assailants, being aware of the vest, directed their fire toward his head.

Common Themes

The Millan Gomez, Velasco Bravo and Gomez Martinez shootings were all similar in that they involved suppressed .380 handguns and were intended to be clean and discreetly conducted events. They stand in stark contrast to many of the cartel killings in Mexico, which tend to be more like the killings of Beltran Guzman and involve massive firepower and very little precision or discretion. Even though the Millan Gomez killing got messy, and the shooter was caught, it was intended to be a very quiet, surgical hit — until Murphy's law kicked in for the assassin.

It is notable that the killing of the four police officials all occurred in proximity to their homes, and that all four attacks were conducted during an arrival or departure at the home. It has long been common for terrorists and criminal kidnappers or assassins to focus on the home or office of their prospective target, because these are known locations that the potential victim frequently visits with some regularity. Also, homes are often preferable to offices, because they usually have less security, and criminals or terrorists can operate around them more easily and with less chance of being caught. Arrivals and departures are prime times for attacks, because the target is generally easier to locate and quickly acquire when on foot or in a car than when in a building.

Furthermore, the objective of preoperational surveillance is to detect the target's patterns and vulnerabilities so that an attack can be planned. Historically, one of the most likely times for an attack is when a potential victim is leaving from or returning to a known location. The most predictable move traditionally is the home-to-office move; however, the team that conducted the surveillance on Velasco Bravo, Gomez Martinez and Millan Gomez apparently found them to be predictable in their evening moves and planned the attacks accordingly. Robles Espinosa was attacked during the more-stereotypical morning move. Attacking in the evening could also give the assailants the cover of darkness. The low-key assassination cell behind the Velasco Bravo, Gomez Martinez and Millan Gomez attacks seemed to prefer that kind of cover. It is also possible that in the Guzman Beltran case, the shopping mall was a known place for him to frequent and that he had established a pattern of visiting there in the evening.

All five of the attacks also occurred in close proximity to vehicles. Millan Gomez, Gomez Martinez and Guzman Beltran were attacked while outside their vehicles; Robles Espinosa and Vellasco Bravo were attacked while in theirs, though neither of the men had an armored vehicle.

Protective Intelligence Lessons

A former federal police officer was arrested in connection with the Millan Gomez case, and he was found to have a list of license plates and home addresses; but such information alone is not enough to plan an assassination. Extensive preoperational surveillance is also required. From the careful planning of the Velasco Bravo, Gomez Martinez and Millan Gomez hits, it is apparent that the targets were under surveillance for a prolonged period of time. The fact that Robles Espinosa was hit during his morning move from home to work also tends to indicate that he had an established pattern that had been picked up by surveillance. Even in the Guzman Beltran killing, one does not amass a team of 20 or 40 assassins at the drop of a hat. Clearly, the operation was planned and the target had been watched.

The fact that surveillance was conducted in each of these cases means that the people conducting that surveillance were forced to expose themselves to detection. Furthermore, preoperational surveillance is normally not that sophisticated, since people rarely look for it. This means that had countersurveillance efforts been used these efforts likely would have been detected, especially since countersurveillance efforts often focus on known, predictable locations such as the home and office.

Another important lesson is that bodyguards and armored cars are no guarantee of protection in and of themselves. Assailants can look for and exploit vulnerabilities — as they did in the Velasco Bravo and Millan Gomez cases — if they are allowed to conduct surveillance at will and are given the opportunity to thoroughly assess the protective security program. Even if there are security measures in place, malefactors may choose to attack in spite of security and, in such a case, will do so with adequate resources to overcome those security measures. If there are protective agents, the attackers will plan to neutralize them first. If there is an armored vehicle, they will find ways to defeat the armor — something easily accomplished with the rocket-propelled grenades, LAW rockets and .50-caliber sniper rifles found in the arsenals of Mexican cartels.

Unfortunately, many people believe that the presence of armed bodyguards — or armed guards combined with armored vehicles — provides absolute security. This macho misconception is not confined to Latin America, but is pervasive there. Frankly, when we consider the size of the assault team employed in the Guzman Beltran hit (even if it consisted of only 20 men) and their armaments, there are very few protective details in the world sufficiently trained and equipped to deal with that level of threat. Executive protection teams and armored cars provide very little protection against dozens of attackers armed with AK rifles and rocket-propelled grenades, especially if the attackers are given free rein to conduct surveillance and plan their attack.

Indeed, many people — including police and executive protection personnel — either lack or fail to employ good observation skills.

These skills are every bit as important as marksmanship — if not more — but are rarely taught or practiced. Additionally, even if a protection agent observes something unusual, in many cases there is no system in place to record these observations and no efficient way to communicate them or to compare them to the observations of others. There is often no process to investigate such observations to determine if they are indicators of something untoward.

The real counter to such a threat is heightened security awareness and a robust countersurveillance program, coupled with careful route and schedule analysis. Routes and traveling times must be varied, surveillance must be looked for and those conducting surveillance must not be afforded the opportunity to operate at will and with impunity. Suspicious events must be catalogued and investigated. Emphasis must also be placed on attack recognition and driver training to provide every possibility of spotting a pending attack and avoiding it before it can be successfully launched. Action is always faster than reaction. And even a highly skilled protection team can be defeated if the attacker gains the tactical element of surprise — especially if coupled with overwhelming firepower.

Ideally, those conducting surveillance must be made uncomfortable or even manipulated into revealing their position when it proves advantageous to countersurveillance teams. Dummy motorcade moves are a fine tool to add into the mix, as is the use of safe houses for alternate residences and offices. Any ploy to confuse, deceive or deter potential scouts that ultimately makes them tip their hand is a valuable trick of the trade employed by protective intelligence practitioners — professionals tasked with the difficult mission of deterring the type of assassinations we have recently seen in Mexico.

16: A Brazen Cartel Killing
June 27, 2008

Igor Labastida Calderon, a commander of the traffic and contraband division in Mexico's Federal Preventive Police investigating the death of Edgar Millan Gomez, was shot dead by a gunman June 26 while he lunched at a Mexico City restaurant. Labastida had worked with Millan on regional security before the latter died in a drug cartel-related killing May 8.

The killing of Labastida, whose role in investigating the Millan killing most likely made him a target, represents yet another cartel-arranged killing of a high-level police official. More seriously, it highlights that the cartels felt confident enough to kill a leading investigator into cartel activity in broad daylight in the seat of Mexican public power, something that would not happen in a strong state.

In the Labastida killing, a gunman exited his car and entered the Anita restaurant in the Argentina Antigua neighborhood of Mexico City, opening fire with two handguns, a .380-caliber pistol and a 9mm. The shooter quickly left, driving away in a Volkswagen Bora. Though several federal police agents were at the restaurant at the time, it appears the gunman was specifically targeting Labastida. Labastida's bodyguard also died in the shooting, while three other federal police officers at Labastida's table were injured.

The killing of Labastida is the fifth in a series of high-profile police killings in Mexico City that started with Roberto Velasco on May 1 and continued with the killings of Millan, Jose Aristeo Gomez and Esteban Robles. These deaths represent a drug cartel offensive against the government that threatens to destabilize Mexico. While is not yet clear which cartel was behind the Labastida attack, the incident probably was connected to the Beltran Leyvas, who recently broke with Sinaloa cartel leader Joaquin "El Chapo" Guzman and were behind Millan's death.

The brazenness of this attack is meant to communicate to Mexican police that no one is safe — whether in their home, where Millan was killed, or in a public space like Labastida. The fact that the killer targeted a group of police with protection in broad daylight shows that security for officials in Mexico remains misdirected even after the recent spate of high-profile killings.

17: Tactical Implications of the Labastida Hit
June 27, 2008

The brazen killing of Igor Labastida Calderon, a commander of the traffic and contraband division in Mexico's Federal Preventive Police, carries important tactical lessons that must be learned if Mexican authorities are to have any hope of keeping any of their charges safe.

Labastida was killed while eating lunch at a restaurant in the Mexican capital. He was accompanied by his bodyguard (who was also killed) and several other police agents, three of whom were wounded in the audacious attack.

The modus operandi in the Labastida assassination stands in stark contrast with the May killings of Edgar Millan Gomez, Roberto Velasco Bravo and Jose Aristeo Gomez Martinez. In each of those three cases, the victims were shot after dark with suppressed .380 pistols and had no executive protection agents present. (Millan Gomez's protective agents had just dropped him off at the door of his residence; they returned to the scene after the shooting and subdued the shooter after Millan Gomez struggled with his assailant, forcing him to fire shots from a second, non-suppressed weapon.) In spite of the foul-up in the Millan Gomez hit, these three operations were designed to be discreet and cleanly conducted.

By killing Labastida Calderon — who was investigating the Millan Gomez killing — the cartel honcho behind it (most likely Arturo Beltran Levya) was sending a message: If you investigate me you will die. The killing also was designed intentionally to send a second message: I can get you any time and any place regardless of protection, and you cannot stop me.

In spite of the different modi operandi between this case and the killings last month, a tactical analysis of the Labastida killing reveals certain similarities. In all these cases, the killers had good intelligence (some of which came from inside sources). Perhaps more important, the killers had the freedom to conduct pre-operational surveillance and plan the assassination without detection or hindrance. Obviously, had their surveillance been detected, additional security measures would have been implemented. As it was, the surveillance was not detected, and the assailants were able to launch the attack and gain tactical surprise on Labastida and his security detail.

The tactical lessons to be taken from this case are very similar to those drawn from the assassinations last month and apparently not heeded.

- Attackers cannot be permitted free rein to conduct surveillance. Had countersurveillance efforts been employed, the target's security details probably would have detected the assailants.

- Personal information of potential targets, such as schedules, must be carefully guarded.

- Large men with large guns and armored cars are no guarantee of protection in and of themselves. Assailants can — and will — look for and exploit vulnerabilities. Even when there are security measures in place, brazen criminals may choose to attack in spite of security. When they do, they will attack with adequate resources to overcome security measures. If there are protective agents, the attackers will neutralize them first. If there is an armored vehicle, they will find ways to defeat the armor — something easily accomplished with the rocket-propelled grenades (RPGs), LAW rockets and .50-caliber sniper rifles found in the arsenals of Mexican cartels.

- Observation skills and attack recognition are critical. They literally mean the difference between life and death.

- VIPs must not wholly rely on their executive protection details to keep them safe. They must take ownership for their own security, even when that means doing uncomfortable things like varying times and routes and not visiting favorite spots on a predictable basis.

As we saw in the May 8 killing of Edgar Guzman Beltran, which was conducted by 40 assailants armed with automatic rifles and RPGs, the cartels can mobilize large, heavily equipped assault teams. There are very few protective details in the world capable of withstanding such an assault. Unless a protective intelligence-focused scheme is employed to protect high-ranking Mexican police officials — an approach that stresses the lessons above — the Mexican government will not be able to keep any of its charges safe.

18: The Fallout from Phoenix
July 2, 2008

Late on the night of June 22, a residence in Phoenix was approached by a heavily armed tactical team preparing to serve a warrant. The members of the team were wearing the typical gear for members of their profession: black boots, black BDU pants, Kevlar helmets and Phoenix Police Department (PPD) raid shirts pulled over their body armor. The team members carried AR-15 rifles equipped with Aimpoint sights to help them during the low-light operation and, like most cops on a tactical team, in addition to their long guns, the members of this team carried secondary weapons — pistols strapped to their thighs.

But the raid took a strange turn when one element of the team began directing suppressive fire on the residence windows while the second element entered — a tactic not normally employed by the PPD. This breach of departmental protocol did not stem from a mistake on the part of the team's commander. It occurred because the eight men on the assault team were not from the PPD at all. These men were not cops serving a legal search or arrest warrant signed by a judge; they were cartel hit men serving a death warrant signed by a Mexican drug lord.

The tactical team struck hard and fast. They quickly killed a man in the house and then fled the scene in two vehicles, a red Chevy Tahoe and a gray Honda sedan. Their aggressive tactics did have consequences, however. The fury the attackers unleashed on the home — firing over 100 rounds during the operation — drew the attention of a nearby Special Assignments Unit (SAU) team, the PPD's real tactical team, which responded to the scene with other officers. An SAU officer noticed the Tahoe fleeing the scene and followed it until it entered an alley. Sensing a potential ambush, the SAU officer chose to establish a perimeter and wait for reinforcements rather than charge down the alley after the suspects. This was fortunate, because after three of the suspects from the Tahoe were arrested, they confessed that they had indeed planned to ambush the police officers chasing them.

The assailants who fled in the Honda have not yet been found, but police did recover the vehicle in a church parking lot. They reportedly found four sets of body armor in the vehicle and also recovered an assault rifle abandoned in a field adjacent to the church.

This Phoenix home invasion and murder is a vivid reminder of the threat to U.S. law enforcement officers that stems from the cartel wars in Mexico.

Violence Crosses the Border

The fact that the Mexican men involved in the Phoenix case were heavily armed and dressed as police comes as no surprise to anyone who has followed security events in Mexico. Teams of cartel enforcers frequently impersonate police or military personnel, often wearing matching tactical gear and carrying standardized weapons. In fact, it is rare to see a shootout or cartel-related arms seizure in Mexico where tactical gear and clothing bearing police or military insignia is not found.

One reason for the prevalent use of this type of equipment is that many cartel enforcers come from military or police backgrounds. By training and habit, they prefer to operate as a team composed of members equipped with standardized gear so that items such as ammunition and magazines can be interchanged during a firefight. This also gives a team member the ability to pick up the familiar weapon of a fallen comrade and immediately bring it into action. This is, of course, the same reason military units and police forces use standardized equipment in most places.

Police clothing, such as hats, patches and raid jackets, is surprisingly easy to come by. Authentic articles can be stolen or purchased through uniform vendors or cop shops. Knockoff uniform items can easily be manufactured in silk screen or embroidery shops by duplicating authentic designs. Even badges are easy to obtain if one knows where to look.

While it now appears that the three men arrested in Phoenix were not former or active members of the Mexican military or police, it is not surprising that they employed military- and police-style tactics. Enforcers of various cartel groups such as Los Zetas, La Gente Nueva or the Kaibiles who have received advanced tactical training often pass on that training to younger enforcers (many of whom are former street thugs) at makeshift training camps located on ranches in northern Mexico. There are also reports of Israeli mercenaries visiting these camps to provide tactical training. In this way, the cartel enforcers are transforming ordinary street thugs into highly-trained cartel tactical teams.

Though cartel enforcers have almost always had ready access to guns, including military weapons such as assault rifles and grenade launchers, groups such as Los Zetas, the Kaibiles and their young disciples bring an added level of threat to the equation. They are highly trained men with soldiers' mindsets who operate as a unit capable of using their weapons with deadly effectiveness. Assault rifles in the hands of untrained thugs are dangerous, but when those same weapons are placed in the hands of men who can shoot accurately and operate tactically as a fire team, they can be overwhelmingly powerful — not only when used against enemies and other intended targets, but also when used against law enforcement officers who attempt to interfere with the team's operations.

Targets

Although the victim in the Phoenix killing, Andrew Williams, was reportedly a Jamaican drug dealer who crossed a Mexican cartel, there are many other targets in the United States that the cartels would like to eliminate. These targets include Mexican cartel members who have fled to the United States for a number of reasons. One is the violent cartel war that has raged in Mexico for the past few years over control of important smuggling routes and strategic locations along those routes. Another is the Calderon administration's crackdown, first on the Gulf cartel and now on the Sinaloa cartel. Pressure from rival cartels and the government has forced many cartel leaders into hiding, and some of them have left Mexico for Central America or the United States.

Traditionally, when violence has spiked in Mexico, cartel figures have used U.S. cities such as Laredo, El Paso and San Diego as rest and recreation spots, reasoning that the general umbrella of safety provided by U.S. law enforcement to those residing in the United States would protect them from assassination by their enemies. As bolder Mexican cartel hit men have begun to carry out assassinations on the U.S. side of the border in places such as Laredo, Rio Bravo, and even Dallas, the cartel figures have begun to seek sanctuary deeper in the United States, thereby bringing the threat with them.

While many cartel leaders are wanted in the United States, many have family members not being sought by U.S. law enforcement. (Many of them even have relatives who are U.S. citizens.) Some family members have also settled comfortably inside the United States, using the country as a haven from violence in Mexico. These families might become targets, however, as the cartels look for creative ways to hurt their rivals.

Other cartel targets in the United States include Drug Enforcement Administration and other law enforcement officers responsible for operations against the cartels, and informants who have cooperated with U.S. or Mexican authorities and been relocated stateside for safety. There are also many police officers who have quit their jobs in Mexico and fled to the United States to escape threats from the cartels, as well as Mexican businessmen who are targeted by cartels and have moved to the United States for safety.

To date, the cartels for the most part have refrained from targeting innocent civilians. In the type of environment in which they operate inside Mexico, cartels cannot afford to have the local population, a group they use as camouflage, turn against them. It is not uncommon for cartel leaders to stage public relations events (they have even held carnivals for children) in order to build goodwill with the general population. As seen with al Qaeda in Iraq, losing the support of the local population is deadly for a militant group attempting to hide within that population.

Cartels have also attempted to minimize civilian casualties in their operations inside the United States, though for a different operational consideration. The cartels believe that if a U.S. drug dealer or a member of a rival Mexican cartel is killed in a place like Dallas or Phoenix, nobody really cares. Many people see such a killing as a public service, and there will not be much public outcry about it, nor much real effort on the part of law enforcement agencies to identify and catch the killers. The death of a civilian, on the other hand, brings far more public condemnation and law enforcement attention.

However, the aggressiveness of cartel enforcers and their brutal lack of regard for human life means that while they do not intentionally target civilians, they are bound to create collateral casualties along the way. This is especially true as they continue to conduct operations like the Phoenix killing, where they fired over 100 rounds of 5.56mm ball ammunition at a home in a residential neighborhood.

Tactical Implications

Judging from the operations of the cartel enforcers in Mexico, they have absolutely no hesitation about firing at police officers who interfere with their operations or who dare to chase them. Indeed, the Phoenix case nearly ended in an ambush of the police. It must be noted, however, that this ambush was not really intentional, but rather the natural reaction of these Mexican cartel enforcers to police pursuit. They were accustomed to shooting at police and military south of the border and have very little regard for them. In many instances, this aggression convinces the poorly armed and trained police to leave the cartel gunmen alone.

The problem such teams pose for the average U.S. cop on patrol is that the average cop is neither trained nor armed to confront a heavily armed fire team. In fact, a PPD source advised STRATFOR that, had the SAU officer not been the first to arrive on the scene, it could have been a disaster for the department. This is not a criticism of the Phoenix cops. The vast majority of police officers and federal agents in the United States simply are not prepared or equipped to deal with a highly trained fire team using insurgent tactics. That is a task suited more for the U.S. military forces currently deployed in Iraq and Afghanistan.

These cartel gunmen also have the advantage of being camouflaged as cops. This might not only cause considerable confusion during a firefight (who do backup officers shoot at if both parties in the fight are dressed like cops?) but also means that responding officers might hesitate to fire on the criminals dressed as cops. Such hesitation could provide the criminals with an important tactical advantage — an advantage that could prove fatal for the officers.

Mexican cartel enforcers have also demonstrated a history of using sophisticated scanners to listen to police radio traffic, and in some cases they have even employed police radios to confuse and misdirect the police responding to an armed confrontation with cartel enforcers.

We anticipate that as the Mexican cartels begin to go after more targets inside the United States, the spread of cartel violence and these dangerous tactics beyond the border region will catch some law enforcement officers by surprise. A patrol officer conducting a traffic stop on a group of cartel members who are preparing to conduct an assassination in, say, Los Angeles, Chicago or northern Virginia could quickly find himself heavily outgunned and under fire. Of course, cops in the United States are far more capable than their Mexican counterparts of dealing with this threat.

In addition to being far better trained, U.S. law enforcement officers also have access to far better command, control and communication networks than their Mexican counterparts. Like we saw in the Phoenix example, this communication network provides cops with the ability to quickly summon reinforcements, air support and tactical teams to deal with heavily armed criminals — but this communication system only helps if it can be used. That means cops need to recognize the danger before they are attacked and prevented from calling for help. As with many other threats, the key to protecting oneself against this threat is situational awareness, and cops far from the border need to become aware of this trend.

19: A Shift in Cartel Tactics?
Jan. 15, 2008

Even after more than a year of expanded security operations across Mexico, nearly all accounts suggest the violence associated with the drug trade there continues to increase. Within the last week, the country has seen intense firefights involving rocket-propelled grenades in cities along the U.S. border, prolonged gun battles in Cancun, mutilated bodies discovered in Acapulco, two severed heads found just blocks away from the international airport in Mexico City and the assassination of three police officers and the wife and daughter of an officer in Tijuana. Especially considering their locations, these incidents should be of particular concern to the more than 100,000 U.S.

high school and college students expected to visit Mexico during the upcoming spring break season.

STRATFOR has followed these trends of violence closely, documenting the many security concerns associated with the country's organized criminal entities. Adding to these worries is the new concern of a prolonged insurgent-style campaign being waged by the country's powerful drug cartels. U.S. counterterrorism sources report that the Gulf cartel in particular has realized that it is incapable of head-to-head engagements with the Mexican military and federal police but is confident that engaging in insurgent-style tactics will give it an advantage.

In many ways, these kinds of tactics already are being used by Mexico's drug-trafficking organizations. Cartel members have demonstrated a strong capability to conduct ambushes and hit-and-run attacks against convoys, highway checkpoints and police and military installations.

More unnerving is the Jan. 12 discovery of a booby-trapped body in a cartel safe house in Cancun. Police responding to a report of a kidnapping became engaged in an extended gun battle with cartel members when the officers approached what turned out to be a safe house containing a cache of assault rifles and grenades. Once the suspects fled the house and the authorities began searching the premises, police reported that the cartel members had pulled the pin on a fragmentation grenade and then placed the grenade in the hand of a dead body.

These kinds of practices are of particular concern to Mexican and U.S. authorities as they consider how the cartels will respond to the increased security environment.

If the possibility of increasing insurgent-style tactics from the cartels is to be examined, however, reasons why the cartels have not engaged in this kind of fighting before must also be explored. For example, it is somewhat surprising that Mexico's drug-trafficking organizations have yet to make use of improvised explosive devices in their attacks against civilian and police targets, especially considering how available inexpensive explosives are in Mexico. Furthermore, the cartels have business relationships with Colombian drug gangs that have expertise and experience in constructing and deploying car bombs; members of Colombian drug cartels often travel to Mexico to meet with cartel members there and work out the details of cocaine shipments from South America. The Kaibiles — Central American special forces — who have joined some of the cartels also presumably have expertise in explosives.

However, most drug cartel enforcers in Mexico come from military or law enforcement backgrounds and are much more familiar with using guns than bombs. Furthermore, the cartels have not had to shift tactics yet, since — despite the increased security presence in many areas — they still largely have been able to rely on bribes and intimidation in order to transport drugs and make money. Yet this does not alleviate the concern that heavier government pressure on the cartels will force them to adopt insurgent-style tactics that could result in greater collateral damage.

It is important to note that any cartel-related insurgency that arises will not lead to a shift in the cartels' goals. Their primary objectives of making a profit and defeating security forces will not expand to include any type of political overthrow. Mexico's drug cartels will continue to focus on their lucrative drug markets.

20: The Cartels Adopt Improvised Incendiary Devices
July 16, 2008

When three cars exploded July 14 in Culiacan, capital of the Mexican state of Sinaloa, police first thought the cars were destroyed by Molotov cocktails. Further investigation yielded evidence suggesting that butane canisters rigged to create an explosive-actuated incendiary device were used — not an entirely new approach in Mexico but one that is rarely seen there. Nevertheless, it does indicate that the drug cartels are incorporating a new weapon into their arsenals.

The three butane gas canisters were detonated remotely in front of a cartel safe house as a rival cartel ambushed the house. The devices were activated using cell phones and a garage door opener. Nobody was killed by the devices, which probably were set by individuals inside the safe house as booby traps. It is unclear who was responsible for detonating them, but it appears that members of the Beltran Leyva cartel (to whom the safe house belonged) had the devices in place before the ambush as part of their defenses. Such booby traps are commonly used in methamphetamine labs in the United States.

These were not vehicle-borne improvised explosive devices (VBIEDs), as some reports have erroneously noted. They were incendiary devices placed in or under the cars. A VBIED employs a car to attack a specific target, and insurgents often use them in Iraq and Afghanistan. The attack on the Indian Embassy in Kabul, Afghanistan, is a good example of the use of a VBIED.

According to the Mexican newspaper El Universal, a U.S. Justice Department official called the Culiacan bombing "narcoterrorism," a term conjuring up images of the late Colombian cartel leader Pablo Escobar's cocaine trafficking cartel, which detonated huge VBIEDs to kill its rivals. But the kinds of devices used in Culiacan on July 14 — blast caps attached to gas canisters, essentially — are very common in other countries, particularly Greece and Russia, and organized-crime groups, insurgent groups and common criminals use these devices the world over.

That Mexican cartels would have adopted the tactic is not surprising given the overall expansion of cartel violence in Mexico. Gunfights with government forces and rival cartels have led to record numbers of deaths. And as these gunfights become more and more violent, cartels are looking for other ways to take out their targets. Using gas canisters to create remotely detonated improvised devices is a much more efficient way to kill a target while limiting (but certainly not eliminating) collateral damage.

The use of grenades and other explosive devices is quite common among cartel members, but the difference between a grenade and an IED or improvised incendiary device is significant. Foot soldiers need only basic training in the use of a grenade, whereas improvised devices using butane canisters require a certain level of expertise to build and rig for remote detonation.

The Culiacan attack used an incendiary device placed in or under a car — a tactic that can be used to kill a specific target or, as in this case, to kill ambushers who might use the car for cover during a firefight. It remains unclear whether the cars (or the gas canisters attached to them) belonged to the safe house or the ambushing cartel members. Either way, this use of improvised incendiary devices indicates that Mexican drug cartels are expanding their arsenals.

21: Mexico Security Memo
Sept. 22, 2008

Independence Day Bombing

The level of daily violence in Mexico crossed a dangerous threshold Sept. 15 with a grenade attack on a crowd of civilians during Mexico's Independence Day celebration in Morelia, Michoacan state. Police say that at the culmination of the celebration, shortly before midnight, an unidentified man threw a fragmentation grenade into the center of the city's central plaza, where approximately 30,000 people had gathered. Several minutes later, a second grenade detonated a few blocks away. Overall, eight people died and up to 100 were wounded as a result of the blasts. The investigation is ongoing, but by most accounts, authorities suspect the attack was conducted by a faction of Michoacan's La Familia crime organization.

It is difficult to overstate the significance of this attack. Up until this point, Mexico's drug war had primarily affected government officials and those involved in the drug trade. Collateral damage occasionally included casualties among civilian bystanders, but, generally, the civilian population had been insulated from the violence. The attack in Morelia, however, represents the first clear case of the indiscriminate killing of civilians.

This attack has many implications — one of which is likely to be that officials in Mexico City will reassess the threat. Whereas the government was dealing with the effects of increasing attacks on police officers before, now authorities must deal with the prospect of additional terrorist-style attacks on civilian targets. However, while authorities are right to prepare for such a scenario, it is by no means certain that such attacks will become the norm across Mexico. First, it is not clear where the attack order originated in the criminal chain of command; in fact, the simplicity of the attack would have required the participation of no more than one or two people, and grenades are not exactly hard to acquire in Mexico. Second, the fact that such attacks have not become the norm already suggests that the country's larger cartels have calculated that it is not in their interest to indiscriminately kill civilians — at least not yet.

Of course, it is possible that the tactics used in the Sept. 15 attack will be used only once, similar to a February improvised explosive device attack in Mexico City. In that case, STRATFOR described the implications of an expansion of the cartels' arsenal, but more than seven months later, it remains an isolated incident. Nevertheless, as long as one group is willing and able to indiscriminately target civilians, it will undoubtedly affect many aspects of the country's security landscape.

Perhaps more important, the Sept. 15 attack highlights just what kind of innovation Mexico's criminal groups are capable of when backed into a corner and serves as a powerful reminder that, as bad as the situation is in Mexico, it can certainly get a lot worse.

Cartel Operations and the United States

The Sept. 15 attack will not only have repercussions in Mexico City but also in Washington, as the United States prepares to increase its investment in the fight against the drug trade by spending $2 billion in counternarcotics aid money to Mexico and Central America through the Merida Initiative. The United States has been involved in the fight against Mexican drug traffickers for years, as the cartels have expanded their reach into the United States. The culmination this past week of Project Reckoning, in which 175 members and associates of the Gulf cartel were arrested in the United States, underscores how Mexican drug traffickers are using their assets north of the border not only for domestic distribution but also for transatlantic trafficking purposes.

This past week also saw warnings of intensifying violence in border cities, particularly Ciudad Juarez. According to a source in the Mexican government, Mexican authorities along the border are preparing for a significant uptick in the violence in Chihuahua state as rival drug gangs are expected to increase their attacks on each other at the end of September and beginning of October.

This kind of cartel activity has become the norm for the United States along the border. The grenade attack in Morelia, however, is a different story. Two days after the attack, the U.S. ambassador to Mexico issued a condemnation of the "narcoterrorists" behind the attack, which STRATFOR believes is the first time a U.S. official has used that term in reference to Mexican drug traffickers. An embassy spokesman told STRATFOR that the attacks certainly crossed the line, but that the ambassador's use of the term "narcoterrorist" was not intended to reflect a shift in thinking in Washington regarding the threat in Mexico.

Nevertheless, it is hard to believe that the prospect of future terrorist-style attacks south of the border will not spark a reassessment by the United States. Although there is currently no evidence to suggest that Mexico will become what Colombia was during the height of Bogota's war against the cartels there — which included frequent car bombs, the bombing of a commercial airliner and the targeting of a vice-presidential candidate — there is no denying that Mexico has experienced a steady escalation in violence. Such a significant step in this escalation is difficult to ignore.

105

22: The Long Road to Security Reform
Oct. 1, 2008

Mexican President Felipe Calderon sent a security reform package to the Mexican Congress on Sept. 30. Mexico's security apparatus is waging a bitter war against drug cartels, and as the death toll rises, Calderon faces increasing pressure to bring the violence under control. However, despite Calderon's concerted efforts, security reform will be extremely difficult to achieve.

Forged in a meeting Calderon held with Mexican security officials and the leaders of all 32 Mexican states, the bill is the latest in a series of reforms. This bill proposes the creation of a national database of criminals and increased penalties for drug-trafficking offenses, while substituting rehabilitation therapy for drug abusers in place of incarceration. The measure also establishes a new department that will oversee anti-corruption efforts in the federal forces and proposes to enhance coordination of state- and municipal-level police forces with federal-level forces.

Calderon's recent initiatives are by no means out of the ordinary for his administration, which has been characterized by a great deal of reform. However, the security situation in Mexico has given the issue new impetus as the violence increases. The death toll for cartel-related violence for 2008 thus far stands at about 3,100, compared to a total death toll of 2,500 in 2007. To put that in context, the total number of U.S. combat deaths in Iraq since the beginning of the war in 2003 is just under 3,400. Mexico stands a good chance of beating that number in 2008 alone.

Public opposition to the rising violence has started growing, and anti-violence groups recently organized a countrywide march that could herald a new era of public unrest in reaction to the violence. This mood was exacerbated by the Sept. 15 attack on Mexican Independence Day celebrations in Morelia, Michoacan state, which displayed a heretofore unseen willingness on the cartels' part to blatantly attack unarmed civilians.

Though Calderon's approval ratings remain high, the people of Mexico also believe that the government is losing the war against the drug cartels.

Despite this impression, the government has certainly scored some successes against the cartels. Through the deployment of around 36,000 troops to different cartel hot spots around the country, Mexico has managed to disrupt some operations. These successes have included the capture of a semi-submersible vessel loaded with nearly six tons of cocaine in July, and the interdiction of 8,000 drums of methamphetamine ingredients in Guadalajara, also in July. But these successes have been partial, and the cartels have clearly started adjusting their tactics, including shifting some of their operations farther down into Central America.

Meanwhile, the cartel-related violence in Mexico has only risen. The fundamental cause of the violence is not only the security efforts Calderon has led against the cartels but also the fracturing of alliances and territorial control among the cartels that the Mexican military's presence has incurred. The violence includes clashes between security forces and cartels — particularly as cartels have increased their targeting of police officers — but also shows the raging struggle for territory among major drug traffickers.

In the midst of this chaos, Calderon is attempting to make a series of reforms that will give Mexico the sort of ideally coordinated and modern police force it needs. But the Mexican government faces a set of determined, violent, organized cartels that have between $40 billion and $100 billion of income per year at their disposal. The cartels actively and effectively use both violence and bribery to control local officials and have the power to completely undermine government initiatives through the corruption of government law enforcement personnel. Thus, not only does the government face challenges from the outside, it also faces deep and abiding corruption in its ranks — corruption that only gets worse as more law enforcement agencies become involved in combating the drug trade.

In the long term, Calderon aims to gradually remove the military from the cartel fight. The military has so far been the main tool that he has used against the cartels. But not only is it logistically difficult and undesirable to keep the military deployed in long-term domestic operations (the military deployment is coming up on its two-year anniversary), Mexico also runs a certain risk of introducing corruption into the military.

But in order to disengage the military from its anti-cartel operations, Calderon must substantially reorganize the federal police. He has begun to do so by merging the Federal Investigative Agency (AFI) and the Federal Preventive Police (PFP). Designed to centralize control over the agencies and put anti-corruption policies into effect, it is a policy that has so far gone poorly — with federal agents even staging public protests in opposition to the merger.

However, although structural shifts such as the AFI-PFP merger will allow the government to make strides in gaining control of the country, the fundamental issue is how to combat corruption. The government must find a way to protect law enforcement agents from being targeted by the cartels, and it must also somehow make honesty more profitable than colluding with the cartels.

Until Calderon can address these fundamental problems, it does not matter how many reform packages he is able to pass through Congress. Ultimately, they will amount to little more than a timely publicity stunt for the government during a time of rising indignation.

23: The Counterintelligence Implications of Foreign Service Nationals
Oct. 29, 2008

Mexican Attorney General Eduardo Medina Mora said Oct. 27 that five officials from the anti-organized crime unit (SIEDO) of the Office of the Mexican Attorney General (PGR) have been arrested for allegedly providing intelligence to the Beltrán Leyva drug- trafficking organization for money. Two of the recently arrested officials were senior SIEDO officers. One of those was Fernando Rivera Hernández, SIEDO's director of intelligence; the other was Miguel Colorado González, SIEDO's technical coordinator.

This episode follows earlier announcements of the arrests in August of SIEDO officials on corruption charges. Medina Mora said that since July, more than 35 PGR agents have been arrested for accepting bribes from cartel members — bribes that, according to Medina Mora, can range from $150,000 to $450,000 a month depending on the quality of information provided.

Mexican newspapers including La Jornada are reporting that information has been uncovered in the current investigation indicating the Beltrán Leyva organization had developed paid sources inside Interpol and the U.S. Embassy in Mexico City, and that the source in the embassy has provided intelligence on Drug Enforcement Administration (DEA) investigations. The source at the U.S. Embassy was reportedly a foreign service national investigator, or FSNI. The newspaper El Universal has reported that the U.S. Marshals Service employed the FSNI in question.

This situation provides us with a good opportunity to examine the role of foreign service national employees at U.S. missions abroad and why they are important to embassy functions, and to discuss the counterintelligence liability they present.

Foreign Service Nationals

U.S. embassies and consulates can be large and complicated entities. They can house dozens of U.S. government agencies and employ hundreds, or even thousands, of employees. Americans like their creature comforts, and keeping a large number of employees comfortable (and productive) requires a lot of administrative and logistical support, everything from motor pool vehicles to commissaries. Creature comforts aside, merely keeping all of the security equipment functioning in a big mission — things like gates, vehicle barriers, video cameras, metal detectors, magnetic locks and residential alarms — can be a daunting task.

In most places, the cost of bringing Americans to the host country to do all of the little jobs required to run an embassy or consulate is prohibitive. Because of this, the U.S. government often hires a large group of local people (called foreign service nationals, or FSNs) to perform non-sensitive administrative functions. FSN jobs can range from low-level menial positions, such as driving the embassy shuttle bus, answering the switchboard or cooking in the embassy cafeteria, to more important jobs such as helping the embassy contract with local companies for goods and services, helping to screen potential visa applicants or translating diplomatic notes into the local language. Most U.S. diplomatic posts employ dozens of FSNs, and large embassies can employ hundreds of them.

The embassy will also hire FSNIs to assist various sections of the embassy such as the DEA attaché, the regional security office, Immigration and Customs Enforcement and the anti-fraud unit of the consular section. FSNIs are the embassy's subject-matter experts on crime in the host country and are responsible for maintaining liaison between the embassy and the host country's security and law enforcement organizations. In a system where most diplomats and attachés are assigned to a post only for two or three years, the FSNs become the institutional memory of the embassy. They are the long-term keepers of the contacts with the host country government and will always be expected to introduce their new American bosses to the people they need to know in the government to get their jobs done.

Because FSNIs are expected to have good contacts and to be able to reach their contacts at any time of the day or night in case of emergency, the people hired for these FSNI positions are normally former senior law enforcement officers from the host country. The senior police officials are often close friends and former classmates of the current host country officials. This means that they can call the chief of police of the capital city at home on a Saturday or the assistant minister of government at 3 a.m. if the need arises.

To help make sure this assistance flows, the FSNI will do little things like deliver bottles of Johnny Walker Black during the

Christmas holidays or bigger things like help the chief of police obtain visas so his family can vacation at Disney World. Visas, in fact, are a very good tool for fostering liaison. Not only can they allow the vice minister to do his holiday shopping in Houston, they can also be used to do things like bring vehicles or consumer goods from the United States back to the host country for sale at a profit.

Since FSNs tend to work for embassies for long periods of time, while the Americans rotate through, there is a tendency for FSNs to learn the system and to find ways to profit from it. It is not uncommon for FSNs to be fired or even prosecuted in local court systems for theft and embezzlement. FSNs have done things like take kickbacks on embassy contracts for arranging to direct the contract to a specific vendor; pay inflated prices for goods bought with petty cash and then split the difference with the vendor who provided the false receipt; and steal gasoline, furniture, computers and nearly anything else that can be found in an embassy.

While this kind of fraud is more commonplace in Third World nations where corruption is endemic, it is certainly not confined there; it can even occur in European capitals. Again, visas are a critical piece of the puzzle. Genuine U.S. visas are worth a great deal of money, and it is not uncommon to find FSNs involved in various visa fraud schemes. FSN employees have gone as far as accepting money to provide visas to members of terrorist groups like Hezbollah. In countries involved in human trafficking, visas have been traded for sexual favors in addition to money. In fairness, the amount that can be made from visa fraud means it is not surprising to find U.S. foreign service officers participating in visa fraud as well.

Liabilities

While it saves money, employing FSNs does present a very real counterintelligence risk. In essence, it is an invitation to a local intelligence service to send people inside U.S. buildings to collect information. In most countries, the U.S. Embassy cannot do a complete background investigation on an FSN candidate without the assistance of the host country government. This means the chances of catching a plant are slim unless the Americans have their own source in the local intelligence service that will out the operation.

In many countries, foreigners cannot apply for a job with the U.S. Embassy without their government's permission. Obviously, this means local governments can approve only those applicants who agree to provide the government with information. In other countries, embassy employment is not that obviously controlled, but there still is a strong possibility of the host country sending agents to apply for jobs along with the other applicants.

It may be just coincidence, but in many countries the percentage of very attractive young women filling clerical roles at the U.S. Embassy appears many times higher than the number of attractive young women in the general population. This raises the specter of "honey traps," or sexual entrapment schemes aimed at U.S. employees. Such schemes have involved female FSNs in the past. In one well known example, the KGB employed attractive female operatives against the Marine Security Guards in Moscow, an operation that led to an extremely grave compromise of the U.S. Embassy there.

Because of these risk factors, FSNs are not allowed access to classified information and are kept out of sections of the embassy where classified information is discussed and stored. It is assumed that any classified information FSNs can access will be compromised.

Of course, not all FSNs report to host country intelligence services, and many of them are loyal employees of the U.S. government. In many countries, however, the extensive power host country intelligence services can wield over the lives of its citizens means that even otherwise loyal FSNs can be compelled to report to the host country service against their wills. Whereas an American diplomat will go home after two or three years, FSNs must spend their lives in the host country and are not protected by diplomatic status or international conventions. This makes them very vulnerable to pressure. Additionally, the aforementioned criminal activity by FSNs is not just significant from a fiscal standpoint. Such activity also leaves those participating in it open to blackmail by the host government if the activity is discovered.

When one considers the long history of official corruption in Mexico and the enormous amounts of cash available to the Mexican drug cartels, it is no surprise that members of the SIEDO, much less an FNSI at the U.S. Embassy, should be implicated in such a case. The allegedly corrupt FNSI most likely was recruited into the scheme by a close friend or former associate who may have been working for the government and who was helping the Beltrán Leyva organization develop its intelligence network.

Limits

It appears that the FSNI working for the Beltrán Leyva organization at the U.S. Embassy in Mexico City worked for the U.S. Marshals Service, not the DEA. This means that he would not have had access to much DEA operational information. An FSNI working for the U.S. Marshals Service would be working on fugitive cases and would be tasked with liaison with various Mexican law enforcement jurisdictions. Information regarding fugitive operations would be somewhat useful to the cartels, since many cartel members have been indicted in U.S. courts and the U.S. government would like to extradite them.

Even if the FSNI involved had been working for the DEA, however, there are limits to how much information he would have been able to provide. First of all, DEA special agents are well aware of the degree of corruption in Mexico, and they are therefore concerned that information passed on to the Mexican government can be passed to the cartels. The special agents also would assume that their FSN employees may be reporting to the Mexican government, and would therefore take care to not tell the FSN anything they wouldn't want the Mexican government — or the cartels — to know.

The type of FSNI employee in question would be tasked with conducting administrative duties such as helping the DEA attaché with liaison and passing name checks and other queries to various jurisdictions in Mexico. The FSN would not be privy to classified DEA cable traffic, and would not sit in on sensitive operational meetings.

In the intelligence world, however, there are unclassified things that can be valuable intelligence. These include the names and home addresses of all the DEA employees in the country, for example, or the types of cars the special agents drive and the confidential license plates they have for them.

Other examples could be the FSNI being sent to the airport to pick up a group of TDY DEA agents and bringing them to the embassy. Were the agents out-of-shape headquarters-types wearing suits and doing an inspection, or fit field agents from a special operations group coming to town to help take down a high-value target? Even knowing that the DEA attaché has suddenly changed his schedule and is now working more overtime can indicate that something is up. Information that the attaché has asked the FSNI about the police chief in a specific jurisdiction, for example, could also be valuable to a drug-trafficking organization expecting a shipment to arrive at that jurisdiction.

In the end, it is unlikely that this current case resulted in grave damage to DEA operations in Mexico. Indeed, the FSNI probably did far less damage to counternarcotics operations than the 35 PGR employees who have been arrested since July. But the vulnerabilities of FSN employees are great, and there are likely other FSNs on the payroll of the various Mexican cartels.

As long as the U.S. government employs FSNs it will face the security liability that comes with them. In general, however, this liability is offset by the utility they provide and the systems put in place to limit the counterintelligence damage they can cause.

24: Worrying Signs from Border Raids
Nov. 12, 2008

Last week the Mexican government carried out a number of operations in Reynosa, Tamaulipas, aimed at Jaime "El Hummer" Gonzalez Duran, one of the original members of the brutal cartel group known as Los Zetas. According to Mexican government officials, Gonzalez Duran controlled the Zetas' operations in nine Mexican states.

The Nov. 7 arrest of Gonzalez Duran was a major victory for the Mexican government and will undoubtedly be a major blow to the Zetas. Taking Gonzalez Duran off the streets, however, is not the only aspect of these operations with greater implications. The day before Gonzalez Duran's arrest, Mexican officials searching for him raided a safe house, where they discovered an arms cache that would turn out to be the largest weapons seizure in Mexican history. This is no small feat, as there have been several large hauls of weapons seized from the Zetas and other Mexican cartel groups in recent years.

The weapons seized at the Gonzalez Duran safe house included more than 500 firearms, a half-million rounds of ammunition and 150 grenades. The cache also included a LAW rocket, two grenade launchers and a small amount of explosives. Along with the scores of assorted assault rifles, grenades and a handful of gaudy gold-plated pistols were some weapons that require a bit more examination: namely, the 14 Fabrique Nationale (FN) P90 personal defense weapons and the seven Barrett .50-caliber sniper rifles contained in the seizure.

Matapolicias

As previously noted, the FN Five-Seven pistol and FN P90 personal defense weapon are very popular with the various cartel enforcer groups operating in Mexico. The Five-Seven and the P90 shoot a 5.7 x 28mm round that has been shown to be effective in penetrating body armor as well as vehicle doors and windows. Because of this ability to punch through body armor, cartel enforcers call the weapons "matapolicias," Spanish for "cop killers." Of course, AK-47 and M16-style assault rifles are also effective at penetrating body armor and vehicles, as are large-caliber hunting rifles such as the 30.06 and the .308. But the advantage of the Five-Seven and the P90 is that they provide this penetration capability in a much smaller — and thus far more concealable — package.

The P90 is a personal defense weapon designed to be carried by tank crew members or combat support personnel who require a compact weapon capable of penetrating body armor. It is considered impractical for such soldiers to be issued full-size infantry rifles or even assault rifles, so traditionally these troops were issued pistols and submachine guns. The proliferation of body armor on the modern battlefield, however, has rendered many pistols and submachine guns that fire pistol ammunition ineffective. Because of this, support troops needed a small weapon that could protect them from armored troops; the P90 fits this bill.

In fact, the P90 lends itself to anyone who needs powerful, concealable weapons. Protective security details, some police officers and some special operations forces operators thus have begun using the P90 and other personal defense weapons. The P90's power and ability to be concealed also make it an ideal weapon for cartel enforcers intent on conducting assassinations in an urban environment — especially those stalking targets wearing body armor.

The Five-Seven, which is even smaller than the P90, fires the same fast, penetrating round. Indeed, cartel hit men have killed several Mexican police officers with these weapons in recent months. However, guns that fire the 5.7 x 28mm cartridge are certainly not the only firearms used in attacks against police — Mexican cops have been killed by many other types of weapons.

Reach Out and Touch Someone

While the P90 and Five-Seven are small and light, and use a small, fast round to penetrate armor, the .50-caliber cartridge fired by a Barrett sniper rifle is the polar opposite: It fires a huge chunk of lead. By way of comparison, the 5.7 x 28mm cartridge is just a little more than 1.5 inches long and has a 32-grain bullet. The .50-caliber Browning Machine Gun (BMG) cartridge is actually 12.7 x 99mm, measures nearly 5.5 inches long and fires a 661-grain bullet. The P90 has a maximum effective range of 150 meters (about 165 yards), whereas a Barrett's listed maximum effective range is 1,850 meters (about 2,020 yards) — and there are reports of coalition forces snipers in Afghanistan scoring kills at more than 2,000 meters (about 2,190 yards).

The .50-BMG round not only will punch through body armor and normal passenger vehicles, it can defeat the steel plate armor and the laminated ballistic glass and polycarbonate windows used in lightly armored vehicles. This is yet another reminder that there is no such thing as a bulletproof car. The round is also capable of penetrating many brick and concrete block walls.

We have heard reports for years of cartels seeking .50-caliber sniper rifles made by Barrett and other U.S. manufacturers. Additionally, we have noted many reports of seizures from arms smugglers in the United States of these weapons bound for Mexico, or of the weapons being found in Mexican cartel safe houses — such as the seven rifles seized in Reynosa. Unlike the P90s, however, we cannot recall even one instance of these powerful weapons being used in an attack against another cartel or against a Mexican government target. This is in marked contrast to Ireland, where the Irish Republican Army used .50-caliber Barrett rifles obtained from the United States in many sniper attacks against British troops and the Royal Ulster Constabulary.

That Mexican cartels have not used these devastating weapons is surprising. There are, in fact, very few weapons in the arsenals of cartel enforcers that we have not seen used. Firefights can feature everything from hand grenades to LAW rockets to rocket-propelled grenades. Even though most inter-cartel warfare has occurred inside densely populated Mexican cities such as Tijuana, Ciudad Juarez and Nuevo Laredo — places where it would be very difficult to find a place to take a shot longer than a few hundred meters, much less a

117

couple thousand — the power of the Barrett could be very effective for taking out targets wearing body armor, riding in armored vehicles, located inside the safe house of a rival cartel or even inside a government building. Also, unlike improvised explosive devices, which the cartels have avoided using for the most part, the use of .50-caliber rifles would not involve a high probability of collateral damage.

This indicates that the reason the cartels have not used these weapons is to be found in the nature of snipers and sniping.

Snipers

Most military and police snipers are highly trained and very self-disciplined. Being a sniper requires an incredible amount of practice, patience and preparation. Aside from rigorous training in marksmanship, the sniper must also be trained in camouflage, concealment and movement. Snipers are often forced to lie immobile for hours on end. Additional training is required for snipers operating in urban environments, which offer their own set of challenges to the sniper; though historically, as seen in battles like Stalingrad, urban snipers can be incredibly effective.

Snipers commonly deploy as part of a team of two, comprising a shooter and a spotter. This means two very self-disciplined individuals must be located and trained. The team must practice together and learn how to accurately estimate distances, wind speed, terrain elevation and other variables that can affect a bullet's trajectory. An incredible amount of attention to detail is required for a sniper team to get into position and for their shots to travel several hundred meters and accurately, consistently strike a small target.

In spite of media hype and popular fiction, criminals or terrorists commit very few true sniper attacks. For example, many of our sniper friends were very upset that the media chose to label the string of murders committed by John Mohammed and Lee Boyd Malvo as the "D.C. Sniper Case." While Mohammed and Malvo did use concealment, they commonly shot at targets between 50 and 100 meters (about 55 yards to 110 yards) away. Therefore, calling Mohammed and Malvo snipers was a serious insult to the genuine article. The assassinations of President John F. Kennedy and Martin Luther King Jr., as well as the killing of Dr. Bernard Slepian, also have been dubbed sniper attacks, but they actually were all shootings committed at distances of less than 100 meters.

Of course, using a Barrett at short ranges (100 meters or less) is still incredibly effective and does not require a highly trained sniper — as a group of Bureau of Alcohol, Tobacco, Firearms and Explosives special agents found out in 1993 when they attempted to serve search and arrest warrants at the Branch Davidian compound in Waco, Texas. The agents were met with .50-caliber fire that ripped gaping holes through the Chevrolet Suburbans they sought cover behind. Many of the agents wounded in that incident were hit by the shrapnel created as the .50-caliber rounds punched through their vehicles.

While it is extremely powerful, the Barrett is also a long, heavy weapon. If the sniper lacks training in urban warfare, it might prove very difficult to move around with the gun and also to find a concealed place to employ it. This may partially explain why the Mexican cartels have not used the weapons more.

Moreover, while the Zetas originally comprised deserters from the Mexican military and over the years have shown an ability to conduct assaults and ambushes, we have not traditionally seen them deploy as snipers. Today, most of the original Zetas are now in upper management and no longer serve as foot soldiers.

The newer men brought into the Zetas include some former military and police officers along with some young gangster types; most of them lack the level of training possessed by the original Zetas. While the Zetas have also brought on a number of former Kaibiles, Guatemalan special operations forces personnel, most of them appear to be assigned as bodyguards for senior Zetas. This may mean we are not seeing the cartels employ snipers because their rank-and-file enforcers do not possess the discipline or training to function as snipers.

Potential Problems

Of course, criminal syndicates in possession of these weapons still pose a large potential threat to U.S. law enforcement officers, especially when the weapons are in the hands of people like Gonzalez Duran and his henchmen. According to an FBI intelligence memo dated Oct. 17 and leaked to the media, Gonzalez Duran appeared to have gotten wind of the planned operation against him. He reportedly had authorized those under his command to defend their turf at any cost, to include engagements with U.S. law enforcement agents. It is important to remember that a chunk of that turf was adjacent to the U.S. border and American towns, and that Reynosa — where Gonzalez Duran was arrested and the weapons were seized — is just across the border from McAllen, Texas.

Armed with small, powerful weapons like the P90, cartel gunmen can pose a tremendous threat to any law enforcement officer who encounters them in a traffic stop or drug raid. Over the past several years, we have noted several instances of U.S. Border Patrol agents and other U.S. law enforcement officers being shot at from Mexico. The thought of being targeted by a weapon with the range and power of a .50-caliber sniper rifle would almost certainly send chills up the spine of any Border Patrol agent or sheriff's deputy working along the border.

Armed with assault rifles, hand grenades and .50-caliber sniper rifles, cartel enforcers have the potential to wreak havoc and outgun U.S. law enforcement officers. The only saving grace for U.S. law enforcement is that many cartel enforcers are often impaired by drugs or alcohol and tend to be impetuous and reckless. While the cartel gunmen are better trained than most Mexican authorities, their training does not stack up to that of most U.S. law enforcement officers. This was illustrated by an incident on Nov. 6 in Austin, Texas, when a police officer used his service pistol to kill a cartel gunman who fired on the officer with an AK-47.

While the arrest of Gonzalez Duran and the seizure of the huge arms cache in Reynosa have taken some killers and weapons off the street, they are only one small drop in the bucket. There are many heavily armed cartel enforcers still at large in Mexico, and the violence is spreading over the border into the United States. Law enforcement officers in the United States therefore need to maintain a keen awareness of the threat.

25: The Barrio Azteca Trial and the Prison Gang-Cartel Interface
Nov. 19, 2008

On Nov. 3, a U.S. District Court in El Paso, Texas, began hearing a case concerning members of a criminal enterprise that calls itself Barrio Azteca (BA). The group members face charges including drug trafficking and distribution, extortion, money laundering and murder. The six defendants include the organization's three bosses, Benjamin Alvarez, Manuel Cardoza and Carlos Perea; a sergeant in the group, Said Francisco Herrera; a lieutenant, Eugene Mona; and an associate, Arturo Enriquez.

The proceedings represent the first major trial involving BA, which operates in El Paso and West Texas, New Mexico and Arizona. The testimony is revealing much about how this El Paso-based prison gang operates, and how it interfaces with Mexican drug cartel allies that supply its drugs.

Mexico's cartels are in the business of selling drugs like marijuana, cocaine and heroin in the United States. Large amounts of narcotics flow north while large amounts of cash and weapons flow south. Managing these transactions requires that the cartels have a physical presence in the United States, something a cartel alliance with a U.S. gang can provide.

Of course, BA is not the only prison gang operating in the United States with ties to Mexico. Prison gangs can also be called street gangs — they recruit both in prisons and on the street. Within the United

121

States, there are at least nine well-established prison gangs with connections to Mexican drug cartels; Hermanos de Pistoleros Latinos, the Mexican Mafia and the Texas Syndicate are just a few such groups. Prison gangs like BA are very territorial and usually cover only a specific region, so one Mexican cartel might work with three to four prison or street gangs in the United States. Like BA, most of the U.S. gangs allied with Mexican cartels largely are composed of Mexican immigrants or Mexican-Americans. Nevertheless, white supremacist groups, mixed-race motorcycle gangs and African-American street gangs also have formed extensive alliances with Mexican cartels.

Certainly, not all U.S. gangs the Mexican cartels have allied with are the same. But examining how BA operates offers insights into how other gangs — like the Latin Kings, the Texas Syndicate, the Sureños, outlaw motorcycle gangs, and transnational street gangs like MS-13 — operate in alliance with the cartels.

Barrio Azteca Up Close

Spanish for "Aztec Neighborhood," BA originated in a Texas state penitentiary in 1986, when five inmates from El Paso organized the group as a means of protection in the face of the often-brutal ethnic tensions within prisons. By the 1990s, BA had spread to other prisons and had established a strong presence on the streets of El Paso as its founding members served their terms and were released. Reports indicate that in the late 1990s, BA had begun working with Joaquin "El Chapo" Guzman's Sinaloa Federation drug- trafficking organization, which at the time controlled drug shipments to Ciudad Juarez, El Paso's sister city across the Rio Grande.

According to testimony from several different witnesses on both sides of the current trial, BA now works only with the Juarez cartel of Vicente Carrillo-Fuentes, which has long controlled much of Mexico's Chihuahua state and Ciudad Juarez, and broke with the Sinaloa Federation earlier in 2008. BA took sides with the Juarez cartel, with which it is jointly running drugs across the border at the Juarez plaza.

BA provides the foot soldiers to carry out hits at the behest of Juarez cartel leaders. On Nov. 3, 10 alleged BA members in Ciudad Juarez were arrested in connection with 12 murders. The suspects were armed with four AK-47s, pistols and radio communication equipment — all hallmarks of a team of hit men ready to carry out a mission.

According to testimony from the ongoing federal case, which is being brought under the Racketeer Influenced and Corrupt Organizations (RICO) Act, drugs are taken at a discount from the supplier on the Mexico side and then distributed to dealers on the street. These distributors must then pay "taxes" to BA collectors to continue plying their trade. According to testimony from Josue Aguirre, a former BA member turned FBI informant, BA collects taxes from 47 different street-level narcotics operations in El Paso alone. Failure to pay these taxes results in death. One of the murder charges in the current RICO case involves the death of an El Paso dealer who failed to pay up when the collectors arrived to collect on a debt.

Once collected, the money goes in several different directions. First, BA lieutenants and captains, the midlevel members, receive $50 and $200 per month respectively for compensation. The bulk of BA's profit is then transferred using money orders to accounts belonging to the head bosses (like Alvarez, Cardoza and Perea) in prison. Cash is also brought back to Ciudad Juarez to pay the Juarez cartel, which provided the drugs in the first place.

BA receives discounts on drugs from the Juarez cartel by providing tactical help to its associates south of the border. Leaders of Carrillo Fuentes' organization in Juarez can go into hiding in El Paso under BA protection if their lives are in danger in Juarez. They can also order BA to track down cartel enemies hiding in El Paso. Former BA member Gustavo Gallardo testified in 2005 that he was sent to pick up a man in downtown El Paso who had cheated the Juarez cartel of money. Once Gallardo dropped him off at a safe house in El Paso, another team took the man — who was bound with rope and duct tape — to Ciudad Juarez, where Gallardo assumes he was killed.

BA and the World of Prison Gangs

Prison gangs are endemic to prison systems, where safety for inmates comes in numbers. Tensions (usually along racial lines) among dangerous individuals regularly erupt into deadly conflict. Prison gang membership affords a certain amount of protection against rival groups and offers fertile recruiting ground.

Once a prison gang grows its membership (along with its prestige) and establishes a clear hierarchy, its leader can wield an impressive amount of power. Some even wind up taking over prisons, like the antecedents of Russian organized crime did.

It might seem strange that members on the outside send money and answer to bosses in prison, since the bosses are locked up. But these bosses wield a great deal of influence over gang members in and out of prison. Disobedience is punishable by death, and regardless of whether a boss is in prison, he can order a hit on a member who has crossed him. Prison gang members also know that if they end up in prison again — a likely outcome — they will once again be dependent on the help of the boss to stay alive, and can perhaps even earn some money while doing time.

BA's illegal activities mean its members constantly cycle in and out of prison. Many BA members were involved in smaller, local El Paso street gangs before they were imprisoned. Once in prison, they joined BA with the sponsorship of a "godfather" who walks the recruit through the process. BA then performs a kind of background check on new recruits by circulating their name throughout the organization. BA is particularly interested in any evidence that prospective members have cooperated with the police.

Prison authorities are certainly aware of the spread of BA, and they try to keep Mexican nationals separated from known BA members, who are mostly Mexican-American, to prevent the spread of the gang's influence. BA has organizations in virtually every penitentiary in Texas, meaning that no matter where a BA member is imprisoned, he will have a protection network in place. BA members with truly extensive prison records might personally know the leader of every prison chapter, thus increasing the member's prestige. Thus, the constant cycling of members from the outside world into prison does not inhibit BA, but makes its members more cohesive, as it allows the prison system to increase bonds among gang members.

Communication challenges certainly arise, as exchanges between prisoners and those on the outside are closely monitored. But BA seems to have overcome this challenge. Former BA member Edward Ruiz testified during the trial that from 2003 to 2007, he acted as a clearinghouse for jailed members' letters and packages, which he then distributed to members on the outside. This tactic ensured that all prison communications would be traceable to just one address, thus not revealing the location of other members.

BA also allegedly used Sandy Valles New, who worked in the investigations section of the Office of the Federal Public Defender in El Paso from 1996 to 2002, to pass communications between gang members inside and outside prison. She exploited the access to — and the ability to engage in confidential communications with — inmates that attorneys enjoy, transmitting information back and forth between BA members inside and outside prison. Taped conversations reveal New talking to one of the bosses and lead defendants, Carlos Perea, about her fear of losing her job and thus not being able to continue transmitting information in this way. She also talked of crossing over to Ciudad Juarez to communicate with BA members in Mexico.

While BA had inside sources like New assisting it, the FBI was able to infiltrate BA in return. Josue Aguirre and Johnny Michelleti have informed on BA activities to the FBI since 2003 and 2005, respectively. Edward Ruiz, the mailman, also handed over stacks of letters to the FBI.

BA and the Mexican Cartels

As we indicated earlier, BA is only one of dozens of prison gangs operating along the U.S.-Mexican border that help Mexican drug-trafficking organizations smuggle narcotics across the border and then distribute them for the cartels. Mexican drug-trafficking organizations need groups that will do their bidding on the U.S. side of the border, as the border is the tightest choke point in the narcotics supply chain.

Getting large amounts of drugs across the border on a daily basis requires local connections to bribe border guards or border town policemen. Gangs on the U.S. side of the border also have contacts who sell drugs on the retail level, where markups bring in large profits. The current trial has revealed that the partnership goes beyond narcotics to include violence as well. In light of the high levels of violence raging in Mexico related to narcotics trafficking, there is a genuine worry that this violence (and corruption) could spread inside the United States.

One of the roles that BA and other border gangs fill for Mexican drug-trafficking organizations is that of enforcer. Prison gangs wield tight control over illegal activity in a specific territory. They keep tabs on people to make sure they are paying their taxes to the gang and not affiliating with rival gangs. To draw an analogy, they are like the local police who know the situation on the ground and can enforce specific rules handed down by a governmental body — or a Mexican cartel.

Details emerging from the ongoing trial indicate that BA works closely with the Juarez cartel and has contributed to drug-related violence inside the United States. While the killing of a street dealer by a gang for failure to pay up on time is common enough nationwide and hardly unique to Mexican drug traffickers, apprehending offenders in El Paso and driving them to Ciudad Juarez to be held or killed does represent a very clear link between violence in Mexico and the United States.

BA has proved its ability to strike within the United States. According to a STRATFOR source, BA is connected to Los Zetas — the U.S.-trained Mexican military members who deserted to traffic drugs — through a mutual alliance with the Juarez cartel. The Zetas possess a high level of tactical skill that could be passed along to BA, thus increasing its effectiveness.

The Potential for Cross-Border Violence

The prospect of enhanced cross-border violence is frightening, but the violence itself is not new. So far, Mexican cartels and their U.S. allies have focused on those directly involved in the drug trade. Whether this restraint will continue is unclear. Either way, collateral damage is always a possibility.

Previous incidents, like one that targeted a drug dealer in arrears in Phoenix and others that involved kidnappings and attacks against U.S. Border Patrol agents, indicate that violence has already begun creeping over from Mexico. So far, violence related to drug trafficking has not caused the deaths of U.S. law enforcement officials and/or civilians, though it has come close to doing so.

Another potential incubator of cross-border violence exists in BA's obligation to offer refuge to Juarez cartel members seeking safety in the United States. Such members most likely would have bounties on their heads. The more violent Mexico (and particularly Ciudad Juarez) becomes, the greater the risk Juarez cartel leaders face — and the more pressure they will feel to seek refuge in the United States. As more Juarez cartel leaders cross over and hide with BA help, the cartel's enemies will become increasingly tempted to follow them and kill them in the United States. Other border gangs in California, Arizona and New Mexico probably are following this same trajectory.

Two primary reasons explain why Mexican cartel violence for the most part has stopped short of crossing the U.S. border. First, the prospect of provoking U.S. law enforcement does not appeal to Mexican drug-trafficking organizations operating along the border. They do not want to provoke a coordinated response from a highly capable federal U.S. police force like the Drug Enforcement Administration, Bureau of Alcohol, Tobacco, Firearms and Explosives, or FBI. By keeping violence at relatively low levels and primarily aimed at other gang members and drug dealers, the Mexican drug-trafficking organizations can lessen their profile in the eyes of these U.S. agencies. Conversely, any increase in violence and/or the killing of U.S. police or civilians would dramatically increase federal scrutiny and retaliation.

The second reason violence has not crossed the border wholesale is that gangs like BA are in place to enforce the drug-trafficking organizations' rules. The need to send cartel members into the United States to kill a disobedient drug dealer is reduced by having a tight alliance with a border gang that keeps drugs and money moving smoothly and carries out the occasional killing to maintain order.

But the continued integrity of BA and its ability to carry out the writ of larger drug-trafficking organizations in Mexico might not be so certain. The Nov. 3 trial will undermine BA activity in the crucial trafficking corridor of El Paso/Ciudad Juarez.

The indictment and possible incarceration of the six alleged BA members would not damage the gang so badly — after all, BA is accustomed to operating out of prison, and there must certainly be members on the outside ready to fill in for their incarcerated comrades. But making BA's activities and modus operandi public should increase scrutiny on the gang and could very well lead to many more arrests.

In light of the presence of at least two FBI informants in the gang, BA leaders have probably moved into damage control mode, isolating members jeopardized by the informants. This will disrupt BA's day-to-day operations, making it at least temporarily less effective. STRATFOR sources say BA members on both sides of the border have been ordered to lie low until the trial is over and the damage can be fully assessed. This is a dangerous period for gangs like BA, as their influence over their territory and ability to operate is being reduced.

Weakening BA by extension weakens the Juarez cartel's hand in El Paso. While BA no doubt will survive the investigations the trial probably will spawn, given the high stakes across the border in Mexico, the Juarez cartel might be forced to reduce its reliance on BA. This could prompt the Juarez cartel to rely on its own members in Ciudad Juarez to carry out hits in the United States and to provide its own security to leaders seeking refuge in the United States. It could also prompt it to turn to a new gang facing less police scrutiny. Under either scenario, BA's territory would be encroached upon. And considering the importance of controlling territory to prison gangs

— and the fact that BA probably still will be largely intact — this could lead to increased rivalries and violence.

The Juarez cartel-BA dynamic could well apply to alliances between U.S. gangs and Mexican drug-trafficking organizations, such as Hermanos de Pistoleros Latinos in Houston, the Texas Syndicate and Tango Blast operating in the Rio Grande Valley and their allies in the Gulf cartel; the Mexican Mafia in California and Texas and its allies in the Tijuana and Sinaloa cartels; and other gangs operating in the United States with ties to Mexican cartels like Mexikanemi, Norteños and the Sureños.

Ultimately, just because BA or any other street gang working with Mexican cartels is weakened does not mean that the need to enforce cartel rules and supply chains disappears. This could put Mexican drug-trafficking organizations on a collision course with U.S. law enforcement if they feel they must step in themselves to take up the slack. As their enforcers stateside face more legal pressure, the cartels' response therefore bears watching.

26: Mexico in Crisis: An Introduction
Dec. 8, 2008

As the year draws to a close, the STRATFOR team has been re-evaluating the stability of several key countries in the international system. In many cases the results have been pessimistic (even by our often jaundiced standards). This effort has given rise to our Countries in Crisis series, and STRATFOR now begins the publication of that series' second installment: an overview of Mexico.

The Mexican state is undergoing the most severe challenges it has faced since the 1910-1920 Mexican Revolution. Unlike the deep and overlapping complexities that threaten to shatter the first country in our series, Ukraine, Mexico's problems can be boiled down to illicit drugs. The country's geography almost dictates that Mexico's City's writ will be ignored across wide tracts of the country, and current efforts to bring law and order to the Mexican frontier are threatening the central functionality of the state itself. In 2008 alone, Mexico has already suffered more deaths from drug-related violence than all coalition deaths in Iraq since the war's beginning in 2003.

STRATFOR will delve deeply into the Mexican crisis in two parts, with a supplemental addendum. First, we will dissect the economic and political trends that run alongside the cartel wars, highlighting where there is hope that Mexico may yet avoid the fate of degenerating into a failed state and where such hope is unwarranted. Second, we will look at the geographic, institutional and security factors that have caused and exacerbated Mexico's cartel wars. Finally, we will present our 2008 cartel report, an annual publication that will serve as an addendum to the Countries in Crisis series. The report will chronicle in detail the continuing evolution of the drug war in 2008, showing how Mexican cartels have evolved and spread their influence not only throughout Mexico but also across the border into the United States and into the wider world.

27: Mexico in Crisis (Part 1):
A Critical Confluence of Events
Dec. 9, 2008

Mexico appears to be a country coming undone. Powerful drug cartels use Mexico for the overland transshipment of illicit drugs — mainly cocaine, marijuana and methamphetamine — from producers in South America to consumers in the United States. Violence between competing cartels has grown over the past two years as they have fought over territory and as the Mexican army has tried to secure the embattled areas, mainly on the country's periphery. It is a tough fight, made even tougher by endemic geographic, institutional and technical problems in Mexico that make a government victory hard to achieve. The military is stretched thin, the cartels are becoming even more aggressive and the people of Mexico are growing tired of the violence.

At the same time, the country is facing a global economic downturn that will slow Mexico's growth and pose additional challenges to national stability. Although the country appears to be in a comfortable fiscal position for the short term, the outlook for the country's energy industry is bleak, and a decline in employment could prompt social unrest. Complications also loom in the political sphere as Mexican parties campaign ahead of 2009 legislative elections and jockey for position in preparation for the 2012 presidential election.

Economic Turmoil

As the international financial crisis roils economies around the world, Mexico has been hit hard. Tightly bound to its northern neighbor, Mexico's economy is set to shrink alongside that of the United States, and it will be an enormous challenge for the Mexican government to face in the midst of a devastating war with the drug cartels.

The key to understanding the Mexican economy is an appreciation of Mexico's enormous integration with the United States. As a party to the North American Free Trade Agreement and one of the largest U.S. trading partners, Mexico is highly vulnerable to the vagaries of the U.S. economy. The United States is the largest single source of foreign direct investment in Mexico. Even more important, the United States is the destination of more than 80 percent of Mexico's exports. A slowdown in economic activity and consumer demand in the United States thus translates directly into a slowdown in Mexico.

In addition to the sale of most Mexican goods in the U.S. markets, the United States is a major source of revenue for Mexico through remittances, and together these sources of income provide around a quarter of Mexico's gross domestic product (GDP). When Mexican immigrants send money home from the United States, it makes up a substantial portion of Mexico's external revenue streams. Remittances to Mexico totaled US$23.9 billion in 2007, according to the Mexican

Central Bank. The slowdown in the U.S. housing sector has brought remittances down during the course of 2008 from highs in the middle of 2007. As of the end of September 2008, remittances for the year were down by $672.6 million from the same period in 2007.

The decline in remittances is being matched by a slowdown in Mexico's economy across the board. The Mexican government estimates that Mexico's GDP will slow from 3.2 percent growth in 2007 to 1.8 percent in 2008. Given that the U.S. economy is sliding into recession at the same time, this is likely only the beginning of the Mexican slowdown, and growth is expected to bottom out at 0.9 percent in 2009.

With growing pressure on the rest of the economy, the prospect of rising unemployment is perhaps the most daunting challenge. So far, unemployment and underemployment in Mexico have risen from 9.77 percent in December 2007 to 10.82 percent in October 2008, (some 27 percent of the workforce is employed in the informal sector). But slowed growth and declining demand in the United States is sure to cause further declines in employment in Mexico. As happened in the wake of Mexico's 1982 debt crisis, Mexicans may seek to return to a certain degree of subsistence farming in order to make it through the tough times, but that is nowhere near an ideal solution. The government has proposed a $3.4 billion infrastructure buildup plan to be implemented in 2009 that will seek to boost jobs (and demand for industrial goods) throughout Mexico, although it is not clear how quickly this can take effect or how many jobs it might create.

Further compounding the employment issue is the possibility of Mexican immigrants returning from the United States as jobs disappear to the north. STRATFOR sources have already reported a slightly higher-than-normal level of immigrants returning to Mexico, and although it is too early to plot the trajectory of this trend, there is little doubt that job opportunities are evaporating in the United States. As migrants return to Mexico, however, there are very few jobs waiting for them there, either. This presents the very real possibility that the available jobs will be in the black markets, and specifically with the drug cartels. Demand for drugs persists despite economic downturns, and the business of the cartels continues unabated. Indeed, for the cartels, the economic downturn could be an excellent recruitment opportunity.

The turmoil in U.S. financial markets has directly damaged the value of the Mexican peso and has caused a loss of wealth among Mexican companies. Mexican businesses have lost billions of dollars (exact figures are not available at this time) to bad currency bets. Mexican companies in search of extra financing have had trouble floating corporate paper, which has forced the government to offer billions of dollars worth of guarantees. The upside to this is that a weaker currency will increase the attractiveness of Mexican exports to the United States vis-à-vis China (for a change), which will boost the export sector to a certain degree.

The fluctuating peso has also forced the Mexican central bank to inject about $14.8 billion into currency markets to stabilize the peso. Nevertheless, the peso has devalued by approximately 22.6 percent since the beginning of 2008. Partially as a result of the currency devaluation, inflation appears to be rising slightly. The government has reported a 12-month inflation rate of 6.2 percent, through mid-November. This is actually fairly low for a developing nation, but it is the highest inflation has been in Mexico since 2001.

Mexico's financial sector is highly exposed to the international credit market, with about 80 percent of Mexico's banks owned by foreign companies, and the banking sector has been unstable in recent months. Foreign capital has, to a certain degree, fled Mexican investments and banks as capital worldwide veered away from developing to developed markets, in response to the global financial crisis. The result is a decline in investments across the board, and there was a sharp decline in the purchase of Mexican government bonds. After a four-week fall in bond purchases, the Mexican government announced a $1.1 billion bond repurchase package Dec. 2 in an attempt to increase liquidity in the capital markets and lower interest rates. Although investors were not responsive, it is an indication that the government is taking its countercyclical duties seriously.

As the government seeks to counter falling employment and other economic challenges, it will need to lean heavily on its available resources. The central bank holds $83.4 billion in foreign reserves, as of Nov. 28, and can continue to use the money to implement monetary stabilization. Mexico also maintains oil stabilization funds that total more than $7.4 billion, which provides a small fiscal cushion. The 2009 Mexican federal budget calls for the first budget deficit in years — amounting to 1.8 percent of GDP — and has increased spending by 13 percent from the previous year's budget, to $231 billion.

Some 40 percent of this budget relies on oil revenues generated by Mexican state-owned oil company Petroleos Mexicanos (Pemex). Despite the fall in oil prices, Mexico has managed to secure its energy income through a series of hedged oil-sales contracts. These contracts will sustain the budget through the duration of 2009 with prices set from $70 to $100 per barrel. Mexico is a major exporter of oil — ranked the sixth largest producer and the 10th largest exporter. The energy industry is critical for the economy, just as it is for the government.

In the long term, however, Mexico's energy industry is crippled. Due to a history of restrictive energy regulations, oil production is falling precipitously (primarily at Mexico's gigantic offshore Cantarell oil field), with government reports indicating that production averaged 2.8 million barrels per day (bpd) between January and September, which is far from Mexico's target production of 3 million bpd. Thus, even if Mexico has secured the price of its oil through 2009, it cannot guarantee its production levels in the short term, and perhaps not in the long term.

To try to boost the industry's prospects, the Mexican government has passed an energy reform plan that will allow Pemex to issue contract agreements to foreign companies for joint exploration and production projects. The government has also decided to assume some of Pemex's debt in order to ease the company's access to international credit in light of the tight international credit market.

These changes could help Mexico pull its oil production rate out of the doldrums. However, most of Mexico's untapped reserves are located either in deep complex formations or offshore — environments in which Pemex is at best a technical laggard — making extraction projects expensive and technically difficult. With the international investment climate constrained by capital shortages, foreigners barred from sharing ownership of the oil they produce and the price of oil falling, it is not yet clear how interested foreign oil companies will be in such partnerships.

The decline in the energy sector has the potential to produce a sustained fiscal crisis in the two- to three-year time frame, even assuming that other aspects of the economic environment (nearly all of which are beyond Mexico's control) rectify themselves. The slack in government revenue will have to be taken up through increased taxes on other industries or on individuals, but it is not yet clear how such a replacement source of revenue might be created.

The overall political implications of the financial crisis will be reflected in a decline in employment and the standard of living of average Mexicans. In a country where political expression takes the form of paralyzing protest, the economic downturn could spell near-disaster for the administration of Mexican President Felipe Calderon.

The Shifting Political Landscape

In power since 2000, the ruling National Action Party (PAN) has enjoyed a fairly significant level of support for Calderon both within the legislature — where it lacks a ruling majority — and in the population at large, particularly given the razor-thin margin with which Calderon won his office in 2006. The Calderon administration has launched a number of reform efforts targeting labor, energy and, of course, security.

Although the PAN has maintained an alliance with the Institutional Revolutionary Party (PRI) for much of Calderon's administration, this is a unity that is unlikely to persist, given that both parties have begun to lay out their campaigns for the 2012 presidential election.

For the ruling party, there are a number of looming challenges on the political scene. Mexico has seen a massive spike in crime and drug-related violence coincide with the first eight years of rule by Calderon's PAN after 71 straight years of rule by the PRI. To make things worse, the global financial crisis has begun to impact Mexico — through no fault of its own — and the impact on employment could be devastating. Given the confluence of events, it is almost guaranteed that Calderon and the PAN will suffer political losses going forward, weakening the party's ability to move forward with decisive action.

So far, Calderon has been receiving credit for his all-out attack on the drug cartels, and his approval ratings are near 60 percent. As the economy weakens and the death toll mounts, however, this positive outlook could easily falter.

The challenge will not likely come from the PAN's 2006 rival, the Revolutionary Democratic Party (PRD). The PRD gained tremendous media attention when party leader Andres Manuel Lopez Obrador lost the presidential election to Calderon and proceeded to stage massive demonstrations protesting his loss. Since then, the PRD has adopted a less-radical stance, and the far-left elements of the party have begun to part ways with the less radical elements. This split within the PRD could weaken the party as it moves forward.

The weakening of the PRD is auspicious for Mexico's third party, the PRI, which has been playing a very careful game. The PRI has engaged in partnerships with the PAN in opposition (for the most part) to the leftist PRD. In doing so, the PRI has taken a strong role in the formation of legislation. However, the PRI's prospects for the 2012 presidential election have begun to improve, with the party's popularity on the rise. As of late October, the PRI was polling extremely well — at the expense of both the PAN and the PRD — with a 32.4 percent approval rating, compared to the PAN's 24.5 percent and the PRD's 10.8 percent.

In the short term, the June 2009 legislative elections will be a litmus test for the political gyrations of Mexico, a warm-up for the 2012 elections and the next stage of political challenges for Calderon. As the PRI positions itself in opposition to the PAN — and particularly if the party gains more seats in the Mexican legislature

— it will become increasingly difficult for the government to reach compromise solutions to looming challenges. Calderon is somewhat protected by his high approval ratings, which will make overt moves against him politically questionable for the PRI or the PRD.

Although a great deal could change (and quickly), these dynamics highlight the potential changes in political orientation for Mexico over the next three years. In the short term, the political situation remains relatively secure for Calderon, which is critical for a president who is balancing the need for substantial economic resuscitation with an ongoing war on domestic organized crime.

Mexico's most critical challenge is the convergence of events it now faces. The downturn in the economy, the political dynamics or the deteriorating security situation, each on its own, might not pose an insurmountable problem for Mexico. What could prove insurmountable is the confluence of all three, which appears to be in the making.

28: Mexico in Crisis (Part 2): A War of Attrition is a Limited Strategy
Dec. 11, 2008

Mexico's primary challenge in its fight against the drug cartels is its geography. The country's northern border region is made up of desert, separating the western and eastern coastal transportation networks and population centers. Great distances and inhospitable terrain — much of it arid or mountainous — make government control of the country extremely challenging.

The government does not control the slopes of the Sierra Madre Oriental or the Sierra Madre Occidental, which run north-south up each coast and are the primary drug-trafficking routes. Nor does it control the northern desert that borders the United States, which, like the fabled Wild West in the United States, is essentially a frontier where laws written in Mexico City are difficult to enforce.

The northern border region is fundamentally defined by its proximity to the United States, which is the primary source of trade revenue, tourism, remittances, jobs (for those who brave the border crossing) and foreign direct investment. Of course, the United States is also the world's biggest market for illicit drugs. Southeastern Mexico is equally frontier-like, with dense jungles on the eastern edge of the Mexico-Guatemala border and in the mountains of the Chiapas highlands. Though closer to Mexico City, the southern region is extremely poor, ethnically diverse and still hosts the Zapatista National Liberation Army, a remnant of the Mexican Revolution in the early 20th century.

Not incidentally, the revolution, which began in 1910, involved a near-identical challenge for the central government in terms of territorial control, with rebels of Emiliano Zapata's Liberation Army of the South in southern Mexico and Pancho Villa's army in the north. The geographical similarities between the revolutionary-era strongholds and those of today's drug cartels underscore how historically difficult it is for the government to control its territory. The absence of natural geographic connections such as interlinking rivers, which would provide easy and rapid transit for federal security forces, mean that the Mexican central government must overcome mountains, deserts and jungles to assert its authority in the hinterlands.

Today, the cartels take full advantage of the government's lack of control in the northern and southern parts of the country. Drug traffickers move cocaine into southern Mexico after traversing Central America, on the way north from the cocoa-growing Andean countries of South America. To the north, and along the transportation corridors of the two coasts, Mexican drug cartels enjoyed limited government interference during the decades of the Institutional Revolutionary Party (PRI) rule and established de facto kingdoms where their word was law and drugs moved efficiently northward — into the United States.

In 2006, however, the tide turned for the drug traffickers when newly elected Mexican President Felipe Calderon rode to power on

MEXICO'S GEOGRAPHY

Pacific Ocean

Gulf of California

Sierra Madre Occidental

Mexican High Plateau

Sierra Madre Oriental

Sierra Madre Del Sur

Mexico City

Chiapas Highlands

UNITED STATES

Gulf of Mexico

CUBA

GUATEMALA

BELIZE

HONDURAS

0 mi   200   400

campaign promises of crushing the cartels. The task would not be easy for Calderon. Corruption permeates every level of Mexico's law enforcement institutions — whose members are continuously under the threat of death by the cartels — and local (and even federal) police are unable to maintain the rule of law. This has left much of Mexico's border region utterly lawless.

With local and federal law enforcement compromised — and faced with a well-trained, wealthy, heavily armed and pernicious enemy — Calderon concluded that the only way to defeat Mexican organized crime was to deploy the military. But despite the military's superior firepower and combat capabilities (compared to domestic security forces), it is neither big enough to cover the necessary territory nor is it designed for domestic law enforcement. Long, drawn-out military operations also stress an already troubled government budget. And the environment in which the military must operate is a hostile one. As it pursues the cartels, the Mexican military is more like an occupying power chasing local insurgents than an agency of the central government enforcing the rule of law. Moreover, its relatively untarnished reputation in a country rife with corruption is not guaranteed to endure. The longer it stays engaged with the cartels the greater its chances of being corrupted. The reality, of course, is that Mexico has few other options.

Institutional Problems

During the 71 years of rule by the PRI and the subsequent six-year presidency of the National Action Party's Vicente Fox, the Mexican government made limited moves against the cartels. For most of PRI's rule, the cartels were nowhere near as strong as they have become in the past decade, so politicians could afford to let them be, for the most part. Lacking pressure during this time, the cartels grew increasingly powerful, establishing complex business networks throughout their regions and into the international drug markets. As business began to pick up, so did the influence of the cartels. The increasing cash flow gave the cartels higher operating budgets, which made it easier to buy

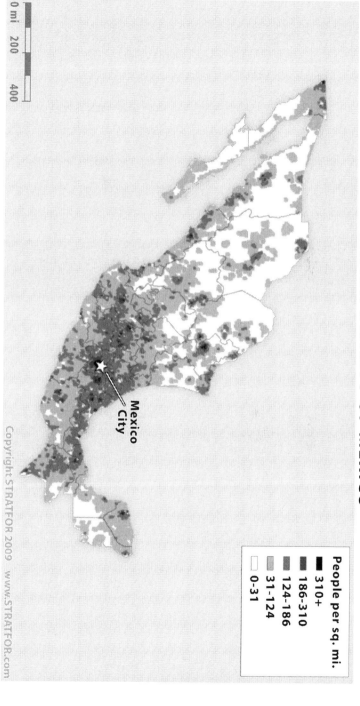

POPULATION DENSITY OF MEXICO

Mexico
City

People per sq. mi.
- 310+
- 186-310
- 124-186
- 31-124
- 0-31

0 mi   200   400

cooperation from local authorities and also raised the stakes in the drug-trafficking industry.

As the cartels became more powerful the level of violence also began to rise, and by 2006 Calderon's government decided to make its move. By this time, however, the drug cartels were so entrenched that they had become the law of the land in their respective territories. Local and federal law enforcement authorities had become corrupt, and the influx of military troops had the effect of destabilizing these relationships — as the planners intended — and wreaking havoc on the business of the cartels. With the dissolution of their networks, the cartels began fighting back, leveraging their established links in the government and aggressively defending their turf.

The problem of corruption boils down to the lure of money and the threat of death. Known by the phrase plata o plomo (which literally translates to "silver or lead," with the implied meaning, "take a bribe or take a bullet"), the choice given to law enforcement and government officials puts them under the threat of death if they do not permit (or, as is often the case, facilitate) cartel operations. With the government historically unable to protect all of its personnel from these kinds of threats — and certainly unable to match the cartels' deep pockets — Mexico's law enforcement officials have become almost universally unreliable. Death threats have increased as the government has intensified its anti-cartel operations, resulting in high turnover and difficulties recruiting new personnel — especially qualified personnel. (The city of Juarez has been without a police chief since mid-summer, after previous chiefs were killed or fled to the United States. Similar fates have befallen local law enforcement agencies in nearly every Mexican state.)

In terms of ready cash, Mexican organized crime can beat any offer the government can make. The Mexican cartels bring in somewhere between $40 billion and $100 billion per year. The Oct. 27 announcement that 35 employees of the anti-organized crime unit (SIEDO) in the Office of the Mexican Attorney General (PGR) had been arrested and charged with corruption illustrates the fact that not even the upper reaches of government are safe from infiltration by the cartels. In this example, top officials were paid up to $450,000 per month to pass information along to a cartel involved in cocaine trafficking. This kind of money is a huge temptation in a country where annual salaries for public servants run from $10,000 for local police officers to $48,000 for senators and $220,000 for the president. Organized crime can target key individuals in the Mexican government and convince them to provide information with a combination of lucrative offers and physical threats if they do not comply.

When it comes to carrying through on death threats, the cartels have proven themselves to be quite efficient. The assassinations of Edgar Millan Gomez, Igor Labastida Calderon and other federal police officials in Mexico City earlier this year are cases in point. Hitting high-level officials in the capital of the country sends a bold message to government officials. On a local and more pernicious level, the cartels have mounted a concerted offensive against state and municipal police. In the past year they have murdered a total of 500 police officers, and in some towns, the chief of police and the entire police force have been arrested on corruption charges.

Death threats are a serious problem for Mexican authorities because Mexico simply does not have the capacity to protect all of its law enforcement personnel and government officials. Effective protective details require high levels of skill, and Mexico's manpower deficiencies make it difficult to find people to fill these positions — especially since the candidates would largely be Mexican law enforcement personnel who are themselves the targets.

And without comprehensive protection, there is very little incentive for law enforcement personnel to hold out against cartel influence. After all, once the cartels have established themselves as the law of the land, it is much easier for local police to let sleeping dogs lie than it is to pick fights with the biggest dog on the block — with no hope of sufficient backup from the central government.

The consistent loss of personnel through charges of corruption and death is an inherent weakness for Mexico. It makes the preservation of institutional knowledge difficult, further eroding the effectiveness of the government's security efforts. Additionally, the loss of local police chiefs, mayors and state and federal police officials to death, prosecution or resignation disrupts continuity of authority and makes stability on the operational level impossible. Furthermore, the process is self-perpetuating. Those who replace dead or corrupt officials are often less experienced and less vetted and are more likely to be lost to corruption or assassination.

High turnover and corruption also hurts intelligence gathering and reduces situational awareness. Maintaining sources in the field is an important tactic in any war, but those sources require consistent handling by law enforcement personnel they trust — and rapid shifts in personnel destroy that trust. Indeed, corruption and turnover most often drive intelligence capabilities backward, springing leaks and funneling information from the government to the cartels instead of the other way around.

Even the constitution is a source of institutional insecurity, limiting the time in office of the president and legislators to one term. Ironically, while these provisions were put in place to prevent the entrenchment of leaders in positions of power (indeed, this was one of the driving issues of the Mexican Revolution), they actually contribute to the corruption, since leaders do not face the challenge of seeking re-election and enduring voter scrutiny. Though it strengthens the party apparatus by putting the emphasis on the party's plan rather than the individual's ambitions, Mexico's state- and federal-level politicians are lame ducks upon entering office. This frees them to settle political favors and personal matters without needing to explain it to voters on election day.

Federal Law Enforcement Integration

The challenges of the cartel war have prompted the Calderon administration to reorganize and combine the country's two federal law enforcement agencies, the Federal Preventive Police (PFP) and the Federal Investigations Agency (AFI), into what will simply be known as the Federal Police. The two independent agencies have traditionally held different responsibilities and reported to two different secretaries in the president's Cabinet.

The PFP has been the more physical force, essentially a large domestic police agency charged with providing general public safety such as maintaining order at protests and stopping riots. The AFI, on the other hand, was modeled after the U.S. Federal Bureau of Investigation — an agency that focuses more on investigating criminal activity than battling it in the streets. On many counternarcotics deployments during the past two years, both PFP and AFI have been deployed, with PFP generally handling highway checkpoints and vehicle searches while AFI investigates crime scenes and pursues leads. Since both are federal law enforcement agencies, their areas of responsibilities overlap, but each has maintained its own separate culture and command structure.

With the intensifying drug war over the last two years, it became apparent that Mexico's primary security threat was organized crime and the violence that went along with it. Mexico's cartels are very brutal (and so require the heavy hand of the PFP), but they are also very well organized and conspiratorial (requiring the investigative expertise of the AFI). In the past, the two agencies would often work the same case without coordinating their activities, which resulted in a lack of information-sharing and prolonged investigations. The Calderon administration concluded that fighting the cartels requires a federal police force able to provide physical security and conduct investigative work seamlessly.

So the government implemented a plan to integrate the PFP and AFI — a plan that, while considered complete on paper, is far from complete in practice. Such bureaucratic transitions inevitably take much time and effort and result in short-term inefficiencies (which can be a problem with a cartel war raging). To date, bureaucratic rivalries appear to have prevented any real unity at all. Despite the paper agreement, the PFP and AFI remain split in practice, making their own arrests and pursuing their own cases with limited interaction with each other. In September 2008, AFI agents protested the fact that they were being made to report to PFP commanders in the

Public Security Secretariat. PFP eventually removed the AFI agents from the case, clearly demonstrating the interagency rivalries.

Moreover, it is not clear how the decision will impact corruption in the agencies. On the one hand, having centralized control over a single institution streamlines the corruption-monitoring process. On the other hand, with only one federal security institution, there is no second party to provide an independent outside check on corruption. Furthermore, if there is only one agency and it is corrupt or suffering from attacks, then all of Mexico's federal police are weakened. Additionally, maintaining two agencies also allows for each to be insulated from the corruption and weaknesses of the other.

It is clear that a formal union of two independent police agencies cannot be institutionalized overnight. But the pressure is great to speed up the process. Calderon has set a tentative deadline of complete integration by 2012 (which is also the year of the next presidential election). The idea is for the Federal Police to ultimately take the lead in the campaign against the cartels instead of the military.

Beyond the problems of bureaucratic reorganization, Mexico's federal law enforcement agencies face a number of logistical and technical challenges. Technical deficiencies will be addressed to some degree by the U.S. Merida Initiative, which will grant approximately $900 million to Mexico over the next two years for equipment and training. This will give Mexico the opportunity to pick up technologies like ion spectrometry equipment (narcotic-sensing technology) that has proved to be useful in marijuana seizures. There is also a great deal of room to improve information collection, storage and analysis. There is no centralized database with criminal records for local, state or federal police agencies. Law enforcement agencies also lack sufficient secure-communications and drug-detection capabilities, which means that police activities can be monitored by the cartels and domestic drug shipments are more difficult to detect.

But even if Mexico could create the most effective and efficient bureaucratic structure and obtain the very latest technologies for its security forces, there is no real way to offset the crippling corruption that permeates federal law enforcement. And with the increasing ferocity of the drug cartels, there is no end in sight to the pressure they can and will place on Mexico's law enforcement personnel. The underlying causes of institutional corruption in Mexico — coercion and bribery — are deeply intertwined in the country's political culture and will take decades, perhaps generations, to root out. This means that the government will not reach its goal of transitioning the drug war into the hands of law enforcement any time soon, which in turn will have consequences for the military as it struggles against the cartels. Fundamentally, the security forces need reform (and quickly) before the military succumbs to the same pressures that have crippled the federal police.

The Mexican Military

Before Calderon sent the army after the drug lords in 2006, drug smuggling was rampant in Mexico, but the cartels controlled their respective territories, where corruption reigned and peace prevailed (more or less). There were occasional cartel-on-cartel skirmishes but they tended to be short-lived. The historic lack of government pressure eventually created more wealth and power for the cartels to fight over and the violence began to rise. When Calderon sent in federal troops, they effectively stirred up the hornet's nest. Drug-related murders throughout Mexico skyrocketed as cartels competed for the loosely held territory of their faltering rivals.

Calderon is not the first Mexican president to utilize the military to combat the cartels, but he has dramatically changed the way the military contributes to the government's counternarcotics mission. Calderon's predecessors relied primarily on the Special Forces Airmobile Group (GAFE), which was specially trained and equipped to conduct uniquely challenging operations on short notice. These missions included the 2003 arrest of Osiel Cardenas Guillen, former leader of the Gulf cartel, and the 2002 capture of Benjamin Arellano Felix, head of the Tijuana cartel.

But operations involving GAFE or High Command GAFE (the most elite of Mexico's special forces) were single-target, one-off

CARTEL-RELATED DEATHS IN MEXICO

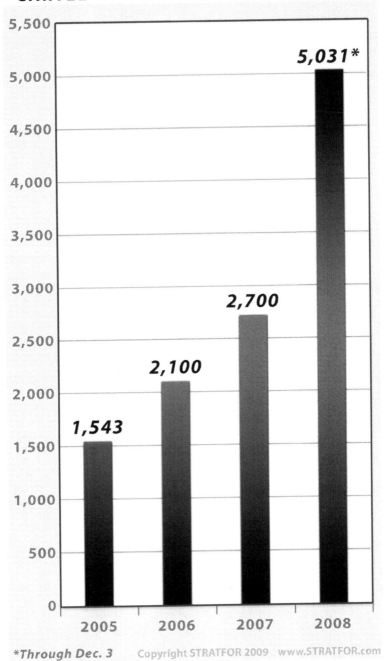

*Through Dec. 3   Copyright STRATFOR 2009   www.STRATFOR.com

missions. Since 2006, Calderon has deployed troops — including both special forces units and regular infantry battalions — for the first time on long-term missions designed to impose stability and unravel the entire cartel system. The mission has become, in a sense, as much counterinsurgency as counternarcotics, with federal forces operating far afield with limited knowledge of the local landscape or people. In some ways, this is very similar to the challenges U.S. forces face in Iraq and Afghanistan.

Mexico's domestic national security policy under Calderon has been formulated at the Cabinet level, with the Interior Secretariat (SEGOB) taking the lead. Despite Interior Secretary Juan Camilo Mourino's death in a Nov. 4 plane crash in Mexico City (thought to be caused by pilot error), security policy will likely continue to emanate from the secretariat. SEGOB works with the Defense Secretariat, the Public Security Secretariat and the PGR in coordinating the deployment of federal forces (both military and law enforcement).

Nearly all large-scale deployments are joint operations with federal police and troops patrolling together, which combines the brute strength of military force with the investigative abilities of the federal police. The cooperation is not perfect, and there are plenty of examples of poor coordination. Many of the major raids and arrests have been carried out by GAFE to the exclusion of federal law enforcement. GAFE then transfers detainees into the custody of the attorney general's office for prosecution. Often, federal law enforcement is cut out of sensitive operations — presumably because the army has intelligence that could be compromised if exposed to corrupt federal police.

Calderon's first military deployment against the cartels involved 6,500 troops dispatched to Michoacan (Calderon's home state) in December 2006. Michoacan was the center of a surge of violence that had left 500 dead in drug-related incidents that year (many of the deaths were stunningly gruesome, including beheadings and dismemberments). The following month, Calderon deployed 3,300 troops to Baja California state and 1,000 troops to Guerrero state. Since then, troops have been sent in to quell violence in 14 other states, with total deployments holding steady for the past six months at approximately 35,000. Though the deployment numbers are a closely held secret, we also estimate that roughly 10,000 federal police also have been sent to these trouble spots.

Mexican army infantry and special forces are fighting the bulk of the military's ground war against the cartels. Special forces are involved in precision raids on strategic locations while the infantry conducts patrols (often with federal police officers), establishes road checkpoints and engages in search-and-destroy missions on marijuana and opium poppy cultivation operations. Upon arriving in an area of operations, the troops begin by vetting the local police. This requires, at the very least, a temporary disarmament of police officers, and sometimes the local corruption is so deep that the officers are permanently relieved of their weapons. The Mexican navy has been similarly utilized for offshore operations such as the 2006 sealing off of Michoacan's coastline in conjunction with simultaneous ground operations. When necessary, military units coordinate with authorized federal police to perform investigations that the military is not allowed or prepared to conduct.

Calderon's strategy for the first 12 months of the military's counter-cartel operations involved, almost exclusively, targeting the Gulf cartel in strongholds in and around Tamaulipas and Michoacan states. The goal during this period appears to have been to dismantle Gulf before focusing on other cartels. In the process, however, the Sinaloa cartel began to make moves to fill in the gaps left by Gulf. Although violence spun out of control in Sinaloa territory, almost no troops were sent there during the first year (Sinaloa territory has little important commerce or industry and was a lower priority, while Gulf operates near the Monterrey-Nuevo Laredo shipping corridor, through which more than 60 percent of Mexican exports to the United States pass). During these first 12 to 15 months, the counter-cartel strategy was dictated by the territory controlled by the Gulf cartel.

Now it appears that the strategy is to go after multiple cartels and to manage the violence in population centers. After 12 to 15 months of operations against Gulf, the cartel was significantly weaker and violence was beginning to flare in other areas, including large population centers like Juarez and Tijuana. At that point, the government began spreading deployments more broadly, quickly dispatching troops as needed to "put out fires." One of the primary factors in the shift in strategy was public opinion. Residents and mayors of large cities like Tijuana and Juarez were becoming increasingly fed up with the growing violence. Eager to demonstrate to the populace and state governments that it still had a handle on the situation, the federal government began to react more directly to these concerns, sending troops not against a particular cartel but to the latest violent hot spot. So far, while the federal government has succeeded in maintaining positive approval ratings, it has stretched the military very thin in the process.

Essentially, the military moved from using a sledgehammer on a single target to using a series of small hammers on many targets. Results have been less than satisfactory. Earlier in the campaign, army deployments would initially result in an immediate and noticeable decrease in violence. This is no longer the case. Since March, when the military moved in to stabilize Juarez — where violence was rapidly spinning out of control — the army has had fewer troops available and has had to rely on the local police for help. The violence continued even after the troops arrived.

The Juarez operation was a turning point in the federal government's strategy, and it is a good example of how public opinion drove the government toward a high-profile response that would not, in the end, significantly improve the security situation. The operation represented the first large-scale deployment in which an insufficient number of soldiers and federal police were forced to compensate for the manpower shortage by enlisting the help of local law enforcement. Naturally, the situation was complicated by the fact that one reason the troops were there in the first place was to investigate the local police for links to organized crime. As a result, many police protested or went on strike, and to this day the city's security situation remains tenuous. Juarez was the first clear sign that the government was not deploying enough forces to meet the military's expanded mission.

One of the biggest problems the military has had to confront is Mexico's sheer size. The country's 200,000-strong military (all branches, with the army at about 144,000) — consisting mostly of conscripts — is simply not big enough to dominate Mexico's 761,606 square miles of territory or pursue an estimated 500,000 people involved in the illicit drug trade. Some 35,000 federal troops are deployed at any one time. In the northern border area, where 16,000 troops are deployed, drug traffickers have a tremendous amount of open land at their disposal, where they have established a vast network of routes and safe houses (the northern border area spans nearly 250,000 square miles and is about the size of Texas). Law enforcement efforts in this environment are extremely difficult, since the cartels have the ability to rapidly shift transit routes and change their patterns of behavior to avoid detection (although they will usually pass through towns in which they are capable of establishing control). The 16,000 troops on the northern border face a similar situation that U.S. Marines confronted in Iraq's Anbar province, where a frustrating game of "whack a mole" became the prevailing coalition tactic. Even with U.S. cooperation, there are simply too few Mexican troops along the U.S.-Mexico border to comprehensively combat cartel activities inside Mexico.

A second challenge that the Mexican military must deal with is even more basic: It was not designed for this kind of mission. Like most standing armies, Mexico's army is not trained or equipped to enforce the country's domestic laws. It lacks not only the civil authority but also the expertise necessary to conduct investigations and impose order. Even though the military does deploy with federal law enforcement, which has some civil expertise, the degree to which the military must operate without the help of local police (i.e., those who know the territory) is a crippling hindrance.

The military is thus being forced to adapt rapidly to a kind of warfare that can be easily termed asymmetric. Organized criminal assailants in Mexico, like insurgents in Iraq and Afghanistan, are difficult to distinguish from innocent civilians and can mount attacks then quickly blend into the population. And with no way to rely on local

MEXICO'S MILITARY REGIONS AND ZONES

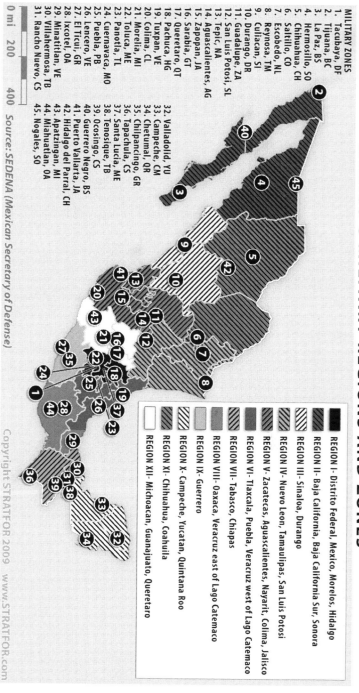

MILITARY ZONES

1. Tacubaya, DF
2. Tijuana, BC
3. La Paz, BS
4. Hermosillo, SO
5. Chihuahua, CH
6. Saltillo, CO
7. Escobedo, CO
8. Reynosa, TM
9. Culiacan, SI
10. Durango, DR
11. Guadalupe, ZA
12. San Luis Potosi, SL
13. Tepic, NA
14. Aguascalientes, AG
15. Zapopan, JA
16. Sarabia, GT
17. Queretaro, QT
18. Pachuca, HG
19. Tuxpan, VE
20. Colima, CL
21. Morelia, MI
22. Toluca, ME
23. Panotla, TL
24. Cuernavaca, MO
25. Puebla, PB
26. Lencero, VE
27. El Ticul, GR
28. Ixcotel, OA
29. Minatitlan, VE
30. Villahermosa, TB
31. Rancho Nuevo, CS
32. Valladolid, YU
33. Campeche, CM
34. Chetumal, QR
35. Chilpancingo, GR
36. Tapachula, CS
37. Santa Lucia, ME
38. Tenosique, TB
39. Ocosingo, CS
40. Guerrero Negro, BS
41. Puerto Vallarta, JA
42. Hidalgo del Parral, CH
43. Apatzingan, MI
44. Miahuatlan, OA
45. Nogales, SO

REGION I- Distrito Federal, Mexico, Morelos, Hidalgo
REGION II- Baja California, Baja California Sur, Sonora
REGION III- Sinaloa, Durango
REGION IV- Nuevo Leon, Tamaulipas, San Luis Potosi
REGION V- Zacatecas, Aguascalientes, Nayarit, Colima, Jalisco
REGION VI- Tlaxcala, Puebla, Veracruz west of Lago Catemaco
REGION VII- Tabasco, Veracruz east of Lago Catemaco
REGION VIII- Oaxaca, Chiapas
REGION IX- Guerrero
REGION X- Campeche, Yucatan, Quintana Roo
REGION XI- Chihuahua, Coahuila
REGION XII- Michoacan, Guanajuato, Queretaro

0 mi   200   400   *Source: SEDENA (Mexican Secretary of Defense)*

expertise, accurate and timely intelligence is extremely limited. Viewed as an occupying force, federal troops have a difficult time gaining the trust of local inhabitants and developing effective human-intelligence networks, which are key to a successful counterinsurgency.

Despite these challenges, the strategies and policies implemented so far have led to unprecedented successes against drug traffickers. The military is responsible for most of these successes. Over the last two years, the Mexican navy has reduced the maritime trafficking of illicit drugs by 65 percent. The military's increased monitoring of airspace (along with new radars and restrictions of where flights are allowed to land) has led to a 90 percent reduction in aerial trafficking of cocaine from Colombia. In essence, the military has proved thus far to be the only institution in Mexico that has the capability to significantly interfere with organized crime in the country.

Despite these significant successes over the last two years, the army, with its limited number of troops, has not been able to prevent the drug-related death toll from rising (the toll stood at 1,543 in 2005 and will surpass 5,000 in 2008). Indeed, if anything, the security situation has deteriorated throughout Mexico, in part because the government is so focused on the cartels at the expense of ordinary criminals. As a result, violent crimes such as murder, armed robbery and assault are on the rise all over the country.

The Long Hard Slog

There is no simple solution to the problem of Mexico's drug cartels. Even dismantling the cartel apparatus would be a short-term remedy to a permanent problem. As long as there is a demand for drugs in the United States, there will be enterprising individuals who will try to traffic them through the United States' southern neighbor.

The trick, then, is to build solid enough institutions in Mexico to replace — or at least counteract — the influence of the drug traffickers. The military can dismantle corrupt police departments, but the system for establishing an effective judicial or other civic authority in their place does not appear to be comprehensive enough to achieve any lasting reform. The military can purge corrupt individuals from the ranks of local law enforcement, but the basic problem of plata o plomo persists. And there appears to be a decreasing capacity to implement an economic development program that would provide alternative employment opportunities for cartel members and make the drug trade less attractive. Essentially, there is no comprehensive reconstruction strategy, and without a self-sustaining equilibrium emerging from military operations, a clear and decisive victory is difficult to achieve even in the best of circumstances.

While Mexican citizens still by and large support the government's mission, battle fatigue is beginning to set in, and their tolerance for violence could waver. Calderon still maintains approval ratings of around 60 percent, but over half of Mexicans polled over the summer believe that the government is losing the war on cartels. If public support moves away from Calderon, the government's war on organized crime will gain yet another enemy.

29: Mexico in Crisis (Addendum): 2008 Cartel Report
Dec. 11, 2008

Mexico's war against drug cartels continues. What began nearly two years ago with President Felipe Calderon's inauguration has since escalated in nearly every way possible. The past 12 months, in particular, have seen some significant developments as a result of Calderon's campaign. Weapons and drugs have been seized, key members of drug cartels have been arrested and greater cooperation has been established between Mexico and the United States. Despite the genuine hurdles presented by Mexico's bureaucratic infighting and rampant corruption, there is simply no denying that the government has disrupted the cartels' operations in meaningful ways.

One result of these achievements has been greater volatility in the balance of power among the various drug-trafficking organizations in Mexico. During at least the past five years, the criminal environment had been characterized by bipolar domination, with the Gulf cartel on one hand and the Sinaloa cartel on the other. Mexican security forces' relentless focus on the Gulf cartel has damaged the organization's capabilities, leaving a vacuum of power that other cartels have sought to fill. It is still too early to determine which cartels will be left on top once the dust has settled, but what is clear is that this past year has been a year of flux for the cartels.

The year has also seen a shift in the geography of drug trafficking in the Western Hemisphere, nearly all of which is attributable to the situation in Mexico. One of these shifts involves the increasing importance of Central America. After the Mexican government implemented greater monitoring and control of aircraft entering the country's airspace, airborne shipments of cocaine from Colombia decreased by an estimated 95 percent. Maritime trafficking has decreased more than 60 percent. Consequently, Mexican traffickers have expanded their presence in Central American countries as they have begun to rely increasingly on land-based shipping routes to deliver drugs from South American producers. In addition — and likely as a result of the more difficult operating environment — Mexican drug-trafficking groups have also increased their operations in South America to begin providing drugs to markets there and in Europe.

One apparent paradox for the Calderon administration has been that, even while the government has clearly succeeded in damaging the cartels, the country's security situation has continued to deteriorate at what appears to be an unstoppable rate. The total number of drug-related homicides has continued to increase while the violence has continued to escalate in several ways, including high-level assassinations, beheadings, use of a growing arsenal of cartel weapons and the indiscriminate killing of civilians.

The deteriorating security situation certainly has the attention of the Calderon administration. The government is considering the

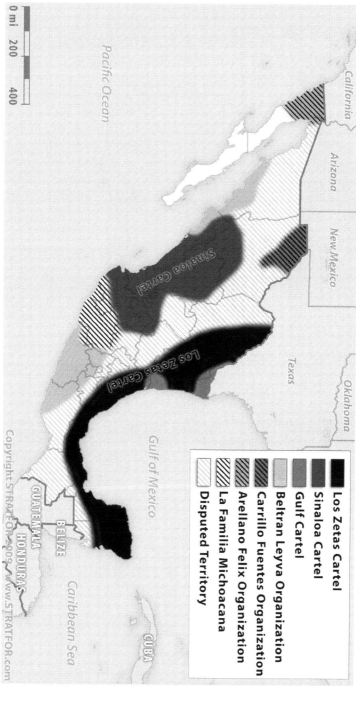

AREAS OF CARTEL INFLUENCES

Legend:
- Los Zetas Cartel
- Sinaloa Cartel
- Gulf Cartel
- Beltran Leyva Organization
- Carrillo Fuentes Organization
- Arellano Felix Organization
- La Familia Michoacana
- Disputed Territory

Sinaloa Cartel

Los Zetas Cartel

Pacific Ocean

Gulf of Mexico

Caribbean Sea

California

Arizona

New Mexico

Texas

Oklahoma

GUATEMALA

BELIZE

HONDURAS

CUBA

0 mi   200   400

Copyright STRATFOR 2009 www.STRATFOR.com

implications of increasing casualties, not only among security forces but also among civilians. In addition, the initial strategy of relying on the military only over the short term appears increasingly unfeasible, as police reforms have proved far more difficult to achieve than the administration anticipated. Despite the costs, Calderon has shown no sign of letting up. Assistance from the United States will begin increasing as the Merida Initiative is implemented, but there is only so much that Washington can do given Mexico's reluctance to allow the United States to establish a stronger security presence on its territory.

Membership and Organization

Gulf Cartel

As recently as a year ago, the Gulf cartel was considered the most powerful drug-trafficking organization in Mexico. After nearly two years of taking the brunt of the Mexican government's efforts, it is an open question at this point whether the cartel is even intact.

The Gulf cartel's headquarters and main area of operation historically has been the northeastern Mexican state of Tamaulipas. Through its use of Los Zetas, who operated for years as the cartel's notorious paramilitary enforcement arm, Gulf trafficked large quantities of narcotics across the Texas border into the United States. The group's symbolic leader is Osiel Cardenas Guillen, who led the cartel until his arrest in 2003. There are conflicting reports on who is presently in charge of the cartel. Some suggest it is Cardenas' brother, Antonio Ezequiel "Tony Tormenta" Cardenas Guillen. These reports conflict with our previous assessment that the cartel is likely led by Jorge "El Coss" Costilla Sanchez. In any case, both men are thought to play a major role in the organization, and they may be sharing leadership responsibilities.

Los Zetas were the primary reason for Gulf's power. Following the extradition of Osiel Cardenas Guillen to the United States in 2007, rumors surfaced that Los Zetas were distancing themselves

GULF CARTEL

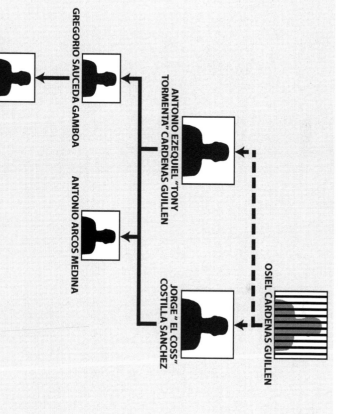

OSIEL CARDENAS GUILLEN

ANTONIO EZEQUIEL "TONY TORMENTA" CARDENAS GUILLEN

JORGE "EL COSS" COSTILLA SANCHEZ

GREGORIO SAUCEDA GAMBOA

ANTONIO ARCOS MEDINA

HECTOR SAUCEDA GAMBOA

from Gulf. Reports of Zeta activity from this past year suggest that the split was complete by spring 2008. Though details on the current relationship between Los Zetas and Gulf are murky, it appears the two groups continue to work together, but that Los Zetas no longer take orders from Gulf.

Los Zetas

During the past 12 months, Los Zetas have remained a power to be reckoned with throughout Mexico. They operate under the command of leader Heriberto "El Lazca" Lazcano. Miguel "Z-40" Trevino Morales is believed to be the organization's No. 2. Trevino reportedly oversees much of the Zetas' operations in the southern portions of the country. Daniel "El Cachetes" Perez Rojas, who was arrested this past year in Guatemala, was responsible for the group's activities in Central America and reportedly answered directly to Lazcano. The November arrest of Jaime "El Hummer" Gonzalez Duran, the organization's third-in-command, was another significant blow to the organization, as Gonzalez was believed responsible for Zeta operations in nine states. It is unclear at the moment who has replaced Perez and Gonzalez in the Zeta hierarchy.

Since their split with Gulf, Los Zetas have contracted themselves to a variety of drug- trafficking organizations throughout the country, most notably the Beltran Leyva organization. Los Zetas also control large swaths of territory in southern Mexico, much of which formerly belonged to the Gulf cartel, and they have a presence in the interior states of Aguascalientes, San Luis Potosi and Zacatecas. Zetas are also present in disputed territories such as Durango, Sonora, Sinaloa, Jalisco, Guerrero and Michoacan due to their alliance with the Beltran Leyva organization, though these areas are not considered to be under their control.

Following the government's crackdowns, Los Zetas have expanded from strictly drug trafficking to other criminal activities, including extortion, kidnapping for ransom and human smuggling. Los Zetas' human smuggling operations are based out of Quintana Roo and

ZETAS

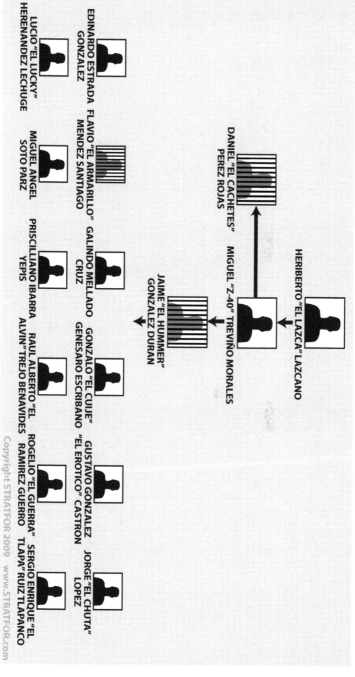

HERIBERTO "EL LAZCA" LAZCANO

MIGUEL "Z-40" TREVIÑO MORALES

DANIEL "EL CACHETES" PEREZ ROJAS

JAIME "EL HUMMER" GONZALEZ DURAN

EDINARDO ESTRADA GONZALEZ

FLAVIO "EL ARMARILLO" MENDEZ SANTIAGO

GALINDO MELLADO CRUZ

GONZALO "EL CUIJE" GENESARO ESCRIBANO

GUSTAVO GONZALEZ "EL EROTICO" CASTRON

JORGE "EL CHUTA" LOPEZ

LUCIO "EL LUCKY" HERENANDEZ LECHUGE

MIGUEL ANGEL SOTO PARZ

PRISCILIANO IBARRA YEPIS

RAUL ALBERTO "EL ALVIN" TREJO BENAVIDES

ROGELIO "EL GUERRA" RAMIREZ GUERRO

SERGIO ENRIQUE "EL TLAPA" RUIZ TLAPANCO

Yucatan states, where mostly Cuban and Central American immigrants enter Mexico on their way to the United States. Los Zetas maintain a vast network of safe houses and access to counterfeit immigration documents — which facilitate the illegal movement of drugs or people. At an average cost of $10,000 per person, human smuggling has become a lucrative business for the organization.

Beltran Leyva Organization

The Beltran Leyva family has a long history in the narcotics business. Until this past year, the organization was part of the Sinaloa Federation, for which it controlled access to the U.S. border in Sonora state (among other responsibilities). By the time Alfredo Beltran Leyva was arrested in January, however, the Beltran Leyva organization's alliance with Sinaloa was over. (It is rumored his arrest resulted from a Sinaloa betrayal.)

Before this year, the Beltran Leyva brothers served as high-ranking members of the organization with many people under their command and plenty of infrastructure to branch out on their own. Under the leadership of Arturo Beltran Leyva, the organization moved quickly to secure strategic narcotics transport routes in the states of Sinaloa, Durango, Sonora, Jalisco, Michoacan, Guerrero and Morelos. This attempt to conquer territory from their former Sinaloa partners sparked a wave of violence. The Beltran Leyva brothers' Colombian cocaine supplier, Ever Villafane Martinez, was arrested in Morelos state in August. Since then, however, the organization has pursued a relationship with Victor and Dario Espinoza Valencia of Colombia's Norte del Valle cartel, though the details of this relationship are unclear.

The Beltran Leyva organization has quickly become one of the most powerful drug- trafficking organizations in Mexico. Not only has it proved capable of trafficking drugs and going toe-to-toe with the Sinaloa cartel, it also has demonstrated a willingness to order targeted assassinations of high-ranking government officials. The most notable of these was the May 9 assassination of acting federal police

BELTRAN LEYVA ORGANIZATION

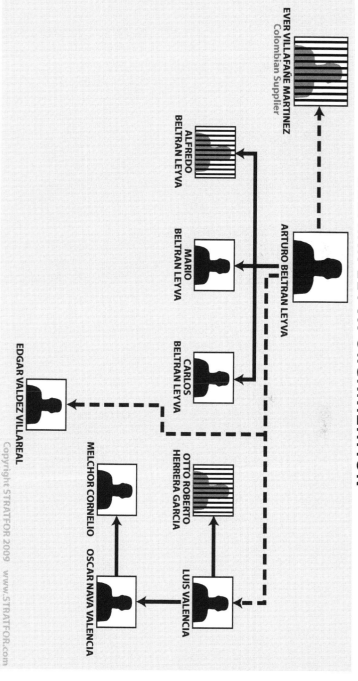

EVER VILLAFAÑE MARTINEZ
Colombian Supplier

ALFREDO BELTRAN LEYVA

MARIO BELTRAN LEYVA

ARTURO BELTRAN LEYVA

CARLOS BELTRAN LEYVA

EDGAR VALDEZ VILLAREAL

MELCHOR CORNELIO

OTTO ROBERTO HERRERA GARCIA

OSCAR NAVA VALENCIA

LUIS VALENCIA

director Edgar Millan Gomez. The Beltran Leyva organization also occasionally has secured the cooperation of other drug-trafficking organizations such as Los Zetas, Gulf, the Juarez cartel and a faction of the Arellano Felix organization (AFO) in Tijuana. However, these alliances are tentative at best and appear to have been forged mainly to counter the powerful influence of Joaquin "El Chapo" Guzman Loera's Sinaloa cartel.

Sinaloa Cartel

Joaquin "El Chapo" Guzman Loera is the most wanted drug lord in Mexico. Despite the turbulence it has experienced this past year, his Sinaloa cartel is perhaps the most capable drug-trafficking organization in Mexico. This turbulence involved the loss of the Vicente Carrillo Fuentes organization in Ciudad Juarez as well as the split with the Beltran Leyva organization. Guzman has maintained his long-standing alliances with his high-ranking lieutenants, Ismael "El Mayo" Zambada Garcia and Ignacio "El Nacho" Coronel Villareal. These two have continued to work with Guzman, even as he has come under attack from nearly every other cartel in Mexico.

The Sinaloa cartel also has come under increasing attack this past year from the Mexican government, which has deployed several thousand troops to Sinaloa state. The increased security presence has so far been too limited to significantly affect the Sinaloa cartel's operations, though some of its money laundering operations and other parts of its infrastructure have been shut down.

The Sinaloa cartel's loss of partners in Mexico does not appear to have impacted its ability to smuggle drugs from South America to the United States. On the contrary, based on seizure reports, the Sinaloa cartel appears to be the most active smuggler of cocaine. It has also demonstrated the ability to establish operations in previously unknown areas, such as Central America and South America, even as far south as Peru, Paraguay and Argentina. It also appears to be most active in diversifying its export markets; rather than relying solely on

SINALOA CARTEL: EL CHAPO

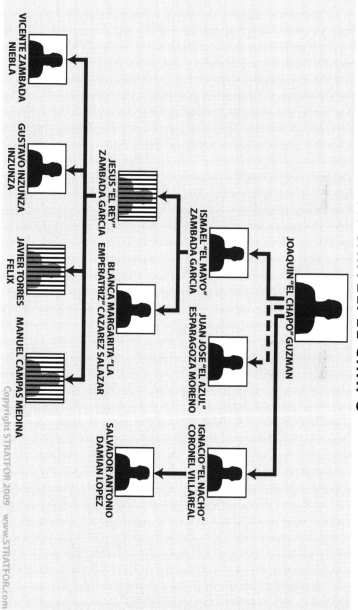

JOAQUIN "EL CHAPO" GUZMAN

ISMAEL "EL MAYO" ZAMBADA GARCIA

JUAN JOSE "EL AZUL" ESPARAGOZA MORENO

IGNACIO "EL NACHO" CORONEL VILLAREAL

SALVADOR ANTONIO DAMIAN LOPEZ

JESUS "EL REY" ZAMBADA GARCIA

BLANCA MARGARITA "LA EMPERATRIZ" CAZAREZ SALAZAR

VICENTE ZAMBADA NIEBLA

GUSTAVO INZUNZA INZUNZA

JAVIER TORRES FELIX

MANUEL CAMPAS MEDINA

SINALOA FEDERATION 2007

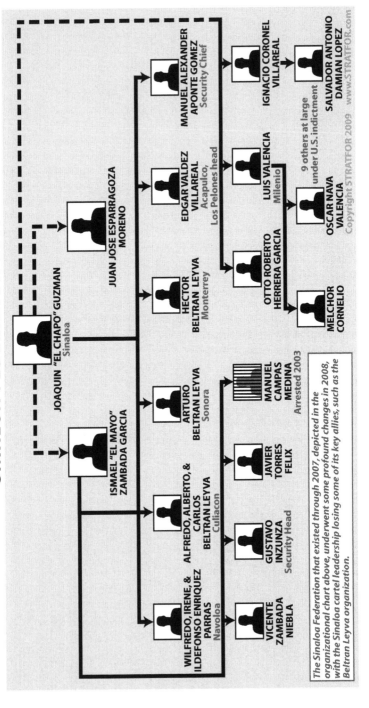

JOAQUIN "EL CHAPO" GUZMAN
Sinaloa

ISMAEL "EL MAYO" ZAMBADA GARCIA

JUAN JOSE ESPARRAGOZA MORENO

WILFREDO, IRENE, & ILDEFONSO ENRIQUEZ PARRAS
Navoloa

ALFREDO, ALBERTO, & CARLOS BELTRAN LEYVA
Culiacon

ARTURO BELTRAN LEYVA
Sonora

HECTOR BELTRAN LEYVA
Monterrey

EDGAR VALDEZ VILLAREAL
Acapulco, Los Pelones head

MANUEL ALEXANDER APONTE GOMEZ
Security Chief

IGNACIO CORONEL VILLAREAL

SALVADOR ANTONIO DAMIAN LOPEZ

VICENTE ZAMBADA NIEBLA

GUSTAVO INZUNZA
Security Head

JAVIER TORRES FELIX

MANUEL CAMPAS MEDINA
Arrested 2003

OTTO ROBERTO HERRERA GARCIA

LUIS VALENCIA
Milenio

MELCHOR CORNELIO

OSCAR NAVA VALENCIA

9 others at large under U.S. indictment

The Sinaloa Federation that existed through 2007, depicted in the organizational chart above, underwent some profound changes in 2008, with the Sinaloa cartel leadership losing some of its key allies, such as the Beltran Leyva organization.

www.STRATFOR.com
Copyright STRATFOR 2009

U.S. consumers, it has made an effort to supply distributors of drugs in Latin American and European countries.

Vicente Carrillo Fuentes Organization/Juarez Cartel

The Vicente Carrillo Fuentes organization, also known as the Juarez cartel, is based out of Ciudad Juarez, Chihuahua state, across the border from El Paso, Texas. It also has a presence in much of northern Chihuahua state and parts of Nuevo Leon and Sonora states.

The cartel is led by Vicente Carrillo Fuentes, brother of original leader Amado Carrillo. Believed to be second-in-command is his nephew, Vicente Carrillo Leyva. The Juarez cartel has had a long-standing alliance with the Beltran Leyva brothers, based on family and business ties. This past year, however, Carrillo Fuentes has turned to Los Zetas to aid in the defense of Juarez.

Over the past year, the Juarez cartel has been locked in a vicious battle with its former partner, the Sinaloa cartel, for control of Juarez. The fighting between them has left more than 2,000 dead in Chihuahua state so far this year. The Juarez cartel relies on two enforcement arms to exercise control over both sides of the border: La Linea, a group of current and former Chihuahua police officers, is prevalent on the Mexican side, while the large street gang Barrio Azteca operates in Texas, in cities such as El Paso, Dallas and Austin.

Arellano Felix Organization/Tijuana Cartel

The AFO, also known as the Tijuana cartel, has been weakened almost beyond recognition over the past year due to the efforts of both U.S. and Mexican law enforcement to capture several high-ranking leaders. The most symbolic was the October arrest of Eduardo "El Doctor" Arellano Felix, the only original Arellano Felix brother who had evaded capture.

Fighting among the various factions of the cartel itself has led to hundreds of deaths in the Tijuana area over the past 12 months and

ARELLANO FELIX ORGANIZATION

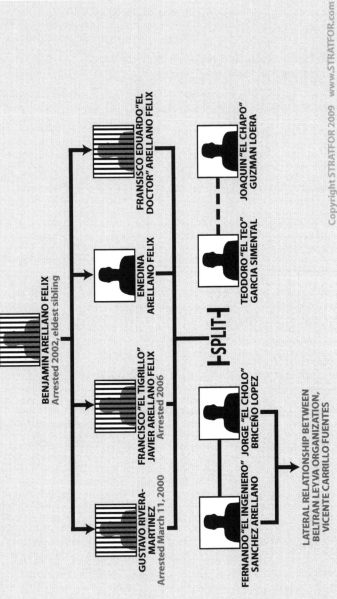

BENJAMIN ARELLANO FELIX
Arrested 2002, eldest sibling

GUSTAVO RIVERA-MARTINEZ
Arrested March 11, 2000

FRANCISCO "EL TIGRILLO" JAVIER ARELLANO FELIX
Arrested 2006

ENEDINA ARELLANO FELIX

FRANSISCO EDUARDO "EL DOCTOR" ARELLANO FELIX

—SPLIT—

FERNANDO "EL INGENIERO" SANCHEZ ARELLANO

JORGE "EL CHOLO" BRICEÑO LOPEZ

TEODORO "EL TEO" GARCIA SIMENTAL

JOAQUIN "EL CHAPO" GUZMAN LOERA

LATERAL RELATIONSHIP BETWEEN BELTRAN LEYVA ORGANIZATION, VICENTE CARRILLO FUENTES

Copyright STRATFOR 2009   www.STRATFOR.com

resulted in the splitting of the cartel into two factions. One is led by Fernando "El Ingeniero" Sanchez Zamora, a nephew of the original Arellano Felix brothers. Eduardo Teodoro "El Teo" Garcia Sementa, who served as an enforcer under the Arellano Felix brothers, controls the rival faction. Disagreements over authority reportedly led to much of the violence between the two factions in the first half of 2008. The violence peaked on April 26 when three separate and prolonged gun battles erupted on the streets of Tijuana, leaving 13 people dead and five wounded.

The most recent wave of violence, which claimed more than 100 lives over a two-week period in October, was again attributed to fighting between the two factions. In this case, however, El Teo's offensive received the support of the Sinaloa cartel, which would benefit greatly from the access to the United States that control of Tijuana would provide.

Calderon's Success Story

Since taking office in December 2006, Mexican President Felipe Calderon has undertaken extraordinary measures in pursuit of the country's powerful drug-trafficking organizations. The policies enacted by Calderon saw some progress during his first year in office, although it has only been during the past year that the continued implementation of these policies has produced meaningful results in the fight against the cartels.

One important result has been the large quantities of illegal drugs and weapons seized by federal authorities. In November 2007, customs officials in Manzanillo, Colima state, seized 26 tons of cocaine from a Hong Kong-flagged ship that had sailed from Colombia. The seizure was the largest in Mexican history, more than double the previous record of 11 tons recovered that October in Tamaulipas state. In July 2007, the Mexican navy captured a self-propelled, semi submersible vessel loaded with nearly 5 tons of cocaine off the coast of Oaxaca state, the first such capture by Mexican authorities. Also in July, federal police near Guadalajara, Jalisco state, uncovered the

169

largest synthetic drug production facility ever found in the country, recovering some 8,000 barrels of ephedrine and acetone, two key ingredients in the manufacture of crystal methamphetamine.

The Mexican government also has pursued the cartels' leadership successfully. Important members of nearly all the country's drug-trafficking organizations have been arrested over the last 12 months, although the highest-ranking kingpins continue to evade capture. Perhaps most symbolic was the October arrest of Eduardo Arellano Felix, considered the last original member of Tijuana's Arellano Felix crime family. The arrest of several key Arellano Felix lieutenants — including Ricardo Estrada Perez in October, Jose Filiberto Parras Ramas in July and Gustavo Rivera Martinez in March — has resulted in fractures in the organization. Arrests also played a role in damaging the Sinaloa cartel, particularly the parts controlled by the Beltran Leyva family, as Alfredo Beltran Leyva was captured in January. Los Zetas have also suffered losses, including the commander of Central American Zeta operations, Daniel "El Cachetes" Perez Rojas. Even more significant, however, was the November arrest of Jaime "El Hummer" Gonzalez, who was captured during a raid in Reynosa, Tamaulipas state. As mentioned, Gonzalez is believed to rank third in the Zeta chain of command.

Calderon's administration has also made important progress in working with the United States. Given Mexico's historical wariness of Washington, this relationship represents a careful balancing act for Calderon, who must consider the domestic political cost of allowing greater American influence in Mexico while relying on the United States for resources, training and intelligence sharing. During his first months in office, Calderon moved quickly to grant a request from Washington to expand the number of Drug Enforcement Administration (DEA) offices in Mexico and to acquire new forensic technology from the Bureau of Alcohol, Tobacco, Firearms and Explosives to better track gun purchases. One major triumph of his administration during the past year has been securing the Merida Initiative, a U.S. counternarcotics assistance plan that is projected to give Mexico some $900 million over two years in the form of equipment and training. The sharing of intelligence between Washington and Mexico City has played a key role in many of Mexico's successes, including the Mexican navy's interdiction of the semi submersible. Another important piece of the relationship with Washington has been the tremendous increase in extraditions of drug-trafficking suspects to the United States. Since taking office, Calderon has granted more than 150 extradition requests, more than double the rate when he took office. This approach makes it far more difficult for drug traffickers to continue operating their businesses from behind bars.

One measure of the impact of the Mexican government's successes would be a decline in the flow of drugs coming into the United States. It is, of course, impossible to know the true amount of illegal drugs entering the country, but one indicator is the street price of these substances, especially cocaine. The U.S. Office of National Drug Control Policy reported in November 2007 that the average price of powder cocaine in many American cities increased nearly 50 percent over the year. This suggests that a decreased supply through Mexico has driven the price up.

Another indication that it is becoming increasingly difficult to traffic drugs in and out of Mexico is the revelation that many drug traffickers have turned to other illegal activities to supplement their incomes. For example, over the last 12 months, many members of Los Zetas — once the most powerful and experienced drug-trafficking operators in Mexico — have become increasingly involved in extortion and kidnapping for ransom in states such as Oaxaca, Veracruz, Tabasco and Campeche. In Oaxaca, for example, several Zetas were arrested this past year for forcing local businesses to pay protection fees to avoid theft or attacks, a development that business owners said was fairly recent. In Veracruz, a group of Zetas has sought to exert its influence over local criminal groups by demanding that they provide a portion of their proceeds to the Zetas, a development that sparked a slight increase in violence over the past year. This does not mean that the Zetas have left the drug trade, but rather that a more difficult operating environment has led them to pursue additional revenue sources.

A Year of Flux

One result of these unprecedented achievements has been greater volatility in the balance of power among the various drug-trafficking organizations. The capture of key cartel members and the downfall of cartels themselves have made 2008 a year of flux for the drug traffickers.

During at least the last five years, the Mexican drug trade had been characterized by a bipolar domination, with the Gulf cartel on one hand and the Sinaloa federation on the other. The turf battles between these two rivals were one of the primary causes of the increasing violence in 2006 and 2007.

When Calderon began deploying large numbers of military troops and federal police in pursuit of the cartels, the first big target was Gulf and Los Zetas. The national strategy appeared to be to target only one cartel at a time. The armed forces, then, descended in 2007 on Gulf strongholds in Tamaulipas state, while the Sinaloa cartel's base of operations went relatively untouched. The result of this relentless focus on Gulf produced some early results that have continued this past year. Not only has Gulf suffered the capture of several high-ranking lieutenants in Mexico but its smuggling and distribution networks in the United States were dealt a severe blow with the culmination in September of "Project Reckoning." During this operation, conducted by multiple law enforcement agencies and jurisdictions, some 175 members and associates of the Gulf cartel in the United States were arrested.

The damage done to Gulf has presented opportunities to other criminal groups over the past 12 months, leading to even greater turf battles and power struggles. Unlike in previous years, however, this violence has not been confined to Gulf and Sinaloa. Instead, there have been two main causes of the battles: splits within these organizations and a resurgence of previously obsolete cartels.

Fractures inside the Sinaloa cartel have been perhaps the most noteworthy new dimension in the cartel war. Until this year, Sinaloa cartel leader Joaquin "El Chapo" Guzman Loera had maintained an alliance with the Beltran Leyva crime family. By the end of 2007, the relationship had become strained. It is unclear what exactly caused the split, but some reports indicate that the two sides so bitterly oppose each other that Guzman provided information to the authorities that led to the arrest of Alfredo Beltran Leyva in January. In retaliation, the Beltran Leyva organization killed Guzman's son four months later.

This past year, the Sinaloa cartel also lost its long-standing alliance with the Carrillo Fuentes organization — also known as the Juarez cartel — leaving Sinaloa's once-large federation in shambles. The Carrillo Fuentes organization was considered the most powerful drug cartel in Mexico during much of the 1990s. However, ever since the death of cartel leader Amado Carrillo Fuentes in 1997, the cartel became relatively obsolete. After its break with Sinaloa this past year, however, there were indications that the Carrillo Fuentes organization was once again a force to be reckoned with. This resurgence likely accounts for the extraordinary spike in violence that began during the summer of 2008 in Ciudad Juarez and the rest of Chihuahua state.

Similarly, the AFO showed renewed activities this past year after being essentially dormant since its peak in the late 1990s. However, several waves of violence in the Tijuana area among various AFO factions, combined with the arrest of several key cartel lieutenants, suggest that AFO is on its last legs.

The Gulf cartel has also struggled to remain intact this past year, as a large number of reports surfaced that its enforcement arm, Los Zetas, had severed ties with the Gulf leadership and begun operating autonomously. Similar reports had sporadically arisen during 2007 and before, though the most recent reports suggest that the distance between Los Zetas and Gulf has increased over the past year. As a result, Los Zetas have reportedly been working with a wide range of drug-trafficking organizations, including the Beltran Leyva organization and the Juarez cartel.

The increased turbulence in inter-cartel relations has produced unprecedented levels of violence that show no sign of abating. Thus, it is premature to predict which cartels will remain on top once the dust

INTER-CARTEL ALLIANCES

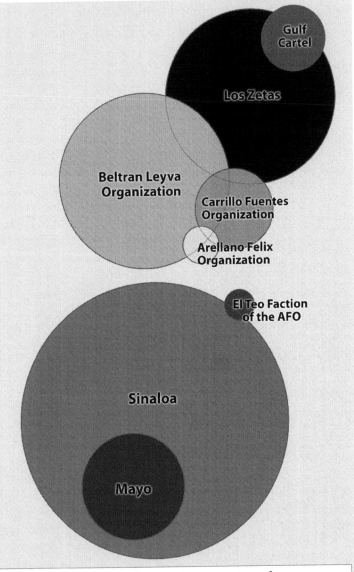

Major Mexican drug cartels operate on a system of interdependence and collaboration, with some organizations overlapping among several groups to varying degrees. The graphic above represents that interconnectedness. The size of the circles signifies the scope of the cartel.*

*Not drawn to scale.

has settled. Historically, the Mexican drug trade has been controlled by two large and competing drug cartels, each of which has had a base of operations in a Mexican city along the U.S. border. A similar situation is certainly possible, though changes in the country's security environment and shifting areas of cartel operations might add new dimensions to the country's criminal landscape.

A Changing Geography

This past year has seen a unique shift in the geography of the drug trade in the Western Hemisphere, nearly all of which can be attributed to the situation in Mexico. The United States remains the primary destination of drugs produced in South American countries such as Peru, Bolivia and Colombia, and Mexico continues to serve as the primary transshipment route. However, the path between South America and Mexico is shifting.

At the beginning of 2007, the two main trafficking platforms for South American drugs bound for Mexico were clandestine aircraft and ships. Land-based trafficking through Central America was minimal. A combination of poor roads, a large number of border crossing checkpoints and unpredictable criminal groups made such shipments slow and vulnerable. By the beginning of 2008, however, there were indications that Mexican drug-trafficking groups had moved to establish a presence in Guatemala and Honduras and that Central America was becoming of greater strategic interest to the northward movement of narcotics. Several months later, it has become more clear just how important Central America is for drug smuggling.

There are several reasons for this shift. The main cause appears to be the greater difficulty of airborne shipment. In early 2007, the Mexican government reduced the number of airports in the Yucatan Peninsula that would be allowed to receive flights from South and Central America. At the same time, several new radars were installed that gave authorities a much better awareness of unauthorized aircraft entering Mexican airspace. The result has been a more than 90 percent decrease in aerial trafficking of cocaine from Colombia to

Mexico, according to estimates by Colombian officials. Greater information sharing with the United States has also made maritime drug shipments more susceptible to capture. Consequently, maritime drug shipments have declined 65 percent over two years, according to estimates by the Mexican navy.

Drug-trafficking organizations have used a variety of strategies to make up for the greater scrutiny. Customs officials at the Mexico City International Airport, for example, have cited an increase in seizures of cocaine being smuggled on commercial flights. Colombian drug traffickers continue to build semi submersible vessels to bring multi-ton shipments of cocaine to Mexico's shores. The most noteworthy shift, however, has been the presence of Mexican drug traffickers in Central America.

A bloody firefight in March in Guatemala's Zacapa province involving several Mexican drug traffickers was the first sign that Mexican cartels were stepping up their battles for control of turf outside Mexico. Reports later surfaced that high-ranking members of the Gulf and Sinaloa cartels might be hiding in Guatemala or Honduras. These suspicions were confirmed when Guatemalan authorities announced the arrest of Daniel "El Cachetes" Perez Rojas, who was considered at the time the second-highest-ranking member of Los Zetas. Several months later, authorities in Panama arrested several Mexican citizens who were believed to be recruiting local criminal organizations to assist the Sinaloa cartel in managing large shipments of cocaine. The fact that the spike in violence in Guatemala was short-lived suggests that it did not take long for the turf wars to become settled and the business of drug trafficking to begin.

The modus operandi for Central American drug smuggling is varied. In August, authorities in Panama, Costa Rica and Nicaragua uncovered a network of safe houses operated by the Sinaloa cartel, which moved large quantities of cocaine via trucks, boats and horses across rivers, lakes, rugged terrain and highways. Other smugglers in Costa Rica have relied on so-called go-fast boats to move drugs in short trips along the country's Caribbean coast, stashing the shipments at various locations along the journey. In October, Nicaraguan authorities arrested several members and associates of the Sinaloa cartel and identified a network of safe houses and staging points used for smuggling drugs. The safe houses were all located along highways that connect the country's southern and northern border, suggesting that overland smuggling remains a popular platform.

Mexican drug traffickers have also expanded their presence in South America over the past year. Perhaps most notable has been the discovery of a network of Mexican synthetic drug producers in Argentina and their murky relationship with a Sinaloa cartel representative in Paraguay. The details are still unclear, but it appears that restrictions on the sale of ephedrine in Mexico drove a group of methamphetamine producers to Argentina, where precursor chemicals are easier to acquire. Some of the drugs produced are sold in Argentina while others are shipped to Mexico via Paraguay for eventual distribution in the United States. In another case, a group of Mexican and Peruvian drug traffickers working for the Sinaloa cartel were arrested in Lima while preparing to send a multi-ton shipment of cocaine to Holland.

The presence of Mexican cartels in Central and South America illustrates two important points. First, there is no question that it is now Mexican groups that are the central figures in the drug trade in the Western Hemisphere. Up until a decade ago, Colombia-based cartels were clearly the most powerful members involved in the drug trade. The closure of the Caribbean smuggling corridor, however, has led to Mexican drug traffickers exercising a monopoly on the drug trade, as nearly all U.S.-bound cocaine enters through Mexico. Nothing demonstrates this better than the fact that it is the Mexican traffickers — not the Colombian producers — who are conquering new turf and even expanding to other markets.

The second point is that the drug trade does not necessarily have to revolve around U.S. consumers. The United States, of course, remains the world's largest consumer of cocaine. However, expanding markets in Latin America and Europe could produce a more profound shift in drug-trafficking routes. There is currently no evidence that this is occurring, but Mexican drug traffickers have demonstrated a

DRUG SUPPLY ROUTES

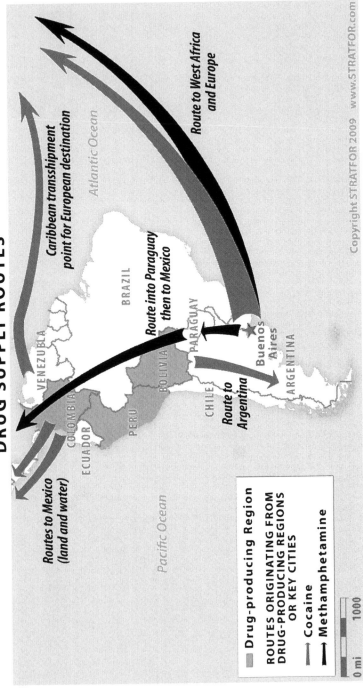

Copyright STRATFOR 2009   www.STRATFOR.com

willingness to pursue other markets when faced with a more difficult operating environment.

A Deteriorating Security Situation

One apparent paradox for the Calderon administration has been that, even while the government has clearly succeeded in damaging the cartels, the country's security situation continues to deteriorate at what appears to be an unstoppable rate.

The most obvious sign of this deteriorating security situation is that the total number of drug-related homicides continues to climb dramatically. The nearly 2,700 killings that occurred in 2007 made it the deadliest year up to that point in the country's drug war. However, 2007 has paled in comparison to 2008, when the 2007 total was surpassed in the first seven months. The death toll currently sits at more than 5,000. At this rate, the country may well finish 2008 with twice the number registered in 2007.

In addition to the rise in the number of killings, the violence has escalated in other important ways that are more difficult to measure. First, Mexican drug violence is just as brutal as ever. Beheadings have now become a regular occurrence, with the most noteworthy incident from this past year being the 12 decapitated bodies of alleged drug dealers found outside Merida, Yucatan state. In the past, most beheadings took place after the victim had been killed. Increasingly, however, authorities report that victims are beheaded alive.

A second way that the violence has escalated this past year is through the use of intimidation and fear. The discovery of hit lists with the names of police officers has become increasingly common in many Mexican cities along the U.S. border. It also is all too common for the officers named on those lists to be gunned down one by one. In addition, drug-trafficking organizations have now begun displaying large banners over highways in cities around the country. Many of the banners make threats against rivals, or accuse a particular criminal group of being supported by local and federal government officials. In several cases, purported recruiting banners appeared in northern Mexico offering higher pay and better equipment to soldiers and police officers who defect to Los Zetas. While it is possible that these banners were a genuine recruiting attempt, it seems more likely that they were intended to intimidate government officials by causing them to question their forces' loyalty.

Third, the past year has seen an increase in the number of attacks on security forces. Some of the deaths have been the result of targeted assassinations against officers caught off duty or off guard. Other times, unlucky police patrols have stumbled across convoys of drug traffickers who, armed with automatic weapons and rocket-propelled grenades, easily overpower the police. In other cases, however, cartel members have deliberately ambushed police and military convoys to assassinate a specific target or free a fellow cartel member. While the total percentage of police officers and soldiers killed is relatively low — approximately 7 percent of all 2007 homicides — the trend has had a broad impact.

A fourth way violence has intensified is through the assassinations of high-ranking government officials, several of whom have been killed during the past year. The targeted killing in Mexico City in May 2007 of Jose Nemesio Lugo Felix, the general coordinator of information at the National Center for Planning and Analysis to Combat Organized Crime, represented the first such high-profile assassination. Several others followed. Perhaps the most high-profile hit thus far has been that of Edgar Millan Gomez, the country's highest-ranking federal police officer, who died when a lone gunman shot him several times in the lobby of his apartment building. The assailant allegedly was part of a professional assassination gang that had been contracted to kill Millan by members of the Beltran Leyva drug-trafficking organization. While government officials have never been immune to Mexico's drug violence, the incidents demonstrate that Mexican drug-trafficking organizations consider high-ranking officials to be legitimate targets.

Another way that the country's drug violence has escalated involves an expansion of the cartels' arsenals. For example, authorities in Culiacan, Sinaloa state, discovered in July that explosive-actuated improvised incendiary devices had destroyed several cars near a cartel safe house after a firefight. Such devices would be useful to target a specific person or, as in this case, to kill ambushers as they approached a perimeter. Another example involved a failed assassination attempt with an improvised explosive device (IED) in Mexico City in February. In that case, the device detonated prematurely as the bomber was transporting it to the target, who was a Mexico City police official.

Finally, this past year witnessed the first clear case of the indiscriminate killing of civilians. The attack occurred when at least one man threw a fragmentation grenade into a crowd at the culmination of the Independence Day celebration in Morelia, Michoacan state. Several minutes later, a second grenade detonated at a plaza several blocks away. Overall, eight people died and up to 100 were wounded as a result of the blasts. Up until this point, Mexico's drug war had primarily affected security forces, government officials and those involved in the drug trade. Although collateral damage occasionally caused casualties among civilian bystanders, the general civilian population was essentially insulated from the violence. Needless to say, this attack represented a significant development in the country's drug war.

Mexico's deteriorating security situation also has an ongoing impact on the United States as the violence continues to cross the border. No one incident better demonstrates this fact than the June home invasion and assassination of a drug dealer in Phoenix by cartel hit men with assault rifles and wearing Phoenix Police Department raid shirts. The assault had all the makings of a Mexican cartel hit — especially the attackers' willingness to engage police officers if necessary.

Looking to the Future

The threat that drug-related violence in Mexico poses to the United States is an important concern, but the implications of Mexico's war on the cartels are certainly greater south of the border. Indeed, the security situation is a dire concern for the Calderon administration. The government is considering the implications of increasing casualties, not only of security forces but also of civilians. The army and federal police have shown themselves to be capable of inflicting damaging blows on the various cartels, but they have been much less successful at curbing the growing violence.

One reason for this lack of effectiveness involves the increasing responsibilities of the Mexican armed forces, perhaps the most versatile tool Calderon has relied on in the cartel war. In addition to their traditional roles in maritime drug interdiction, marijuana and poppy crop eradication and technical intelligence operations, the armed forces have now been deployed on the ground in nearly every state in the country (with concentrations on the periphery). One key mission for the military has been general public safety operations. In January, when drug gang violence erupted in the border city of Ciudad Juarez, Chihuahua state, some 3,000 troops were deployed to investigate cartel members and help curb the violence.

Juarez is an interesting case study of what happens when too few troops are deployed to such a large metropolitan area. In previous deployments to cities such as Reynosa, sufficient troops were available to secure the roads and disarm the local police and investigate them for links to organized crime. Such military deployments nearly always resulted in an immediate decrease in violence. In Juarez, however, the number of troops deployed was too few to disarm local law enforcement personnel. Consequently, the police remained on duty while they were investigated by the same military personnel with whom they were being asked to cooperate on counternarcotics operations. The result was heightened tensions, poor cooperation and even a few firefights between the frustrated military and the disgruntled police.

Because the military is far more effective and less corrupt than federal and local police, it was inevitable that its role in the counternarcotics mission would evolve and expand. The result has been a classic case of mission creep. As more and more duties were assigned to the armed forces, the troops were stretched too thin to be effective. Estimates of the current number of deployed soldiers are notoriously hard to come by, but 35,000 appears to be the maximum number that Calderon can muster in the field at any one time. In any case, investigating local police forces and assuming law enforcement duties are not missions for which Mexico's military was designed or trained.

To be sure, Calderon has stated that the military solution is only temporary and that the ultimate goal is to reform the federal police so that they can take the lead in pursuing the country's drug cartels. These reforms, though, have been hampered by bureaucratic turf battles between the federal attorney general's office and the public security secretariat. It is unclear how long Calderon originally thought it would take to implement the reforms, but some reports suggest the administration now estimates it will be at least 2012 before the federal police are prepared to take over. Reports also suggest the Calderon administration is planning to field up to 45,000 soldiers at a time until 2012 — a significant increase in military deployments.

Of course, an unexpected drop in violence could make such an escalation unnecessary. There is currently no indication that the violence will soon taper off, but it is also premature to assume that the violence will continue to escalate in the way it has so far. For example, the February IED incident sparked concerns that additional and larger IEDs would soon become regular parts of the cartel arsenal. However, eight months later, it remains an isolated incident. Similarly, it is not at all clear that drug-trafficking organizations will continue to indiscriminately kill civilians, especially given the public backlash that occurred following the Sept. 15 attack.

Despite this caveat, the danger is that the cartels have shown themselves to be remarkably innovative and resilient when backed into a corner. Given their powerful arsenals and deep penetration of the country's security forces, a further escalation in attacks against security forces and government officials seem all but inevitable.

30: Cartel Sources in High Places
Dec. 29, 2008

Mexican army Maj. Arturo Gonzalez Rodriguez was arrested the week of Dec. 21 for allegedly assisting Mexican drug-trafficking organizations for $100,000 per month, the Mexican attorney general's office announced Dec. 26. Gonzalez was assigned to the Presidential Guard Corps, the unit responsible for protecting Mexico's president. Based on statements from a former cartel member turned witness, code-named "Jennifer," the attorney general's office has accused Gonzalez of passing information related to the activities and travel plans of Mexican President Felipe Calderon to the Beltran Leyva organization (BLO). Gonzalez also stands accused of leaking military intelligence, training BLO hit men through a private security company and supplying military weapons to various drug-trafficking organizations, including Los Zetas.

In light of other high-level Mexican government corruption charges over the past months, this case is unsettling but certainly does not come as a surprise.

The revelation that Gonzalez was providing intelligence and materials to drug cartels represents a double blow to the Mexican government. First, the fact that a member of an army unit responsible for protecting the president was passing information about presidential movements to the cartels exposes a potentially fatal gap in Calderon's protective detail. While it is not known what specific information Gonzalez had access to, or what exact details he was passing to the cartels, this is a security breach at the highest level. According to the attorney general's office, the informant Jennifer has said the cartels were tracking the president's movements with the intent of avoiding the high level of government security that surrounds him, but had no specific plan to target Calderon. But capability is more important than intent, as intent can change quickly. Tracking Calderon's movements to avoid him could easily have been altered to targeting Calderon if the need arose.

It is unclear exactly how involved Gonzalez was in the daily movements of Calderon. Because he was on the staff, it is safe to assume that he was at least involved in briefings and the general movements of the president, but this information would not necessarily be enough for the cartel to have been able to assassinate Calderon. Most valuable to such a plot would have been information related to presidential transport strategy, namely, how the guard worked to protect Calderon, how it arranged transportation, and how it gathered intelligence on specific threats. Insights into how the guard operated would have given the cartels a glimpse into Calderon's security vulnerabilities — something far more dangerous to Calderon than simply the knowledge of where the president would be at any given time.

The second aspect of the blow is that Gonzalez apparently had been on the cartel payroll since 2005, during which time he held different positions in the government. As he changed assignments, he was kept on as a cartel asset, and the nature of his involvement with the cartels changed. It is entirely feasible that he fed information on other departments of the army (not just the Presidential Guard Corps) over his three-year relationship with the cartels.

A primary reason for the Mexican government to rely on the military to fight the cartels is because state and local law enforcement are considered far too corrupt to be trusted. One of the military's strengths was its perceived lower level of corruption due to its low-level involvement with the cartels, but this case (along with other military corruption arrests this year) confirms that members of the Mexican military also are prone to corruption.

More details must emerge about Gonzalez's exact role in the Presidential Guard Corps and the nature of the intelligence he passed to the BLO in order to more accurately assess the threat he posed to the president. Even so, the fact remains that the cartels' intelligence capabilities have extended to those charged with protecting Mexico's president — and hence to Mexico's political stability.

31: Diplomacy Among Sinaloa's Cartels?
Jan. 30, 2009

The Los Angeles Times reported Jan. 29 that drug-related killings in Mexico's Sinaloa state dropped from 120 in December 2008 to 40 within the first 29 days of January. The reported cause for this drop in drug-related deaths was a truce between rival cartels. STRATFOR sources have confirmed that several Mexican cartels did indeed hold two sit-down meetings, but that they did not reach any widespread truce. The decrease in violence, however, suggests that a low level of diplomacy may be taking place.

The report of decreased violence in Sinaloa state came three days after El Siglo de Durango, a regional newspaper in Mexico's Durango state, reported that representatives of the El Mayo and Sinaloa groups sat down in December with representatives from the Beltran Leyva, Arellano Felix and Carillo Fuentes groups to discuss a cease-fire, as the unprecedented level of inter-cartel violence in 2008 was bad for business. The Beltran Leyva brothers were once allied with Joaquin "El Chapo" Guzman and his Sinaloa Cartel, but they operated separately in 2008. The two groups' fighting over drug-trafficking routes in western Mexico resulted in running battles that accounted for many of the 5,376 drug-related murders in Mexico in 2008. By May 2008, the Mexican military was called into Sinaloa state to help quell the violence.

Nationwide, violence dropped from historical highs in November to more normal levels in December 2008 and rose again in January, but certain states saw the number of reported deaths decrease in the same period. Just as the number of drug-related killings dropped from December 2008 to the end of January in Sinaloa state, in Juarez they dropped from 150 in December 2008 to 80 during the first 25 days of January. These two areas, hotspots in the Sinaloa cartel's battle with Beltran Leyva (in Sinaloa state) and Carillo-Fuentes (in Juarez), can be viewed as two primary fronts in Mexico's cartel conflicts. The fact that the rate of killings there dropped in January (even though

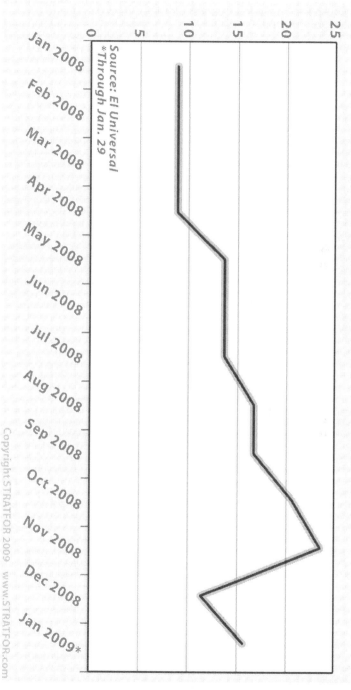

AVERAGE DAILY MURDER RATES IN MEXICO

Source: El Universal
*Through Jan. 29

the national rates were up) offers support for the claims that the cartels have reached a limited cease-fire.

Rumors about cartel cooperation have surfaced before and have quickly dissipated. Occasionally, Mexico's various criminal groups have reached broad truces and alliances, though more often than not these agreements quickly break down. The fierce competition over territory and drug-trafficking gateways along the U.S.-Mexican border offers strong motivation to continue fighting rather than cooperate. Even if the groups reached some sort of agreement, an enduring settlement is unlikely.

However, such a truce would have great significance in the Mexican government's war against the cartels. In 2008, several cartel factions were fighting each other and the Mexican military — a situation that created bloody multi-front wars in which cartels had to divide their resources. If the cartels work out a deal to reduce the fighting among themselves (even if the motivation is only to improve business), it would mean that they could reroute resources that otherwise would be used to fight each other. This means they would have more money to use to bribe officials, more resources to focus on intelligence-gathering operations and lower prices for the narcotics that they traffic. A truce among the cartels would make an already challenging situation for the Mexican military even more complicated, as the military would no longer be able to use the "divide and conquer" tactic in its war against the cartels. While a drop in overall violence would be welcomed by the Mexican government, a long-lasting cartel peace would carry its own risks for the government.

Ultimately, cooperation could also become a strategy for the cartels to combat the government. If the cartels could move from not fighting each other to actively collaborating on undermining the government, they could pose a serious threat to the Mexican state. As mentioned above, many factors make this type of broad cooperation rather unlikely — honor among thieves is a fickle thing — but there are incentives for cooperation as well.

32: A New Weapon in the Cartel Arsenal
Feb. 10, 2009

Grenades used in three recent attacks in Monterrey, Mexico, and Pharr, Texas, all originated from the same lot delivered from South Korea, a STRATFOR source has indicated. That the grenade used in the third attack reportedly came from Mexico indicates that, in addition to the well-known path of weapons flowing from the United States into Mexico, arms also are flowing from Mexico into the United States.

The first of the three attacks targeted the U.S. Consulate in Monterrey, Mexico. Gunmen rammed their car into the consulate's front gates at night in October 2008, firing automatic rifles and tossing a grenade that failed to detonate. In the second incident, again in Monterrey, gunmen attacked a local TV station on Jan. 12 in an attempt to intimidate the news agency into cutting back reporting on cartel activities. The feared group Los Zetas, one of Mexico's deadliest and most professional drug-trafficking organizations — which originally came from the ranks of Mexico's special forces — reportedly was behind both attacks.

In the third attack, three Hispanic men on Jan. 31 tossed a grenade into a night club near Pharr, Texas — a border town about 140 miles from Monterrey — but the grenade did not explode. The attackers might have been targeting three off-duty police officers who were in the club at the time. Police are still searching for the culprits, whom a STRATFOR source has indicated might have belonged to the Bandidos motorcycle gang. The Bandidos have ties to Mexican cartels, as well as a reputation for violence.

The Bandidos gang and groups like it are known to have used improvised explosive devices like pipe bombs. These are less reliable and less effective than military-grade grenades (even though several of the grenades used in the three recent attacks failed to detonate).

Mexico's military is known to use South Korean grenades. High levels of corruption in Mexico make it very likely that members of the Mexican military sold the grenades to Los Zetas. While internal investigations might be able to plug some of the leaks that permitted this transaction, cartels' willingness to pay top dollar for such weapons translates into a huge temptation for poorly paid military personnel. The illegal sale of grenades and other weapons and ordnance, like armor-piercing rounds, to the cartels can therefore be expected to continue.

Gangs north of the border are known to collaborate closely with cartels in Mexico in drug trafficking, human trafficking and kidnapping. While the flow of arms from north to south with the assistance of gangs on the U.S. side has been well-documented, the flow of arms from south to north — specifically grenades — is a new discovery. U.S. officials already have expressed some concern over being outgunned by well-armed Mexican killing squads that use high-powered, automatic weapons. The addition of grenades to the arsenals of gangs north of the border represents even more of a threat to U.S. law enforcement.

33: The Third War
Feb. 18, 2009

Mexico has pretty much always been a rough-and-tumble place. In recent years, however, the security environment has deteriorated rapidly, and parts of the country have become incredibly violent. It is now common to see military weaponry such as fragmentation grenades and assault rifles used almost daily in attacks.

In fact, just last week we noted two separate strings of grenade attacks directed against police in Durango and Michoacan states. In the Michoacan incident, police in Uruapan and Lazaro Cardenas were targeted by three grenade attacks during a 12-hour period. Then on Feb. 17, a major firefight occurred just across the border from the United States in Reynosa, when Mexican authorities attempted to apprehend several armed men seen riding in a vehicle. The men fled to a nearby residence and engaged the pursuing police with gunfire, hand grenades and rocket-propelled grenades (RPGs). After the incident, in which five cartel gunmen were killed and several gunmen, cops, soldiers and civilians were wounded, authorities recovered a 60mm mortar, five RPG rounds and two fragmentation grenades.

Make no mistake, considering the military weapons now being used in Mexico and the number of deaths involved, the country is in the middle of a war. In fact, there are actually three concurrent wars being waged in Mexico involving the Mexican drug cartels. The first is the battle being waged among the various Mexican drug cartels seeking control over lucrative smuggling corridors, called plazas. One such battleground is Ciudad Juarez, which provides access to the Interstate 10, Interstate 20 and Interstate 25 corridors inside the United States. The second battle is being fought between the various cartels and Mexican government forces who are seeking to interrupt smuggling operations, curb violence and bring the cartel members to justice.

Then there is a third war being waged in Mexico, though because of its nature it is a bit more subdued. It does not get the same degree of international media attention generated by the running gun battles and grenade and RPG attacks. However, it is no less real, and in many ways it is more dangerous to innocent civilians (as well as foreign tourists and business travelers) than the pitched battles between the cartels and the Mexican government. This third war is the war being waged on the Mexican population by criminals who may or may not be involved with the cartels. Unlike the other battles, where cartel members or government forces are the primary targets and civilians are only killed as collateral damage, on this battlefront, civilians are squarely in the crosshairs.

The Criminal Front

There are many different shapes and sizes of criminal gangs in Mexico. While many of them are in some way related to the drug cartels, others have various types of connections to law enforcement — indeed, some criminal groups are composed of active and retired cops. These various types of criminal gangs target civilians in a number of ways, including robbery, burglary, carjacking, extortion, fraud and counterfeiting. But of all the crimes committed by these gangs, perhaps the one that creates the most widespread psychological and emotional damage is kidnapping, which also is one of the most underreported crimes. There is no accurate figure for the number of kidnappings that occur in Mexico each year. All of the data regarding kidnapping is based on partial crime statistics and anecdotal accounts and, in the end, can produce only best-guess estimates. Despite this lack of hard data, however, there is little doubt — based even on the low end of these estimates — that Mexico has become the kidnapping capital of the world.

One of the difficult things about studying kidnapping in Mexico is that the crime not only is widespread and affects almost every corner of the country, but it also is executed by a wide range of actors who possess varying levels of professionalism — and very different motives. At one end of the spectrum are the high-end kidnapping gangs that abduct high-net-worth individuals and demand ransoms in the millions of dollars. Such groups employ teams of operatives who carry out specialized tasks such as collecting intelligence, conducting surveillance, snatching the target, negotiating with the victim's family and establishing and guarding the safe houses.

At the other end of the spectrum are gangs that roam the streets and randomly kidnap targets of opportunity. These gangs are generally less professional than the high-end gangs and often will hold a victim for only a short time. In many instances, these groups hold the victim just long enough to use the victim's ATM card to drain his or her checking account, or to receive a small ransom of perhaps several hundred or a few thousand dollars from the family. This type of opportunistic kidnapping is often referred to as an "express kidnapping." Sometimes express kidnapping victims are held in the trunk of a car for the duration of their ordeal, which can sometimes last for days if the victim has a large amount in a checking account and a small daily ATM withdrawal limit. Other times, if an express kidnapping gang discovers it has grabbed a high-value target by accident, the gang will hold the victim longer and demand a much higher ransom. Occasionally, these express kidnapping groups will even "sell" a high-value victim to a more professional kidnapping gang.

Between these extremes there is a wide range of groups that fall somewhere in the middle. These are the groups that might target a bank vice president or branch manager rather than the bank's CEO, or that might kidnap the owner of a restaurant or other small business rather than a wealthy industrialist. The presence of such a broad spectrum of kidnapping groups ensures that almost no segment of the population is immune from the kidnapping threat. In recent years, the sheer magnitude of the threat in Mexico and the fear it generates has led to a crime called virtual kidnapping. In a virtual kidnapping, the victim is not really kidnapped. Instead, the criminals seek to convince a target's family that a kidnapping has occurred, and then use threats and psychological pressure to force the family to pay a quick ransom. Although virtual kidnapping has been around for several years, unwitting families continue to fall for the scam, which is a source of easy money. Some virtual kidnappings have even been conducted by criminals using telephones inside prisons.

As noted above, the motives for kidnapping vary. Many of the kidnappings that occur in Mexico are not conducted for ransom. Often the drug cartels will kidnap members of rival gangs or government officials in order to torture and execute them. This torture is conducted to extract information, intimidate rivals and, apparently in some cases, just to have a little fun. The bodies of such victims are frequently found beheaded or otherwise mutilated. Other times, cartel gunmen will kidnap drug dealers who are tardy in payments or who refuse to pay the "tax" required to operate in the cartel's area of control.

Of course, cartel gunmen do not kidnap only their rivals or cops. As the cartel wars have heated up, and as drug revenues have dropped due to interference from rival cartels or the government, many cartels have resorted to kidnapping for ransom to supplement their cash flow. Perhaps the most widely known group that is engaging in this is the Arellano Felix Organization (AFO), also known as the Tijuana cartel. The AFO has been reduced to a shadow of its former self, its smuggling operations dramatically impacted by the efforts of the U.S. and Mexican governments, as well as by attacks from other cartels and from an internal power struggle. Because of a steep decrease in smuggling revenues, the group has turned to kidnapping and extortion in order to raise the funds necessary to keep itself alive and to return to prominence as a smuggling organization.

In the Line of Fire

There is very little chance the Mexican government will be able to establish integrity in its law enforcement agencies, or bring law and order to large portions of the country, any time soon. Official corruption and ineptitude are endemic in Mexico, which means that Mexican citizens and visiting foreigners will have to face the threat of kidnapping for the foreseeable future. We believe that for civilians and visiting foreigners, the threat of kidnapping exceeds the threat of being hit by a stray bullet from a cartel firefight. Indeed, things are deteriorating so badly that even professional kidnapping negotiators, once seen as the key to a guaranteed payout, are now being kidnapped themselves. In an even more incredible twist of irony, anti-kidnapping authorities are being abducted and executed.

This environment — and the concerns it has sparked — has provided huge financial opportunities for the private security industry in Mexico. Armored car sales have gone through the roof, as have the number of uniformed guards and executive protection personnel. In fact, the demand for personnel is so acute that security companies are scrambling to find candidates. Such a scramble presents a host of obvious problems, ranging from lack of qualifications to insufficient vetting. In addition to old-fashioned security services, new security-technology companies are also cashing in on the environment of fear, but even high-tech tracking devices can have significant drawbacks and shortcomings.

For many people, armored cars and armed bodyguards can provide a false sense of security, and technology can become a deadly crutch that promotes complacency and actually increases vulnerability. Physical security measures are not enough. The presence of armed bodyguards — or armed guards combined with armored vehicles — does not provide absolute security. This is especially true in Mexico, where large teams of gunmen regularly conduct crimes using military ordnance. Frankly, there are very few executive protection details in the world that have the training and armament to withstand an assault by dozens of attackers armed with assault rifles and RPGs. Private security guards are frequently overwhelmed by Mexican criminals and either killed or forced to flee for their own safety. As we noted in May 2008 after the assassination of Edgar Millan Gomez, acting head of the Mexican Federal Police and the highest-ranking federal cop in Mexico, physical security measures must be supplemented by situational awareness, countersurveillance and protective intelligence.

Criminals look for and exploit vulnerabilities. Their chances for success increase greatly if they are allowed to conduct surveillance at will and are given the opportunity to thoroughly assess the protective security program. We have seen several cases in Mexico in which the criminals even chose to attack despite security measures. In such cases, criminals attack with adequate resources to overcome existing security. For example, if there are protective agents, the attackers will plan to neutralize them first. If there is an armored vehicle, they will find ways to defeat the armor or grab the target when he or she is outside the vehicle. Because of this, criminals must not be allowed to conduct surveillance at will.

Like many crimes, kidnapping is a process. There are certain steps that must be taken to conduct a kidnapping and certain times during the process when those executing it are vulnerable to detection. While these steps may be condensed and accomplished quite quickly in an ad hoc express kidnapping, they are nonetheless followed. In fact, because of the particular steps involved in conducting a kidnapping, the process is not unlike that followed to execute a terrorist attack. The common steps are target selection, planning, deployment, attack, escape and exploitation.

Like the perpetrators of a terrorist attack, those conducting a kidnapping are most vulnerable to detection when they are conducting surveillance — before they are ready to deploy and conduct their attack. As we've noted several times in past analyses, one of the secrets of countersurveillance is that most criminals are not very good at conducting surveillance. The primary reason they succeed is that no one is looking for them.

Of course, kidnappers are also very obvious once they launch their attack, pull their weapons and perhaps even begin to shoot. By this time, however, it might very well be too late to escape their attack. They will have selected their attack site and employed the forces they believe they need to complete the operation. While the kidnappers could botch their operation and the target could escape unscathed, it is simply not practical to pin one's hopes on that possibility. It is clearly better to spot the kidnappers early and avoid their trap before it is sprung and the guns come out.

We have seen many instances of people in Mexico with armed security being kidnapped, and we believe we will likely see more cases of this in the coming months. This trend is due not only to the presence of highly armed and aggressive criminals and the low quality of some security personnel, but also to people placing their trust solely in reactive physical security. Ignoring the very real value of critical, proactive measures such as situational awareness, countersurveillance and protective intelligence can be a fatal mistake.

34: The Long Arm of the Lawless
Feb. 25, 2009

Last week we discussed the impact that crime, and specifically kidnapping, has been having on Mexican citizens and foreigners visiting or living in Mexico. We pointed out that there is almost no area of Mexico immune from crime and violence. As if on cue, on the night of Feb. 21 a group of heavily armed men threw two grenades at a police building in Zihuatanejo, Guerrero state, wounding at least five people. Zihuatanejo is a normally quiet beach resort just north of Acapulco, and the attack has caused the town's entire police force to go on strike. (Police strikes, or threats of strikes, are not uncommon in Mexico.)

Mexican police have regularly been targeted by drug cartels, with police officials sometimes forced to seek safety in the United States, but such incidents have occurred most frequently in areas of high cartel activity like Veracruz state or Palomas. The Zihuatanejo incident is proof of the pervasiveness of violence in Mexico, and demonstrates the impact that such violence quickly can have on an area generally considered safe.

Significantly, the impact of violent Mexican criminals stretches far beyond Mexico itself. In recent weeks, Mexican criminals have been involved in killings in Argentina, Peru and Guatemala, and Mexican criminals have been arrested as far away as Italy and Spain. Their impact — and the extreme violence they embrace — is therefore not limited to Mexico, or even to Latin America. For some years now, STRATFOR has discussed the threat that Mexican cartel violence could spread to the United States, and we have chronicled the spread of such violence to the U.S.-Mexican border and beyond.

Traditionally, Mexican drug-trafficking organizations had focused largely on the transfer of narcotics through Mexico. Once the South American cartels encountered serious problems bringing narcotics directly into the United States, they began to focus more on transporting the narcotics to Mexico. From that point, the Mexican cartels transported them north and then handed them off to U.S. street gangs and other organizations, which handled much of the narcotics distribution inside the United States. In recent years, however, these Mexican groups have grown in power and have begun to take greater control of the entire narcotics-trafficking supply chain.

With greater control comes greater profitability, since the percentages demanded by middlemen are cut out. The Mexican cartels have worked to have a greater presence in Central and South America, and now import from South America into Mexico an increasing percentage of the products they sell. They are also diversifying their routes and have gone global; they now even traffic their wares to Europe. At the same time, Mexican drug-trafficking organizations also have increased their distribution operations inside the United States to expand their profits even further. As these Mexican organizations continue to spread beyond the border areas, their profits and power will extend even further — and they will bring their culture of violence to new areas.

Burned in Phoenix

The spillover of violence from Mexico began some time ago in border towns like Laredo and El Paso in Texas, where merchants and wealthy families face extortion and kidnapping threats from Mexican gangs, and where drug dealers who refuse to pay "taxes" to Mexican cartel bosses are gunned down. But now, the threat posed by Mexican criminals is beginning to spread north from the U.S.-Mexican border. One location that has felt this expanding threat most acutely is Phoenix, some 185 miles north of the border. Some sensational cases have highlighted the increased threat in Phoenix, such as a June 2008 armed assault in which a group of heavily armed cartel gunmen dressed like a Phoenix Police Department tactical team fired more than 100 rounds into a residence during the targeted killing of a Jamaican drug dealer who had double-crossed a Mexican cartel. We have also observed cartel-related violence in places like Dallas and Austin, Texas, but Phoenix has been the hardest hit.

Narcotics smuggling and drug-related assassinations are not the only thing the Mexican criminals have brought to Phoenix. Other criminal gangs have been heavily involved in human smuggling, arms smuggling, money laundering and other crimes. Due to the confluence of these Mexican criminal gangs, Phoenix has now become the kidnapping-for-ransom capital of the United States. According to a Phoenix Police Department source, the department received 368 kidnapping reports last year. As we discussed last week, kidnapping is a highly underreported crime in places such as Mexico, making it very difficult to measure accurately. Based upon experience with kidnapping statistics in other parts of the world — specifically Latin America — it would not be unreasonable to assume that there were at least as many unreported kidnappings in Phoenix as there are reported kidnappings.

At present, the kidnapping environment in the United States is very different from that of Mexico, Guatemala or Colombia. In those countries, kidnapping runs rampant and has become a well-developed industry with a substantial established infrastructure. Police corruption and incompetence ensures that kidnappers are rarely caught or successfully prosecuted.

A variety of motives can lie behind kidnappings. In the United States, crime statistics demonstrate that motives such as sexual exploitation, custody disputes and short-term kidnapping for robbery have far surpassed the number of reported kidnappings conducted for ransom. In places like Mexico, kidnapping for ransom is much more common.

The FBI handles kidnapping investigations in the United States. It has developed highly sophisticated teams of agents and resources to devote to investigating this type of crime. Local police departments are also far more proficient and professional in the United States than in Mexico. Because of the advanced capabilities of law enforcement in the United States, the overwhelming majority of criminals involved in kidnapping-for-ransom cases reported to police — between 95 percent and 98 percent — are caught and convicted. There are also stiff federal penalties for kidnapping. Because of this, kidnapping for ransom has become a relatively rare crime in the United States.

Most kidnapping for ransom that does happen in the United States occurs within immigrant communities. In these cases, the perpetrators and victims belong to the same immigrant group (e.g., Chinese Triad gangs kidnapping the families of Chinese businesspeople, or

Haitian criminals kidnapping Haitian immigrants) — which is what is happening in Phoenix. The vast majority of the 368 known kidnapping victims in Phoenix are Mexican and Central American immigrants who are being victimized by Mexican or Mexican-American criminals.

The problem in Phoenix involves two main types of kidnapping. One is the abduction of drug dealers or their children, the other is the abduction of illegal aliens.

Drug-related kidnappings often are not strict kidnappings for ransom per se. Instead, they are intended to force the drug dealer to repay a debt to the drug-trafficking organization that ordered the kidnapping.

Non-drug-related kidnappings are very different from traditional kidnappings in Mexico or the United States, in which a high-value target is abducted and held for a large ransom. Instead, some of the gangs operating in Phoenix are basing their business model on volume, and are willing to hold a large number of victims for a much smaller individual pay out. Reports have emerged of kidnapping gangs in Phoenix carjacking entire vans full of illegal immigrants away from the coyote smuggling them into the United States. The kidnappers then transport the illegal immigrants to a safe house, where they are held captive in squalid conditions — and often tortured or sexually assaulted with a family member listening in on the phone — to coerce the victims' family members in the United States or Mexico to pay the ransom for their release. There are also reports of the gangs picking up vehicles full of victims at day labor sites and then transporting them to the kidnapping safe house rather than to the purported work site.

Drug-related kidnappings are less frequent than the non-drug-related abduction of illegal immigrants, but in both types of abductions, the victims are not likely to seek police assistance due to their immigration status or their involvement in illegal activity. This strongly suggests that the kidnapping problem greatly exceeds the number of cases reported to police.

Implications for the United States

The kidnapping gangs in Phoenix that target illegal immigrants have found their chosen crime to be lucrative and relatively risk-free. If the flow of illegal immigrants had continued at high levels, there is very little doubt the kidnappers' operations would have continued as they have for the past few years. The current economic downturn, however, means the flow of illegal immigrants has begun to slow — and by some accounts has even begun to reverse. (Reports suggest many Mexicans are returning home after being unable to find jobs in the United States.)

This reduction in the pool of targets means that we might be fast approaching a point where these groups, which have become accustomed to kidnapping as a source of easy money — and their primary source of income — might be forced to change their method of operating to make a living. While some might pursue other types of criminal activity, some might well decide to diversify their pool of victims. Watching for this shift in targeting is of critical importance. Were some of these gangs to begin targeting U.S. citizens rather than just criminals or illegal immigrants, a tremendous panic would ensue, along with demands to catch the perpetrators.

Such a shift would bring a huge amount of law enforcement pressure onto the kidnapping gangs, including pressure from the FBI. While the FBI is fairly hard-pressed for resources given its heavy counterterrorism, foreign counterintelligence and white-collar crime caseload, it almost certainly would be able to reassign the resources needed to respond to such kidnappings in the face of publicity and a public outcry. Such a law enforcement effort could neutralize these gangs fairly quickly, but probably not quickly enough to prevent any victims from being abducted or harmed.

Since criminal groups are not comprised of fools alone, at least some of these groups will realize that targeting soccer moms will bring an avalanche of law enforcement attention upon them. Therefore, it is very likely that if kidnapping targets become harder to find in Phoenix — or if the law enforcement environment becomes too hostile due to the growing realization of this problem — then the groups may shift geography rather than targeting criteria. In such a scenario, professional kidnapping gangs from Phoenix might migrate to other locations with large communities of Latin American illegal immigrants to victimize. Some of these locations could be relatively close to the Mexican border like Dallas, Houston, San Antonio, San Diego or Los Angeles, though they could also include locations farther inland like Chicago, Atlanta, New York, or even the communities around meat and poultry packing plants in the Midwest and mid-Atlantic states. Such a migration of ethnic criminals would not be unprecedented. For some time, Chinese Triad groups from New York have traveled elsewhere on the East Coast, like Atlanta, to engage in extortion and kidnapping against Chinese businessmen.

The issue of Mexican drug-trafficking organizations kidnapping in the United States merits careful attention, especially since criminal gangs in other areas of the country could start imitating the tactics of the Phoenix gangs.

35: Central America:
An Emerging Role in the Drug Trade
March 26, 2009

As part of STRATFOR's coverage of the security situation in Mexico, we have observed some significant developments in the drug trade in the Western Hemisphere over the past year. While the United States remains the top destination for South American-produced cocaine, and Mexico continues to serve as the primary transshipment route, the path between Mexico and South America is clearly changing.

These changes have been most pronounced in Central America, where Mexican drug-trafficking organizations have begun to rely increasingly on land-based smuggling routes as several countries in the region have stepped up monitoring and interdiction of airborne and maritime shipments transiting from South America to Mexico.

The results of these changes have been extraordinary. According to a December 2008 report from the U.S. National Drug Intelligence Center, less than 1 percent of the estimated 600 to 700 tons of cocaine that departed South America for the United States in 2007 transited Central America. The rest, for the most part, passed through the Caribbean Sea or Pacific Ocean en route to Mexico. Since then, land-based shipment of cocaine through Central America appears to have ballooned. Earlier this month, U.S. Ambassador to Guatemala Stephen McFarland estimated in an interview with a Guatemalan newspaper that cocaine now passes through that country at a rate of approximately 300 to 400 tons per year.

Notwithstanding the difficulty associated with estimating drug flows, it is clear that Central America has evolved into a significant transshipment route for drugs, and that the changes have taken place rapidly. These developments warrant a closer look at the mechanics of the drug trade in the region, the actors involved, and the implications for Central American governments — for whom drug-trafficking organizations represent a much more daunting threat than they do for Mexico.

Some Background

While the drug trade in the Western Hemisphere is multifaceted, it fundamentally revolves around the trafficking of South American-produced cocaine to the United States, the world's largest market for the drug. Drug shipment routes between Peru and Colombia — where the vast majority of cocaine is cultivated and produced — and the United States historically have been flexible, evolving in response to interdiction efforts or changing markets. For example, Colombian drug traffickers used to control the bulk of the cocaine trade by managing shipping routes along the Caribbean smuggling corridor directly to the United States. By the 1990s, however, as the United States and other countries began to focus surveillance and interdiction efforts along this corridor, the flow of U.S.-bound drugs was forced into Mexico, which remains the main transshipment route for the overwhelming majority of cocaine entering the United States.

A similar situation has been occurring over the last two years in Central America. From the 1990s until as recently as 2007, traffickers in Mexico received multi-ton shipments of cocaine from South America. There was ample evidence of this, including occasional discoveries of bulk cocaine on everything from small propeller aircraft and Gulfstream jets to self-propelled semi submersible vessels, fishing trawlers and cargo ships. These smuggling platforms had sufficient range and capacity to bypass Central America and ship bulk drugs directly to Mexico.

By early 2008, however, a series of developments in several Central American countries suggested that drug-trafficking organizations — Mexican cartels in particular — were increasingly trying to establish new land-based smuggling routes through Central America for cocaine shipments from South America to Mexico and eventual delivery to the United States. While small quantities of drugs had certainly transited the region in the past, the routes used presented an assortment of risks. A combination of poorly maintained highways, frequent border crossings, volatile security conditions and unpredictable local criminal organizations apparently presented such great logistical challenges that traffickers opted to send the majority of their shipments through well-established maritime and airborne platforms.

In response to this relatively unchecked international smuggling, several countries in the region began taking steps to increase the monitoring and interdiction of such shipments. The Colombian government, for one, stepped up monitoring of aircraft operating in its airspace. The Mexican government installed updated radar systems and reduced the number of airports authorized to receive flights originating in Central and South America. The Colombian government estimates that the aerial trafficking of cocaine from Colombia has decreased by as much as 90 percent since 2003.

Maritime trafficking also appears to have suffered over the past few years, most likely due to greater cooperation and information-sharing between Mexico and the United States. The United States has an immense capability to collect maritime technical intelligence, and an increasing degree of awareness regarding drug trafficking at sea. Two examples of this progress include the Mexican navy's July 2008 capture — acting on intelligence provided by the United States — of a self-propelled semi submersible vessel loaded with more than five tons of cocaine, and the U.S. Coast Guard's February 2009 interdiction of a Mexico-flagged fishing boat loaded with some seven tons of cocaine about 700 miles off Mexico's Pacific coast. Presumably as a result of successes such as these, the Mexican navy reported in 2008 that maritime trafficking had decreased by an estimated 60 percent over the last two years.

While it is impossible to independently corroborate the Mexican and Colombian governments' estimates of the degree to which air- and seaborne drug trafficking has decreased over the last few years, developments in Central America over the past year certainly support their assessments. In particular, STRATFOR has observed that in order to make up for losses in maritime and aerial trafficking, land-based smuggling routes are increasingly being used — not by Colombian cocaine producers or even Central American drug gangs but by the now much more powerful Mexican drug-trafficking organizations.

Mechanics of Central American Drug Trafficking

It is important to clarify that what we are defining as land-based trafficking is not limited to overland smuggling. The methods associated with land-based trafficking can be divided into three categories: overland smuggling, littoral maritime trafficking and short-range aerial trafficking.

The most straightforward of these is simple overland smuggling. As a series of investigations in Panama, Costa Rica and Nicaragua demonstrated last year, overland smuggling operations use a wide variety of approaches. In one case, authorities pieced together a portion of a route being used by Mexico's Sinaloa cartel in which small quantities of drugs entered Costa Rica from Panama via the international point of entry on the Pan-American Highway. The cocaine was often held for several days in a storage facility before being loaded onto another vehicle to be driven across the country on major highways. Upon approaching the Nicaraguan border, however, the traffickers opted to avoid the official port of entry and instead transferred the shipments into Nicaragua on foot or on horseback along a remote part of the border. Once across, the shipments were taken to the shores of the large inland Lake Nicaragua, where they were transferred onto boats to be taken north, at which point they would be loaded onto vehicles to be driven toward the Honduran border. In one case in Nicaragua, authorities uncovered another Sinaloa-linked route that passed through Managua and is believed to have followed the Pan-American Highway through Honduras and into El Salvador.

The second method associated with land-based trafficking involves littoral maritime operations. Whereas long-range maritime trafficking involves large cargo ships and self-propelled semi submersible vessels capable of delivering multi-ton shipments of drugs from South America to Mexico without having to refuel, littoral trafficking tends to involve so-called "go-fast boats" that are used to carry smaller quantities of drugs at higher speeds over shorter distances. This method is useful to traffickers who might want to avoid, for whatever reason, a certain stretch of highway or perhaps even an entire country. According to Nicaraguan military officials, several go-fast boats are suspected of operating off the country's coasts and of sailing outside Nicaraguan territorial waters in order to avoid authorities. While it is possible to make the entire trip from South America to Mexico using only this method — and making frequent refueling stops — it is believed that littoral trafficking is often combined with an overland network.

The third method associated with land-based drug smuggling involves short-range aerial operations. In these cases, clandestine planes make stops in Central America before either transferring their

DRUG TRAFFICKING THROUGH CENTRAL AMERICA

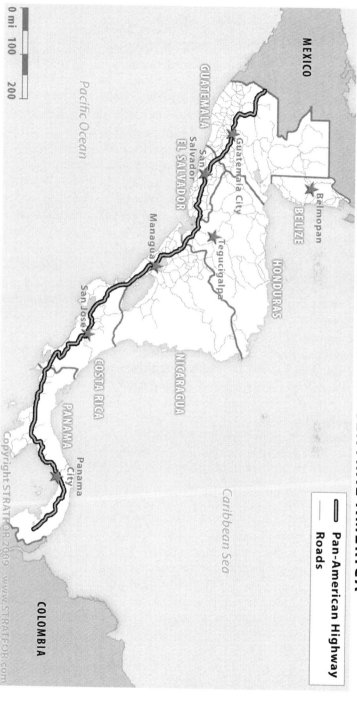

Legend:
- Pan-American Highway
- Roads

MEXICO

BELIZE — Belmopan

GUATEMALA — Guatemala City

EL SALVADOR — San Salvador

HONDURAS — Tegucigalpa

NICARAGUA — Managua

COSTA RICA — San Jose

PANAMA — Panama City

COLOMBIA

Pacific Ocean

Caribbean Sea

0 mi   100   200

Copyright STRATFOR 2009   www.STRATFOR.com

cargo to a land vehicle or making another short flight toward Mexico. Over the past year, several small planes loaded with drugs or cash have crashed or been seized in Honduras, Mexico and other countries in the region. In addition, authorities in Guatemala have uncovered several clandestine airstrips allegedly managed by the Mexican drug-trafficking organization Los Zetas. These examples suggest that even as overall aerial trafficking appears to have decreased dramatically, the practice continues in Central America. Indeed, there is little reason to expect that it would not continue, considering that many countries in the region lack the resources to adequately monitor their airspace.

While each of these three methods involves a different approach to drug smuggling, the methods share two important similarities. For one, the vehicles involved — be they speedboats, small aircraft or private vehicles — have limited cargo capacities, which means land-based trafficking generally involves cocaine shipments in quantities no greater than a few hundred pounds. While smaller quantities in more frequent shipments mean more handling, they also mean that less product is lost if a shipment is seized. More important, each of these land-based methods requires that a drug-trafficking organization maintain a presence inside Central America.

Actors Involved

There are a variety of drug-trafficking organizations operating inside Central America. In addition to some of the notorious local gangs — such as Calle 18 and MS-13 — there is also a healthy presence of foreign criminal organizations. Colombian drug traffickers, for example, historically have been no strangers to the region. However, as STRATFOR has observed over the past year, it is the more powerful Mexico-based drug-trafficking organizations that appear to be overwhelmingly responsible for the recent upticks in land-based narcotics smuggling in Central America.

Based on reports of arrests and drug seizures in the region over the past year, it is clear that no single Mexican cartel maintains a monopoly on land-based drug trafficking in Central America. Los

Zetas, for example, are extremely active in several parts of Guatemala, where they engage in overland and short-range aerial trafficking. The Sinaloa cartel, which STRATFOR believes is the most capable Mexican trafficker of cocaine, has been detected operating a fairly extensive overland smuggling route from Panama to El Salvador. Some intelligence gaps remain regarding, for example, the precise route Sinaloa follows from El Salvador to Mexico or the route Los Zetas use between South America and Guatemala. It is certainly possible that these two Mexican cartels do not rely exclusively on any single route or method in the region. But the logistical challenges associated with establishing even one route across Central America make it likely that existing routes are maintained even after they have been detected — and are defended if necessary.

The operators of the Mexican cartel-managed routes also do not match a single profile. At times, Mexican cartel members themselves have been found to be operating in Central America. More common is the involvement of locals in various phases of smuggling operations. Nicaraguan and Salvadoran nationals, for example, have been arrested in northwestern Nicaragua for operating a Sinaloa-linked overland and littoral route into El Salvador. Authorities in Costa Rica have arrested Costa Rican nationals for their involvement in overland routes through that country. In that case, a related investigation in Panama led to the arrest of several Mexican nationals who reportedly had recently arrived in the area to more closely monitor the operation of their route.

One exception is Guatemala, where Mexican drug traffickers appear to operate much more extensively than in any other Central American country. This may be due, at least in part, to the relationship between Los Zetas and the Guatemalan Kaibiles. Beyond the apparently more-established Zeta smuggling operations there, several recent drug seizures — including an enormous 1,800-acre poppy plantation attributed to the Sinaloa cartel — make it clear that other Mexican drug-trafficking organizations are currently active inside Guatemala. Sinaloa was first suspected of increasing its presence in Guatemala in early 2008, when rumors surfaced that the cartel was trying to recruit local criminal organizations to support its own drug-trafficking operations there. The ongoing Zeta-Sinaloa rivalry at that time triggered a series of deadly firefights in Guatemala, prompting fears that the bloody turf battles that had led to record levels of organized crime-related violence inside Mexico would extend into Central America.

Security Implications in Central America

Despite these concerns and the growing presence of Mexican traffickers in the region, there apparently have been no significant spikes in drug-related violence in Central America outside of Guatemala. Several factors may explain this relative lack of violence.

First, most governments in Central America have yet to launch large-scale counternarcotics campaigns. The seizures and arrests that have been reported so far have generally been the result of regular police work, as opposed to broad changes in policies or a significant commitment of resources to address the problem. More significantly, though, the quantities of drugs seized probably amount to just a drop in the bucket compared to the quantity of drugs that moves through the region on a regular basis. Because seizures have remained low, Mexican drug traffickers have yet to launch any significant reprisal attacks against government officials in any country outside Guatemala. In that country, even the president has received death threats and had his office bugged, allegedly by drug traffickers.

The second factor, which is related to the first, is that drug traffickers operating in Central America likely rely more heavily on bribes than on intimidation to secure the transit of drug shipments. This assessment follows from the region's reputation for official corruption (especially in countries like Nicaragua, Honduras, Panama and Guatemala) and the economic disadvantage that many of these countries face compared to the Mexican cartels. For example, the gross domestic product of Honduras is $12 billion, while the estimated share of the drug trade controlled by the Mexican cartels is estimated to be $20 billion.

Finally, Mexican cartels currently have their hands full at home. Although Central America has undeniably become more strategically important for the flow of drugs from South America, the cartels in Mexico have simultaneously been engaged in a two-front war at home against the Mexican government and against rival criminal organizations. As long as this war continues at its present level, Mexican drug traffickers may be reluctant to divert significant resources too far from their home turf, which remains crucial in delivering drug shipments to the United States.

Looking Ahead

That said, there is no guarantee that Central America will continue to escape the wrath of Mexican drug traffickers. On the contrary, there is reason for concern that the region will increasingly become a battleground in the Mexican cartel war.

For one thing, the Merida Initiative, a U.S. anti-drug aid program that will put some $300 million into Mexico and about $100 million into Central America over the next year, could be perceived as a meaningful threat to drug-trafficking operations. If Central American governments choose to step up counternarcotics operations, either at the request of the United States or in order to qualify for more Merida money, they risk disrupting existing smuggling operations to the extent that cartels begin to retaliate.

Also, even though Mexican cartels may be reluctant to divert major resources from the more important war at home, it is important to recognize that a large-scale reassignment of cartel operatives or resources from Mexico to Central America might not be necessary to have a significant impact on the security situation in any given Central American country. Given the rampant corruption and relatively poor protective security programs in place for political leaders in the region, very few cartel operatives or resources would actually be needed if a Mexican drug-trafficking organization chose to, for example, conduct an assassination campaign against high-ranking government officials.

Governments are not the only potential threat to drug traffickers in Central America. The increases in land-based drug trafficking in the region could trigger intensified competition over trafficking routes. Such turf battles could occur either among the Mexican cartels or between the Mexicans and local criminal organizations, which might try to muscle their way into the lucrative smuggling routes or attempt to grab a larger percentage of the profits.

If the example of Mexico is any guide, the drug-related violence that could be unleashed in Central America would easily overwhelm the capabilities of the region's governments. Last year, STRATFOR considered the possibility of Mexico becoming a failed state. But Mexico is a far stronger and richer country than its fragile southern neighbors, who simply do not have the resources to deal with the cartels on their own.

36: When the Mexican Drug Trade Hits the Border
April 15, 2009

For several years now, STRATFOR has been closely monitoring the growing violence in Mexico and its links to the drug trade. In December, our cartel report assessed the situation in Mexico, and two weeks ago we looked closely at the networks that control the flow of drugs through Central America. This week, we turn our attention to the border to see the dynamics at work there and how U.S. gangs are involved in the action.

The nature of narcotics trafficking changes as shipments near the border. As in any supply chain, shipments become smaller as they reach the retail level, requiring more people to be involved in the operation. While Mexican cartels do have representatives in cities across the United States to oversee networks there, local gangs get involved in the actual distribution of the narcotics.

While there are still many gaps in the understanding of how U.S. gangs interface with Mexican cartels to move drugs around the United States and finally sell them on the retail market, we do know some of the details of gang involvement.

Trafficking vs. Distribution

Though the drug trade as a whole is highly complex, the underlying concept is as simple as getting narcotics from South America to the consuming markets — chief among them the United States, which is the world's largest drug market. Traffickers use Central America and Mexico as a pipeline to move their goods north. The objective of the Latin American smuggler is to get as much tonnage as possible from Colombia, Peru and Bolivia to the lucrative American market and avoid interdictions by authorities along the way.

However, as narcotic shipments near the U.S.-Mexican border, wholesale trafficking turns into the more micro process of retail distribution. In southern Mexico, drug traffickers move product north in bulk, but as shipments cross the U.S. border, wholesale shipments are broken down into smaller parcels in order to hedge against interdiction and prepare the product for the end user. One way to think about the difference in tactics between trafficking drugs in Central America and Mexico and distributing drugs in the United States is to imagine a company like UPS or FedEx. Shipping air cargo from, say, New York to Los Angeles requires different resources than delivering packages to individual homes in southern California. Several tons of freight from the New York area can be quickly flown to the Los Angeles area. But as the cargo gets closer to its final destination, it is broken up into smaller loads that are shipped via tractor trailer to distribution centers around the region, and finally divided further into discrete packages carried in parcel trucks to individual homes.

As products move through the supply chain, they require more specific handling and detailed knowledge of an area, which requires more manpower. The same, more or less, can be said for drug shipments. This can be seen in interdiction reports. When narcotics are intercepted traversing South America into Mexico, they can be measured in tons; as they cross the border into the United States, seizures are reported in kilograms; and by the time products are picked up on the streets of U.S. cities, the narcotics have been divided into packages measured in grams. To reflect this difference, we will refer to the movement of drugs south of the border as trafficking and the movement of drugs north of the border as distributing.

As narcotics approach the border, law enforcement scrutiny and the risk of interdiction also increase, so drug traffickers have to be creative when it comes to moving their products. The constant game of cat-and-mouse makes drug trafficking a very dynamic business, with tactics and specific routes constantly changing to take advantage of any angle that presents itself.

The only certainties are that drugs and people will move from south to north, and that money and weapons will move from north to south. But the specific nature and corridors of those movements are constantly in flux as traffickers innovate in their attempts to stay ahead of the police in a very Darwinian environment. The traffickers employ all forms of movement imaginable, including:

- Tunneling under border fences into safe houses on the U.S. side.

- Traversing the desert on foot with 50-pound packs of narcotics. (Dirt bikes, ATVs and pack mules are also used.)

- Driving across the border by fording the Rio Grande, using ramps to get over fences, cutting through fences or driving through open areas.

- Using densely vegetated portions of the riverbank as dead drops.

- Floating narcotics across isolated stretches of the river.

- Flying small aircraft near the ground to avoid radar.

- Concealing narcotics in private vehicles, personal possessions and in or on the bodies of persons who are crossing legally at ports of entry.

- Bribing border officials in order to pass through checkpoints.

- Hiding narcotics on cross-border trains.

- Hiding narcotics in tractor trailers carrying otherwise legitimate loads.

- Using boats along the Gulf coast.

- Using human "mules" to smuggle narcotics aboard commercial aircraft in their luggage or bodies.

- Shipping narcotics via mail or parcel service.

These methods are not mutually exclusive, and organizations may use any combination at the same time. New ways to move the product are constantly emerging.

Once the narcotics are moved into the United States, drug distributors use networks of safe houses, which are sometimes operated by people with direct connections to the Mexican cartels, sometimes by local or regional gang members, and sometimes by individual entrepreneurs. North of the border, distributors still must maneuver around checkpoints, either by avoiding them or by bribing the officials who work there. While these checkpoints certainly result in seizures, they can only slow or reroute the flow of drugs. Hub cities like Atlanta service a large region of smaller drug dealers who act as individual couriers in delivering small amounts of narcotics to their customers.

It is a numbers game for drug traffickers and distributors alike, since it is inevitable that smugglers and shipments will be intercepted by law enforcement somewhere along the supply chain. Those whose loads are interdicted more often struggle to keep prices low and stay competitive. On the other hand, paying heavy corruption fees or taking extra precautions to ensure that more of your product makes it through also raises the cost of moving the product. Successful traffickers and distributors must be able to strike a balance between protecting their shipments and accepting losses. This requires a high degree of pragmatism and rationality.

Local Gangs

While the Mexican cartels do have people in the United States, they do not have enough people so positioned to handle the increased workload of distributing narcotics at the retail level. A wide range of skill sets is required. Some of the tactics involved in moving shipments across the border require skilled workers, such as pilots, while U.S. gang members along the border serve as middlemen and retail distributors. Other aspects of the operation call for people with expertise in manipulating corrupt officials and recruiting human intelligence sources, while a large part of the process simply involves saturating the system with massive numbers of expendable, low-skilled smugglers who are desperate for the money.

U.S. gangs are crucial in filling the cartel gap north of the border. Members of these border gangs typically are young men who are willing to break the law, looking for quick cash and already plugged into a network of similar young men, which enables them to recruit others to meet the manpower demand. They are also typically tied to Mexico through family connections, dual citizenship and the simple geographic fact that they live so close to the border. However, the U.S. gangs do not constitute formal extensions of the Mexican drug-trafficking organizations. Border gangs developed on their own, have their own histories, traditions, structures and turf, and they remain independent. They are also involved in more than just drug trafficking and distribution, including property crime, racketeering and kidnapping. Their involvement in narcotics is similar to that of a contractor who can provide certain services, such as labor and protection, while drugs move across gang territory, but drug money is not usually their sole source of income.

These gangs come in many shapes and sizes. Motorcycle gangs like the Mongols and Bandidos have chapters all along the southwestern U.S. border and, while not known to actually carry narcotics across the border into the United States, they are frequently involved in distributing smaller loads to various markets across the country to supplement their income from other illegal activities.

Street gangs are present in virtually every U.S. city and town of significant size along the border and are obvious pools of labor for distributing narcotics once they hit the United States. The largest of these street gangs are MS-13 and the Mexican Mafia. MS-13 has an estimated 30,000 to 50,000 members worldwide, about 25 percent of whom are in the United States. MS-13 is unique among U.S. gangs in that it is involved in trafficking narcotics through Central America and Mexico as well as in distributing narcotics in the United States. The Mexican Mafia works with allied gangs in the American Southwest to control large swaths of territory along both sides of the U.S.-Mexican border. These gangs are organized to interact directly with traffickers in Mexico and oversee trans-border shipments as well as distribution inside the United States.

Prison gangs such as Barrio Azteca and the Texas Syndicate reach far beyond the prison fence. Membership in a prison gang typically means that, at one point, the member was in prison, where he joined the gang. But there is a wide network of ex-prisoner gang members on the outside involved in criminal activities, including drug smuggling, which is one of the most accessible ways for a gang member to make money when he is released from prison.

Operating underneath the big gang players are hundreds of smaller city gangs in neighborhoods all along the border. These gangs are typically involved in property theft, drug dealing, turf battles and other forms of street crime that can be handled by local police. However, even these gangs can become involved in cross-border smuggling; for example, the Wonderboys in San Luis, Ariz., are known to smuggle marijuana, methamphetamine and cocaine across the border.

Gangs like the Wonderboys also target illegal immigrants coming across the border and steal any valuable personal items or cash they may have on them. The targeting of illegal immigrants coming into the United States is common all across the border, with many gangs specializing in kidnapping newly arrived immigrants and demanding

GULF INFLUENCE ALONG THE U.S./MEXICO BORDER

1 CALIFORNIA
Varrio Chula Vista
Otay Gang
Mexican Mafia

2 WESTERN ARIZONA (CALIFORNIA-NOGALES)
Wonderboys
Soma 13
West Side
MS-13
North Hollywood
East Side Naked City
Seventh Avenue Gang
Southside 15th Avenue
Barrios los Avenidas
West Coast Crips

3 TUCSON, ARIZONA
Barrio Hollywood
Barrio Libre
Bilby Street Cripts
South Park Family Bloods
Southside Posse Bloods
Mexican Mafia
MS-13

4 EASTERN ARIZONA (NOGALES-NEW MEXICO)
West Side
West Side Pierson Locos
Nogalipos
Surenos
Nortenos
Mexican Mafia
MS-13

5 NEW MEXICO
Mexican Mafia
East Side
Surenos
Nortenos
Syndicato de Nuevo Mexico
Mexican Local Clique
Mexican Clique Killers
Latin Kings
Norte 14
MS-13
Barrio Azteca
18th Street Gang

6 EL PASO, TEXAS - JUAREZ, CHIHUAHUA
Barrio Azteca

7 SOUTH TEXAS (LAREDO-BROWNSVILLE)
Mexican Mafia
Texas Syndicate
Hermandad Pistoleros
Latin Kings
MS-13
Surenos
El Cinco
Tri-City Bombers
Texas Chicano Brotherhood

Source: Local law enforcement

— Transportation Routes

0 mi   200   400

Copyright STRATFOR 2009 www.STRATFOR.com

ransoms from their families. These gangs are responsible for the record level of kidnapping reported in places like Phoenix, where 368 abductions were reported in 2008. Afraid to notify law enforcement out of a fear of being deported, many families of abducted immigrants somehow come up with the money to secure their family member's release.

Drug distribution is by far the most lucrative illicit business along the border, and the competition for money leads to a very pragmatic interface between the U.S. border gangs and the drug cartels in Mexico. Handoffs from Mexican traffickers to U.S. distributors are made based upon reliability and price. While territorial rivalries between drug traffickers have led to thousands of deaths in Mexico, these Mexican rivalries do not appear to be spilling over into the U.S. border gangs, who are engaged in their own rivalries, feuds and acts of violence. Nor do the more gruesome aspects of violence in Mexico, such as torture and beheadings, although there are indications that grenades that were once part of cartel arsenals are finding their way to U.S. gangs. In dealing with the Mexican cartels, U.S. gangs — and cartels in turn — exhibit no small amount of business pragmatism. U.S. gangs can serve more than one cartel, which appears to be fine with the cartels, who really have no choice in the matter. They need these retail distribution services north of the border in order to make a profit.

Likewise, U.S. gangs are in the drug business to make money, not to enhance the power of any particular cartel in Mexico. As such, U.S. gangs do not want to limit their business opportunities by aligning themselves to any one cartel. Smaller city gangs that control less territory are more limited geographically in terms of which cartels they can work with. The Wonderboys in Arizona, for example, must deal exclusively with the Sinaloa cartel because the cartel's turf south of the border encompasses the gang's relative sliver of turf to the north. However, larger gangs like the Mexican Mafia control much broader swaths of territory and can deal with more than one cartel.

The expanse of geography controlled by the handful of cartels in Mexico simply does not match up with the territory controlled by the many gangs on the U.S. side. Stricter law enforcement is one reason

U.S. border gangs have not consolidated to gain control over more turf. While corruption is a growing problem along the U.S. side of the border, it still has not risen to the level that it has in northern Mexico. Another reason for the asymmetry is the different nature of drug movements north of the border. As discussed earlier, moving narcotics in the United States has everything to do with distributing retail quantities of drugs to consumers spread over a broad geographic area, a model that requires more feet on the ground than the trafficking that takes place in Mexico.

Assassins' Gate

Because the drug distribution network in the United States is so large, it is impossible for any one criminal organization to control all of it. U.S. gangs fill the role of middleman to move drugs around, and they are entrusted with large shipments of narcotics worth millions of dollars. Obviously, the cartels need a way to keep these gangs honest.

One effective way is to have an enforcement arm in place. This is where U.S.-based assassins come in. More tightly connected to the cartels than the gangs are, these assassins are not usually members of a gang. In fact, the cartels prefer that their assassins not be in a gang so that their loyalties will be to the cartels, and so they will be less likely to have criminal records or attract law enforcement attention because of everyday gang activity.

Cartels invest quite a bit in training these hit men to operate in the United States. Often they are trained in Mexico, then sent back across to serve as a kind of "sleeper cell" until they are tapped to take out a delinquent U.S. drug dealer. The frequency and ease with which Americans travel to and from Mexico covers any suspicion that might be raised.

The Gaps

The U.S.-Mexican border is a dynamic place, with competition over drug routes and the quest for cash destabilizing northern

Mexico and straining local and state law enforcement on the U.S. side. Putting pressure on the people who are active in the border drug trade has so far only inspired others to adapt to the challenging environment by becoming more innovative and pragmatic.

And there is still so much we do not know. The exact nature of the relationship between Mexican cartels and U.S. gangs is very murky, and it appears to be handled on such an individual basis that making generalizations is difficult. Another intelligence gap is how deeply involved the cartels are in the U.S. distribution network. As mentioned earlier, the network expands as it becomes more retail in nature, but the profit margins also expand, making it an attractive target for cartel takeover. Finally, while we know that gangs are instrumental in distributing narcotics in the United States, it is unclear how much of the cross-border smuggling they control. Is this vital, risky endeavor completely controlled by cartels and gatekeeper organizations based in Mexico, or do U.S. gangs on the distribution side have more say? STRATFOR will continue to monitor these issues as Mexico's dynamic cartels continue to evolve.

37: A Counterintelligence Approach to Controlling Cartel Corruption
May 20, 2009

Rey Guerra, the former sheriff of Starr County, Texas, pleaded guilty May 1 to a narcotics conspiracy charge in federal district court in McAllen, Texas. Guerra admitted to using information obtained in his official capacity to help a friend (a Mexican drug trafficker allegedly associated with Los Zetas) evade U.S. counternarcotics efforts. On at least one occasion, Guerra also attempted to learn the identity of a confidential informant who had provided authorities with information regarding cartel operations so he could pass it to his cartel contact.

In addition to providing intelligence to Los Zetas, Guerra also reportedly helped steer investigations away from people and facilities associated with Los Zetas. He also sought to block progress on investigations into arrested individuals associated with Los Zetas to protect other members associated with the organization. Guerra is scheduled for sentencing July 29; he faces 10 years to life imprisonment, fines of up to $4 million and five years of supervised release.

Guerra is just one of a growing number of officials on the U.S. side of the border who have been recruited as agents for Mexico's powerful and sophisticated drug cartels. Indeed, when one examines the reach and scope of the Mexican cartels' efforts to recruit agents inside the United States to provide intelligence and act on the cartels' behalf, it becomes apparent that the cartels have demonstrated the ability to operate more like a foreign intelligence service than a traditional criminal organization.

Fluidity and Flexibility

For many years now, STRATFOR has followed developments along the U.S.-Mexican border and has studied the dynamics of the cross-border illicit flow of people, drugs, weapons and cash.

One of the most notable characteristics about this flow of contraband is its flexibility. When smugglers encounter an obstacle to the flow of their product, they find ways to avoid it. For example, as we've previously discussed in the case of the extensive border fence in the San Diego sector, drug traffickers and human smugglers diverted a good portion of their volume around the wall to the Tucson sector; they even created an extensive network of tunnels under the fence to keep their contraband (and profits) flowing.

Likewise, as maritime and air interdiction efforts between South America and Mexico have become more successful, Central America has become increasingly important to the flow of narcotics from South America to the United States. This reflects how the drug-trafficking organizations have adjusted their method of shipment and their trafficking routes to avoid interdiction efforts and maintain the northward flow of narcotics.

Over the past few years, a great deal of public and government attention has focused on the U.S.-Mexican border. In response to this attention, the federal and border state governments in the United States have erected more barriers, installed an array of cameras and sensors and increased the manpower committed to securing the border. While these efforts certainly have not hermetically sealed the border, they do appear to be having some impact — an impact magnified by the effectiveness of interdiction efforts elsewhere along the narcotics supply chain.

According to the most recent statistics from the Drug Enforcement Administration, from January 2007 through September 2008 the price per pure gram of cocaine increased 89.1 percent, or from $96.61 to $182.73, while the purity of cocaine seized on the street decreased 31.3 percent, dropping from 67 percent pure cocaine to 46 percent pure cocaine. Recent anecdotal reports from law enforcement sources indicate that cocaine prices have remained high, and that the purity of cocaine on the street has remained poor.

Overcoming Human Obstacles

In another interesting trend that has emerged over the past few years, as border security has tightened and as the flow of narcotics has been impeded, the number of U.S. border enforcement officers arrested on charges of corruption has increased notably. This increased corruption represents a logical outcome of the fluidity of the flow of contraband. As the obstacles posed by border enforcement have become more daunting, people have become the weak link in the enforcement system. In some ways, people are like tunnels under the border wall — i.e., channels employed by the traffickers to help their goods get to market.

From the Mexican cartels' point of view, it is cheaper to pay an official several thousand dollars to allow a load of narcotics to pass by than it is to risk having the shipment seized. Such bribes are simply part of the cost of doing business — and in the big picture, even a low-level local agent can be an incredible bargain.

According to U.S. Customs and Border Protection (CBP), 21 CBP officers were arrested on corruption charges during the fiscal year that ended in September 2008, as opposed to only 4 in the preceding fiscal year. In the current fiscal year (since Oct. 1), 14 have been arrested. And the problem with corruption extends further than just customs or border patrol officers. In recent years, police officers, state troopers, county sheriffs, National Guard members, judges, prosecutors, deputy U.S. marshals and even the FBI special agent in charge of the El Paso office have been linked to Mexican drug-trafficking organizations. Significantly, the cases being prosecuted against these public officials of all stripes are just the tip of the iceberg. The underlying problem of corruption is much greater.

A major challenge to addressing the issue of border corruption is the large number of jurisdictions along the border, along with the reality that corruption occurs at the local, state and federal levels across those jurisdictions. Though this makes it very difficult to gather data relating to the total number of corruption investigations conducted, sources tell us that while corruption has always been a problem along the border, the problem has ballooned in recent years — and the number of corruption cases has increased dramatically.

In addition to the complexity brought about by the multiple jurisdictions, agencies and levels of government involved, there simply is not one single agency that can be tasked with taking care of the corruption problem. It is just too big and too wide. Even the FBI, which has national jurisdiction and a mandate to investigate public corruption cases, cannot step in and clean up all the corruption. The FBI already is being stretched thin with its other responsibilities, like counterterrorism, foreign counterintelligence, financial fraud and bank robbery. The FBI thus does not even have the capacity to investigate every allegation of corruption at the federal level, much less at the state and local levels. Limited resources require the agency to be very selective about the cases it decides to investigate. Given that there is no real central clearinghouse for corruption cases, most allegations of corruption are investigated by a wide array of internal affairs units and other agencies at the federal, state and local levels.

Any time there is such a mixture of agencies involved in the investigation of a specific type of crime, there is often bureaucratic friction, and there are almost always problems with information sharing. This means that pieces of information and investigative leads developed in the investigation of some of these cases are not shared with the appropriate agencies. To overcome this information sharing problem, the FBI has established six Border Corruption Task Forces designed to bring local, state and federal officers together to focus on corruption tied to the U.S.-Mexican border, but these task forces have not yet been able to solve the complex problem of coordination.

Sophisticated Spotting

Efforts to corrupt officials along the U.S.-Mexican border are very organized and very focused, something that is critical to understanding the public corruption issue along the border. Some of the Mexican cartels have a long history of successfully corrupting public officials on both sides of the border. Groups like the Beltran Leyva Organization (BLO) have successfully recruited scores of intelligence assets and agents of influence at the local, state and even federal levels of the Mexican government. They even have enjoyed significant success in recruiting agents in elite units such as the anti-organized crime unit (SIEDO) of the Office of the Mexican Attorney General (PGR). The BLO also has recruited Mexican employees working for the U.S. Embassy in Mexico City, and even allegedly owned Mexico's former drug czar, Noe Ramirez Mandujano, who reportedly was receiving $450,000 a month from the organization.

In fact, the sophistication of these groups means they use methods more akin to the intelligence recruitment processes used by foreign intelligence services than those normally associated with a criminal organization. The cartels are known to conduct extensive surveillance and background checks on potential targets to determine how to best pitch to them. Like the spotting methods used by intelligence agencies, the surveillance conducted by the cartels on potential targets is designed to glean as many details about the target as possible, including where they live, what vehicles they drive, who their family members are, their financial needs and their peccadilloes.

Historically, many foreign intelligence services are known to use ethnicity in their favor, heavily targeting persons sharing an ethnic background found in the foreign country. Foreign services also are known to use relatives of the target living in the foreign country to their advantage. Mexican cartels use these same tools. They tend to target Hispanic officers and often use family members living in Mexico as recruiting levers. For example, Luis Francisco Alarid, who had been a CBP officer at the Otay Mesa, Calif., port of entry, was sentenced to 84 months in federal prison in February for his participation in a conspiracy to smuggle illegal aliens and marijuana into the United States. One of the people Alarid admitted to conspiring with was his uncle, who drove a van loaded with marijuana and illegal aliens through a border checkpoint manned by Alarid.

Like family spy rings (such as the Cold War spy ring run by John Walker), there also have been family border corruption rings. Raul Villarreal and his brother, Fidel, both former CBP agents in San Diego, were arraigned March 16 after fleeing the United States in 2006 after learning they were being investigated for corruption. The pair was captured in Mexico in October 2008 and extradited back to the United States.

'Plata o Sexo'

When discussing human intelligence recruiting, it is not uncommon to refer to the old Cold War acronym MICE (money, ideology, compromise and ego) to explain the approach used to recruit an agent. When discussing corruption in Mexico, people often repeat the phrase "plata o plomo," Spanish for "money or lead" — meaning "take the money or we'll kill you." However, in most border corruption cases involving American officials, the threat of plomo is not as powerful as it is inside Mexico. Although some officials charged with corruption have claimed as a defense that they were intimidated into behaving corruptly, juries have rejected these arguments. This dynamic could change if the Mexican cartels begin to target officers in the United States for assassination as they have in Mexico.

With plomo an empty threat north of the border, plata has become the primary motivation for corruption along the Mexican border. In fact, good old greed — the M in MICE — has always been the most common motivation for Americans recruited by foreign intelligence services. The runner-up, which supplants plomo in the recruitment equation inside the United Sates, is "sexo," or sex. An age-old espionage recruitment tool that fits under the compromise section of MICE, sex has been seen in high-profile espionage cases, including the one involving the Marine security guards at the U.S. Embassy in Moscow. Using sex to recruit an agent is often referred to as setting a "honey trap." Sex can be used in two ways: as a simple payment for services rendered or as a means to blackmail the agent. (The two techniques can be used in tandem.)

It is not at all uncommon for border officials to be offered sex in return for allowing illegal aliens or drugs to enter the country, or for drug-trafficking organizations to use attractive agents to seduce and then recruit officers. Several officials have been convicted in such cases. For example, in March 2007, CBP inspection officer Richard Elizalda, who had worked at the San Ysidro, Calif., port of entry, was sentenced to 57 months in prison for conspiring with his lover, alien smuggler Raquel Arin, to let the organization she worked for bring illegal aliens through his inspection lane. Elizalda also accepted cash for his efforts — much of which he allegedly spent on gifts for Arin — so in reality, Elizalda was a case of "plata y sexo" rather than an either-or deal.

Corruption Cases Handled Differently

When the U.S. government hires an employee who has family members living in a place like Beijing or Moscow, the background investigation for that employee is pursued with far more interest than if the employee has relatives in Ciudad Juarez or Tijuana. Mexico traditionally has not been seen as a foreign counterintelligence threat, even though it has long been recognized that many countries, like Russia, are very active in their efforts to target the United States from Mexico. Indeed, during the Cold War, the KGB's largest rezidentura (the equivalent of a CIA station) was located in Mexico City.

Employees with connections to Mexico frequently have not been that well vetted, period. In one well-publicized incident, the Border Patrol hired an illegal immigrant who was later arrested for alien smuggling. In July 2006, U.S. Border Patrol agent Oscar Ortiz was sentenced to 60 months in prison after admitting to smuggling more than 100 illegal immigrants into the United States. After his arrest, investigators learned that Ortiz was an illegal immigrant himself who had used a counterfeit birth certificate when he was hired. Ironically, Ortiz also had been arrested for attempting to smuggle two illegal immigrants into the United States shortly before being hired by the Border Patrol. (He was never charged for that attempt.)

From an investigative perspective, corruption cases tend to be handled more as one-off cases, and they do not normally receive the same sort of extensive investigation into the suspect's friends and associates that would be conducted in a foreign counterintelligence case. In other words, if a U.S. government employee is recruited by the Chinese or Russian intelligence service, the investigation receives far more energy — and the suspect's circle of friends, relatives and associates receives far more scrutiny — than if he is recruited by a Mexican cartel.

In espionage cases, there is also an extensive damage assessment investigation conducted to ensure that all the information the suspect could have divulged is identified, along with the identities of any other people the suspect could have helped his handler recruit. Additionally, after-action reviews are conducted to determine how the suspect was recruited, how he was handled and how he could have been uncovered earlier. The results of these reviews are then used to help shape future counterintelligence investigative efforts. They are also used in the preparation of defensive counterintelligence briefings to educate other employees and help protect them from being recruited.

The differences in urgency and scope between the two types of investigations are driven by the perception that the damage to national security is greater if an official is recruited by a foreign intelligence agency than if he is recruited by a criminal organization. That assessment may need to be re-examined, given that the Mexican cartels are criminal organizations with the proven sophistication to recruit U.S. officials at all levels of government — and that this has allowed them to move whomever and whatever they wish into the United States.

The problem of public corruption is very widespread, and to approach corruption cases in a manner similar to foreign counterintelligence cases would require a large commitment of investigative, prosecutorial and defensive resources. But the threat posed by the Mexican cartels is different than that posed by traditional criminal organizations, meaning that countering it will require a nontraditional approach.

38: Politics and Narco-Corruption in Michoacan
May 29, 2009

The Mexican organized crime group La Familia had planned to interfere in the country's upcoming July 5 national legislative elections, Mexican media reported May 29, citing sources in Mexican military intelligence and the federal attorney general's office (PGR). La Familia's plan reportedly included financing candidates, coercing voters and transporting voters to polling places in some of the largest cities in the state of Michoacan, including the state capital, Morelia, as well as Uruapan, Lazaro Cardenas, Patzcuaro, Apatzingan and Zitacuaro.

The revelation comes just a few days after a joint operation between PGR and Mexican military forces that resulted in the arrest of more than 30 mayors, judges and other public officials in Michoacan on charges of corruption and links to La Familia. In those cases — the largest single roundup of public officials during the last few years of the country's cartel war — the government charges that La Familia members have used their connections with corrupt public officials to secure a safe operating environment for drug trafficking, retail drug distribution, extortion, kidnapping and other criminal activities.

That a criminal organization such as La Familia had a large number of Mexican public officials on its payroll is not surprising. Even so, this incident illuminates the deeply rooted and widespread nature of organized crime-related official corruption in Mexico.

The extent of organized crime in Mexico ensures that there is no shortage of corrupt officials countrywide. While President Felipe Calderon has pursued a number of anti-corruption initiatives over the last few years targeting such officials, the decision to launch this most recent operation in Michoacan certainly seems like a politically motivated attempt to remind voters ahead of the July 5 legislative elections that Calderon's National Action Party (PAN) remains tough on crime and corruption. So far, the plan seems to have worked. Although the Michoacan state governor and his left-wing opposition Democratic Revolutionary Party (PRD) initially expressed outrage that the arrests took place without the governor's prior knowledge, the PRD leadership eventually backtracked. It clarified that the PRD does support the country's national counternarcotics strategy.

While La Familia is undeniably a powerful player in Michoacan state — and maintains a considerable presence in the neighboring states of Jalisco, Guerrero and Mexico — STRATFOR does not see the group as a significant national or international criminal power. Nonetheless, this case appears to shows that even smaller organized crime groups have not only the intent but also the ability to corrupt public officials at the federal level. Considering that La Familia is just one of many criminal groups in Mexico, it is not a stretch to assume that other groups — such as the much larger Sinaloa and Gulf cartels, the Beltran Leyva organization and Los Zetas — are pursuing even more robust plans to make the country's national elections work in their favor.

Indeed, this case provides a reminder of the deep-seated nature of corruption in Mexico. Two and half years after Calderon took office and began cracking down on drug- trafficking organizations and corruption, the problems are nowhere near going away. And this case shows that corruption goes far beyond just the police and touches all kinds of government officials. Ultimately, fully resolving the problem will involve a long-term effort to address more fundamental issues, including the country's political culture.

39: Economics and the Arms Trade
July 9, 2009

On June 26, the small Mexican town of Apaseo el Alto, in Guanajuato state, was the scene of a deadly firefight between members of Los Zetas and federal and local security forces. The engagement began when a joint patrol of Mexican soldiers and police officers responded to a report of heavily armed men at a suspected drug safe house. When the patrol arrived, a 20-minute firefight erupted between the security forces and gunmen in the house as well as several suspects in two vehicles who threw fragmentation grenades as they tried to escape.

When the shooting ended, 12 gunmen lay dead, 12 had been taken into custody and several soldiers and police officers had been wounded. At least half of the detained suspects admitted to being members of Los Zetas, a highly trained Mexican cartel group known for its use of military weapons and tactics.

When authorities examined the safe house they discovered a mass grave that contained the remains of an undetermined number of people (perhaps 14 or 15) who are believed to have been executed and then burned beyond recognition by Los Zetas. The house also contained a large cache of weapons, including assault rifles and fragmentation grenades. Such military ordnance is frequently used by Los Zetas and the enforcers who work for their rival cartels.

STRATFOR has been closely following the cartel violence in Mexico for several years now, and the events that transpired in Apaseo el Alto are by no means unique. It is not uncommon for the Mexican authorities to engage in large firefights with cartel groups, encounter mass graves or recover large caches of arms. However, the recovery of the weapons in Apaseo el Alto does provide an opportunity to once again focus on the dynamics of Mexico's arms trade.

White, Black and Shades of Gray

Before we get down into the weeds of Mexico's arms trade, let's do something a little different and first take a brief look at how arms trafficking works on a regional and global scale. Doing so will help illustrate how arms trafficking in Mexico fits into these broader patterns.

When analysts examine arms sales they look at three general categories: the white arms market, the gray arms market and the black arms market. The white arms market is the legal, aboveboard transfer of weapons in accordance with the national laws of the parties involved and international treaties or restrictions. The parties in a white arms deal will file the proper paperwork, including end-user certificates, noting what is being sold, who is selling it and to whom it is being sold. There is an understanding that the receiving party does not intend to transfer the weapons to a third party. So, for example, if the Mexican army wants to buy assault rifles from German arms maker Heckler & Koch, it places the order with the company and fills out all the required paperwork, including forms for obtaining permission for the sale from the German government.

Now, the white arms market can be deceived and manipulated, and when this happens, we get the gray market — literally, white arms that are shifted into the hands of someone other than the purported recipient. One of the classic ways to do this is to either falsify an end-user certificate, or bribe an official in a third country to sign an end-user certificate but then allow a shipment of arms to pass through a country en route to a third location. This type of transaction is frequently used in cases where there are international arms embargoes against a particular country (like Liberia) or where it is illegal to sell arms to a militant group (such as the Revolutionary Armed Forces of Colombia, known by its Spanish acronym, FARC). One example of this would be Ukrainian small arms that, on paper, were supposed to go to Cote d'Ivoire but were really transferred in violation of U.N. arms embargoes to Liberia and Sierra Leone. Another example of this would be the government of Peru purchasing thousands of surplus East German assault rifles from Jordan on the white arms market, ostensibly for the Peruvian military, only to have those rifles slip into the gray arms world and be dropped at airstrips in the jungles of Colombia for use by the FARC.

At the far end of the spectrum is the black arms market, where the guns are contraband from the get-go and all the business is conducted under the table. There are no end-user certificates and the weapons are smuggled covertly. Examples of this would be the smuggling of arms from the former Soviet Union (FSU) and Afghanistan into Europe through places like Kosovo and Slovenia, or the smuggling of arms into South America from Asia, the FSU and Middle East by Hezbollah and criminal gangs in the Tri-Border Region.

Nation-states will often use the gray and black arms markets in order to deniably support allies, undermine opponents or otherwise pursue their national interests. This was clearly revealed in the Iran-Contra scandal of the mid-1980s, but Iran-Contra only scratched the surface of the arms smuggling that occurred during the Cold War. Untold tons of military ordnance were delivered by the United States, the Soviet Union and Cuba to their respective allies in Latin America during the Cold War.

This quantity of materiel shipped into Latin America during the Cold War brings up another very important point pertaining to weapons. Unlike drugs, which are consumable goods, firearms are durable goods. This means that they can be useful for decades and are frequently shipped from conflict zone to conflict zone. East German

MPiKMS and MPiKM assault rifles are still floating around the world's arms markets years after the German Democratic Republic ceased to exist. In fact, visiting an arms bazaar in a place like Yemen is like visiting an arms museum. One can encounter century-old, still-functional Lee-Enfield and Springfield rifles in a rack next to a modern U.S. M4 rifle or German HK93, and those next to brand-new Chinese Type 56 and 81 assault rifles.

There is often a correlation between arms and drug smuggling. In many instances, the same routes used to smuggle drugs are also used to smuggle arms. In some instances, like the smuggling routes from Central Asia to Europe, the flow of guns and drugs goes in the same direction, and they are both sold in Western Europe for cash. In the case of Latin American cocaine, the drugs tend to flow in one direction (toward the United States and Europe) while guns from U.S. and Russian organized-crime groups flow in the other direction, and often these guns are used as whole or partial payment for the drugs.

Illegal drugs are not the only things traded for guns. During the Cold War, a robust arms-for-sugar trade transpired between the Cubans and Vietnamese. As a result, Marxist groups all over Latin America were furnished with U.S. materiel either captured or left behind when the Americans withdrew from Vietnam. LAW rockets traced to U.S. military stocks sent to Vietnam were used in several attacks by Latin American Marxist groups. These Vietnam War-vintage weapons still crop up with some frequency in Mexico, Colombia and other parts of the region. Cold War-era weapons furnished to the likes of the Contras, Sandinistas, Farabundo Marti National Liberation Front and Guatemalan National Revolutionary Unity movement in the 1980s are also frequently encountered in the region.

After the civil wars ended in places like El Salvador and Guatemala, the governments and the international community attempted to institute arms buy-back programs, but those programs were not very successful and most of the guns turned in were very old — the better arms were cached by groups or kept by individuals. Some of these guns have dribbled back into the black arms market, and Central and South America are still awash in Cold War weapons.

But Cold War shipments are not the only reason that Latin America is flooded with guns. In addition to the indigenous arms industries in countries like Brazil and Argentina, Venezuela has purchased hundreds of thousands of AK assault rifles in recent years to replace its aging FN-FAL rifles and has even purchased the equipment to open a factory to produce AK-103 rifles under license inside Venezuela. The Colombian government has accused the Venezuelans of arming the FARC, and evidence obtained by the Colombians during raids on FARC camps and provided to the public appears to support those assertions.

More than 90 Percent?

For several years now, Mexican officials have been making public statements that more than 90 percent of the arms used by criminals in Mexico come from the United States. That number was echoed last month in a report by the U.S. Government Accountability Office (GAO) on U.S. efforts to combat arms trafficking to Mexico.

According to the report, some 30,000 firearms were seized from criminals by Mexican officials in 2008. Out of these 30,000 firearms, information pertaining to 7,200 of them, (24 percent) was submitted to the U.S. Bureau of Alcohol, Tobacco, Firearms and Explosives (ATF) for tracing. Of these 7,200 guns, only about 4,000 could be traced by the ATF, and of these 4,000, some 3,480 (87 percent) were shown to have come from the United States.

This means that the 87 percent figure comes from the number of weapons submitted by the Mexican government to the ATF that could be successfully traced and not from the total number of weapons seized by the Mexicans or even from the total number of weapons submitted to the ATF for tracing. The 3,480 guns positively traced to the United States equals less than 12 percent of the total arms seized in 2008 and less than 48 percent of all those submitted by the Mexican government to the ATF for tracing.

In a response to the GAO report, the U.S. Department of Homeland Security (DHS) wrote a letter to the GAO (published as an appendix to the report) calling the GAO's use of the 87 percent statistic "misleading." The DHS further noted, "Numerous problems with the data collection and sample population render this assertion as unreliable."

Trying to get a reliable idea about where the drug cartels are getting their weapons can be difficult because the statistics on firearms seized in Mexico are very confusing. For example, while the GAO report says that 30,000 guns were seized in 2008 alone, the Mexican Prosecutor General's office has reported that between Dec. 1, 2005, and Jan. 22, 2009, Mexican authorities seized 31,512 weapons from the cartels.

Furthermore, it is not prudent to rely exclusively on weapons submitted to the ATF for tracing as a representative sample of the overall Mexican arms market. This is because there are some classes of weapons, such as RPG-7s and South Korean hand grenades, which make very little sense for the Mexicans to pass to the ATF for tracing since they obviously are not from the United States. The ATF is limited in its ability to trace weapons that did not pass through the United States, though there are offices at the CIA and Defense Intelligence Agency that maintain extensive international arms-trafficking databases.

Mexican authorities are also unlikely to ask the ATF to trace weapons that can be tracked through the Mexican government's own databases such as the one maintained by the Mexican Defense Department's Arms and Ammunition Marketing Division (UCAM), which is the only outlet through which Mexican citizens can legally buy guns. If they can trace a gun through UCAM there is simply no need to submit it to ATF.

The United States has criticized Mexico for decades over its inability to stop the flow of narcotics into U.S. territory, and for the past several years Mexico has responded by blaming the guns coming from the United States for its inability to stop the drug trafficking. In this context, there is a lot of incentive for the Mexicans to politicize and play up the issue of guns coming from the United States, and north of the border there are U.S. gun-control advocates who have a vested interest in adding fuel to the fire and gun-rights advocates who have an interest in playing down the number.

Clearly, the issue of U.S. guns being sent south of the border is a serious one, but STRATFOR does not believe that there is sufficient evidence to support the claim that 90 percent (or more) of the cartels' weaponry comes from the United States. The data at present is inclusive — the 90 percent figure appears to be a subsample of a sample, so that number cannot be applied with confidence to the entire country. Indeed, the percentage of U.S. arms appears to be far lower than 90 percent in specific classes of arms such as fully automatic assault rifles, machine guns, rifle grenades, fragmentation grenades and RPG-7s. Even items such as the handful of U.S.-manufactured LAW rockets encountered in Mexico have come from third countries and not directly from the United States.

However, while the 90 percent figure appears to be unsubstantiated by documentable evidence, this fact does not necessarily prove that the converse is true, even if it may be a logical conclusion. The bottom line is that, until there is a comprehensive, scientific study conducted on the arms seized by the Mexican authorities, much will be left to conjecture, and it will be very difficult to determine exactly how many of the cartels' weapons have come from the United States, and to map out precisely how the black, white and gray arms markets have interacted to bring weapons to Mexico and Mexican cartels.

More research needs to be done on both sides of the border in order to understand this important issue.

Four Trends

In spite of the historical ambiguity, there are four trends that are likely to shape the future flow of arms into Mexico. The first of these is militarization. Since 2006 there has been a steady trend toward the use of heavy military ordnance by the cartels. This process was begun in earnest when the Gulf Cartel first recruited Los Zetas, but in order to counter Los Zetas, all the other cartels have had to recruit and train hard-core enforcer units and outfit them with similar weaponry. Prior to 2007, attacks involving fragmentation hand grenades, 40mm grenades and RPGs were somewhat rare and immediately attracted a lot of attention. Such incidents are now quite common, and it is not unusual to see firefights like the June 26 incident in Apaseo el Alto in which dozens of grenades are employed.

Another trend in recent years has been the steady movement of Mexican cartels south into Central and South America. As noted above, the region is awash in guns, and the growing presence of Mexican cartel members puts them in contact with people who have access to Cold War weapons, international arms merchants doing business with groups like the FARC and corrupt officials who can obtain weapons from military sources in the region. We have already seen seizures of weapons coming into Mexico from the south. One notable seizure occurred in March 2009, when Guatemalan authorities raided a training camp in northern Guatemala near the Mexican border that they claim belonged to Los Zetas. In the raid they recovered 563 40mm grenades and 11 M60 machine guns that had been stolen from the Guatemalan military and sold to Los Zetas.

The third trend is the current firearm and ammunition market in the United States. Since the election of Barack Obama, arms sales have gone through the roof due to fears (so far unfounded) that the Obama administration and the Democratic Congress will attempt to restrict or ban certain weapons. Additionally, ammunition companies are busy filling military orders for the U.S. war effort in Iraq and Afghanistan. As anyone who has attempted to buy an assault rifle (or even a brick of .22 cartridges) will tell you, it is no longer cheap or easy to buy guns and ammunition. In fact, due to this surge in demand, it is downright difficult to locate many types of assault rifles and certain calibers of ammunition, though a lucky buyer might be able to find a basic stripped-down AR-15 for $850 to $1,100, or a semiautomatic AK-47 for $650 to $850. Of course, such a gun purchased in the United States and smuggled into Mexico will be sold to the cartels at a hefty premium above the purchase price.

By way of comparison, in places where weapons are abundant, such as Yemen, a surplus fully automatic assault rifle can be purchased for under $100 on the white arms market and for about the same price on the black arms market. This difference in price provides a powerful economic incentive to buy low elsewhere and sell high in Mexico, as does the inability to get certain classes of weapons such as RPGs and fragmentation grenades in the United States. Indeed, we have seen reports of international arms merchants from places like Israel and Belgium selling weapons to the cartels and bringing that ordnance into Mexico through routes other than over the U.S. border. Additionally, in South America, a number of arms smugglers, including Hezbollah and Russian organized-crime groups, have made a considerable amount of money supplying arms to groups in the region like the FARC.

The fourth trend is the increasing effort by the U.S. government to stanch the flow of weapons from the United States into Mexico. A recent increase in the number of ATF special agents and inspectors pursuing gun dealers who knowingly sell to the cartels or straw-purchase buyers who obtain guns from honest dealers is going to increase the chances of such individuals being caught. This stepped-up enforcement will have an impact as the risk of being caught illegally buying or smuggling guns begins to outweigh the profit that can be made by selling guns to the cartels. We believe that these two factors — supply problems and enforcement — will work together to help reduce the flow of U.S. guns to Mexico.

While there has been a long and well-documented history of arms smuggling across the U.S.-Mexican border, it is important to recognize that, while the United States is a significant source of certain classes of weapons, it is by no means the only source of illegal weapons in Mexico. As STRATFOR has previously noted, even if it were possible to hermetically seal the U.S.-Mexican border, the Mexican cartels would still be able to obtain weapons from non-U.S. sources (just as drugs would continue to flow into the United States). The law of supply and demand will ensure that the Mexican cartels will get their ordnance, but it is highly likely that an increasing percentage of that supply will begin to come from outside the United States via the gray and black arms markets.

40: La Familia Expands its Attacks
July 14, 2009

Mexican authorities confirmed July 14 that the 12 men found tortured and shot to death in the town of La Huacana, in Mexico's southeastern state of Michoacan, were federal police agents. The revelation came the same day that gunmen armed with assault rifles in another town in the state opened fire on a federal police building. The previous night, a Mexican federal police agent was wounded during an attack in Lazaro Cardenas, also in Michoacan. In that attack, several men traveling in a vehicle fired assault rifles and threw fragmentation grenades at a group of federal agents returning to a hotel where they had been staying for the past several weeks.

These incidents mark the latest in a series of attacks against federal police in Michoacan state in retaliation for the June 11 arrest of a high-ranking leader of the La Familia Michoacana (LFM) criminal organization. So far, LFM's retaliatory attacks in Michoacan — which have totaled more than 15 over the past four days — have been poorly executed and apparently hastily planned. These latest incidents appear no different. As the possibility of further attacks looms, it is important to consider that even though LFM faces some organizational limitations — and even though STRATFOR does not consider it a top drug-trafficking organization — the group is still a powerful criminal organization able and willing to conduct attacks that stand out for their brazenness and gravity even by Mexico's standards.

LFM stands out among the various drug cartels that operate throughout Mexico for several reasons. Unlike other cartels that have always been focused on drug trafficking, LFM first arose in Michoacan several years ago as a vigilante response to kidnappers and drug gangs — particularly those that produced and trafficked methamphetamines — that operated in the state. With banners and advertisements in local newspapers, LFM made its anti-crime message well known — along with its willingness to use extreme violence against suspected kidnappers, drug traffickers and other criminals.

Before long, however, LFM members were themselves accused of conducting the very crimes they had opposed, including kidnapping for ransom, cocaine and marijuana trafficking, and eventually methamphetamine production. Currently, the group is the largest and most powerful criminal organization in Michoacan — a largely rural state located on Mexico's southeastern Pacific coast — and maintains a significant presence in several surrounding states. The extent to which LFM has succeeded in corrupting public officials across Michoacan testifies to the depth of its involvement in the state.

Beyond its vigilante origins, LFM has also set itself apart from other criminal groups in Mexico based on its almost cult-like ideological and cultural principles. LFM leaders are known to distribute documents to the group's members that include codes of conduct as well as pseudo-religious quotations from a man known as "El Mas Loco" ("the craziest one"), who appears to serve as a sort of inspirational leader for the group.

Outside Michoacan, LFM so far has failed to become a significant national or international player in the drug trade beyond its involvement in methamphetamine trafficking. Geography has hampered the group's ambitions. Developing into a more completely independent drug-trafficking organization would require not only sustained contacts with cocaine and ephedra suppliers overseas, but also a self-secured access point to the United States. This is quite an obstacle for a group based at least 600 miles from the U.S.-Mexican border. So far, only Mexican cartels based on the U.S. border have risen to the top in the drug trade. Until such an access point is secured, LFM will be forced to rely on partnerships and alliances with those drug cartels whose base along the border allows them to control cross-border trafficking.

Another challenge for LFM has been internal. Since the group has been forced to rely on Mexico's other drug cartels — many of which are locked into intense rivalries with each other — it was inevitable that LFM would be drawn into these divisions. Indeed, at present LFM is composed of at least three main factions, one of which has loosely allied itself with the powerful Beltran-Leyva organization, another with the Gulf cartel and another with the Sinaloa cartel. The true extent to which these LFM factions are divided is not known, but the fractures still represent an organizational limitation for the group.

Despite the internal and external constraints on LFM, the group remains a powerful regional organization in the Michoacan area capable of brazen and provocative violence — which is saying something given the milieu of Mexican cartel beheadings and assassinations. LFM's most egregious violent act was the September 2008 grenade attack on civilians in Morelia, Michoacan, during the city's commemoration of Mexico's Independence Day. The incident represents the first clear case of indiscriminate killing of civilians in the history of Mexico's cartel war, setting the LFM strongly apart from Mexico's other drug gangs. Given the wave of LFM retaliatory attacks, this distinction is cause for alarm.

If there is any criminal group in Mexico willing and able to escalate its use of violence, it is LFM. That the group's reach is fairly limited is little comfort for Mexico City, which falls well within LFM's range and will be forced to deal with the deteriorating security situation in Michoacan.

41: The Role of the Mexican Military in the Cartel War
July 29, 2009

U.S. drug czar Gil Kerlikowske is in the middle of a four-day visit this week to Mexico, where he is meeting with Mexican government officials to discuss the two countries' joint approach to Mexico's ongoing cartel war. In prepared remarks at a July 27 press conference with Mexican Attorney General Eduardo Medina Mora, Kerlikowske said Washington is focused on reducing drug use in the United States, supporting domestic law enforcement efforts against drug traffickers and working with other countries that serve as production areas or transshipment points for U.S.-bound drugs.

Absent from his remarks was any mention of the U.S. position on the role of the Mexican military in the country's battle against the drug cartels. Kerlikowske's visit comes amid a growing debate in Mexico over the role that the country's armed forces should play in the cartel war. The debate has intensified in recent weeks, as human rights organizations in Mexico and the United States have expressed concern over civil rights abuses by Mexican troops assigned to counternarcotics missions in various parts of the country.

The director of Mexico's independent National Human Rights Commission, for example, has encouraged the new legislature to re-examine the role of the Mexican military in the country's cartel war, saying that the current approach is clearly not working. The number of citizen complaints against soldiers has increased over the last few years as the troops have become actively engaged in counternarcotics operations, and the commission director has expressed hope for greater accountability on the part of the armed forces.

Citing similar concerns, and the fact that such citizen complaints are handled by the military justice system — which has reportedly not successfully prosecuted a case in years — the independent U.S.-based Human Rights Watch has sent a letter to U.S. Secretary of State Hillary Clinton urging her not to certify Mexico's human rights

record to Congress, which would freeze the disbursement of a portion of the funds for the Merida Initiative, a U.S. counternarcotics aid
package for Mexico.

More important than any possible funding freeze from Washington,
though, is the potential response from the Mexican government.
President Felipe Calderon has emphasized that the use of the military is a temporary move and is necessary until the country's federal
police reforms can be completed in 2012. Legislative leaders from
both main opposition parties complained last week that Calderon's
approach has unnecessarily weakened the armed forces, while the
leader of the Mexican senate — a member of Calderon's National
Action Party — said the legislature will examine the role of the military and seek to balance the needs of the cartel war with the civil
rights of the Mexican people. In addition, the president of Mexico's
supreme court has said the court plans to review the appropriateness
of military jurisdiction in cases involving citizen complaints against
soldiers.

Domestic debate and international criticism of Calderon's use of
the military are not necessarily new. Indeed, Calderon was defending
his approach to representatives of the United Nations back in early
2008. However, the renewed debate, combined with recent changes in
the Mexican legislature, has set the stage for a general re-examination
of the Mexican military's role in the cartel war. And while it is still
unclear exactly where the re-examination will end up, the eventual
outcome could drastically change the way the Mexican government
fights the cartels.

More than Just Law Enforcement

Since taking office in December 2006, Calderon's decision to
deploy more than 35,000 federal troops in security operations
around the country has grabbed headlines. While previous presidents
have used the armed forces for counternarcotics operations in isolated cases, the scope and scale of the military's involvement under
Calderon has reached new heights. This approach is due in no small

part to the staggering level of corruption among federal police. But primarily, the use of the military is a reflection of the many tasks that must be performed under Calderon's strategy, which is far more complex than simply putting boots on the ground and requires more than what traditional law enforcement agencies can provide.

This broad range of tasks can be grouped into three categories:

- The first involves duties traditionally carried out by the armed forces in Mexico, such as technical intelligence collection and maritime and aerial monitoring and interdiction. These tasks are well-suited to the armed forces, which have the equipment, training and experience to perform them. These are also key requirements in the country's counternarcotics strategy, considering that Mexico is the primary transshipment point for South American-produced cocaine bound for the United States, the world's largest market for the drug.

- The second category includes traditional civilian law enforcement and judicial duties. Specifically, this includes actions such as making arrests, prosecuting and convicting defendants and imposing punishment. With the exception of the military routinely detaining suspects and then turning them over to law enforcement authorities, the tasks in this second category have remained mainly in the hands of civilian authorities.

- The final category is more of a gray area. It involves tasks that overlap between Mexico's armed forces and law enforcement agencies, and it is the area over the last few years in which the Mexican military has become increasingly involved. It is also the area that has caused the most controversy, primarily due to the fact that it has brought the troops into closer contact with the civilian population.

Some of the most noteworthy tasks in this final "gray" category include:

- Drug-crop eradication and meth-lab seizures. In addition to being the main transit point for U.S.-bound cocaine, Mexico is also estimated to be the largest producer of marijuana and methamphetamines consumed in the United States. The U.S. National Drug Intelligence Center estimates that more than 17,000 tons of marijuana were produced in Mexico during 2007, most of which was smuggled into the United States. Similarly, seizures of so-called meth superlabs in Mexico over the last few years — some capable of producing hundreds of tons annually — underscore the scale of meth production in Mexico. The destruction of marijuana crops and meth production facilities is a task that has been shared by both the military and law enforcement under Calderon.

- Immigration and customs inspections at points of entry and exit. Thorough inspections of inbound and outbound cargo and people at Mexico's borders have played a key role in some of the more noteworthy drug seizures during the last few years, including the country's largest cocaine seizure at the Pacific port of Manzanillo in November 2007. Similar inspections elsewhere have led to significant seizures of weapons and precursor chemicals used in the production of meth. In many cases, the Mexican armed forces have played a role in either stopping or inspecting suspect cargo.

- Raids and arrests of high-value cartel targets. Beyond simply stopping the flow of drugs and weapons into and out of Mexico, the federal government has also sought to disrupt the powerful organizations that control the drug trade by arresting drug cartel members. Given the federal police's reputation for corruption, highly sensitive and risky operations such as the arrest of high-ranking cartel leaders have more often than not been carried out by the military's elite Special Forces Airmobile Group (GAFE). In most cases, the suspects detained by GAFE units have been quickly handed over to the attorney general's office, though in some cases military personnel have been accused of holding suspects for longer than necessary in order to extract information themselves.

- General public safety and law enforcement. The rise in organized crime-related violence across Mexico over the last few years has been a cause for great concern both within the government and among the population. A central part of the federal government's effort to curb the violence has been the deployment of military forces to many areas, where the troops conduct such actions as security patrols, traffic stops and raids as well as man highway checkpoints. In some cities, the military has been called upon to assume all public-safety and law-enforcement responsibilities, disarming the local police force while looking for police links to organized crime. Another part of this militarization of law enforcement has involved the appointment of military officers — many of whom resign their commission a day before their appointment — to law enforcement posts such as police chief or public safety consultant.

It is this final trend that has led to most of the concerns and complaints regarding the military's role in the cartel war. The federal government has been mindful of these concerns from the beginning and has tried to minimize the criticism by involving the federal police as much as possible. But it has been the armed forces that have provided the bulk of the manpower and coordination that federal police agencies — hampered by rampant corruption and a tumultuous reform process — have not been able to muster.

A Victim of its Own Success

The armed forces' greater effectiveness, rapid deployment capability and early successes in some public security tasks made it inevitable that its role would evolve and expand. The result has been a classic case of mission creep. By the time additional duties were being assigned to the military, its resources had become stretched too thin to be as effective as before. This reality became apparent by early 2008 in public-safety roles, especially when the military was tasked with security operations in cities as large and as violent as Ciudad Juarez.

Even though the Mexican military was not designed or trained for law-enforcement duties or securing urban areas, it had been generally successful in improving the security situation of the smaller cities to which it had been deployed throughout 2007. But by early 2008, when soldiers were first deployed to Ciudad Juarez en masse, it became clear that they simply had too much on their plate. As the city's security environment deteriorated disastrously during the second half of 2008, the military presence there proved incapable of controlling it, an outcome that has continued even today, despite the unprecedented concentration of forces that are currently in the city.

In addition to the military's mission failures, it has also struggled with increasing civil rights complaints from citizens. In particular, soldiers have been accused of unauthorized searches and seizures, rough treatment and torture of suspects (which in some cases have included police officers), and improper rules of engagement, which have led several times to civilian deaths when soldiers mistook them for hostile shooters. In many cities, particularly in northern and western Mexico, exasperated residents have staged rallies and marches to protest the military presence in their towns.

While the military has certainly not acted flawlessly in its operations and undoubtedly bears guilt for some offenses, these complaints are not completely reliable records of the military's performance. For one thing, many cartel enforcers routinely dress in military-style clothing and travel in vehicles painted to resemble military trucks, while many also have military backgrounds and operate using the tactics they were taught. This makes it difficult for residents, during the chaos of a raid, to distinguish between legitimate soldiers and cartel members. More important, however, is the fact that the Mexican drug cartels have been keenly aware of the threat posed to them by the military and of the controversy associated with the military's involvement in the cartel war. For this reason, the cartels have been eager to exploit this vulnerability by paying residents to protest the military presence and spread reports of military abuses.

Outlook

As the Mexican congress and supreme court continue the debate the appropriateness of the military in various roles in the cartel war, it is important to recall what the armed forces have done well. For all its faults and failures, the military remains the most reliable security tool available to the Mexican government. And continued problems with the federal police reforms mean that the military will remain the most reliable and versatile option for the foreseeable future.

Any legislative or judicial effort to withdraw the armed forces from certain tasks will leave the government with fewer options in battling the cartels and, ultimately, in an even more precarious position than it is in now. The loss of such a valuable tool in some areas of the cartel war would force the government to fundamentally alter its strategy in the cartel war, most likely requiring it to scale back its objectives.

42: Confidential Informants:
A Double-Edged Sword
Aug. 19, 2009

Police in El Paso, Texas, announced Aug. 11 that they had arrested three suspects in the May 15 shooting death of Jose Daniel Gonzalez Galeana, a Juarez cartel lieutenant who had been acting as a confidential informant (CI) for the U.S. Immigration and Customs Enforcement (ICE) agency. It was an activity that prompted the Juarez cartel to put out a hit on him, and Gonzalez was shot multiple times outside his home in an upscale El Paso neighborhood. A fourth suspect was arrested shortly after the Aug. 11 announcement. Among the suspects is an 18-year-old U.S. Army soldier stationed at nearby Fort Bliss who the other suspects said had been hired by one of the leaders of the Juarez cartel to pull the trigger on Gonzalez.

The suspects also include two other teenagers, a 17-year-old and a 16-year-old.

The man who recruited the teenagers, Ruben Rodriguez Dorado — also a lieutenant in the Juarez cartel — has also been arrested, and the emerging details of the case paint him as a most interesting figure. After receiving orders from his superiors in the Juarez cartel to kill Gonzalez, Rodriguez was able to freely enter the United States and conduct an extensive effort to locate Gonzalez — he reportedly even paid Gonzalez's cell phone bill in an effort to obtain his address. Armed with the address, he then conducted extensive surveillance of Gonzalez and carefully planned the assassination, which was then carried out by the young gunman he had recruited.

The sophistication of Rodriguez's investigative and surveillance efforts is impressive, and the Gonzalez hit was not the first time he undertook such tasks. According to an affidavit filed in state court, Rodriguez told investigators that he also located and surveilled targets for assassination in Mexico. Perhaps the most intriguing aspect of this case is that the entire time Rodriguez was plotting the Gonzalez assassination he, too, was working as a CI for ICE.

While it is unclear at this point if ICE agents played any part in helping Rodriguez find Gonzalez, at the very least, Rodriguez's status as an ICE informant would certainly have been useful in camouflaging his nefarious activities and could have given him some level of official cover. Although Rodriguez was a legal permanent resident of the United States, having friends in ICE would allow him to cross the border repeatedly without much scrutiny and help deflect suspicion if he were caught while conducting surveillance.

Without having access to the information Rodriguez was providing to ICE, it is very difficult for us to assess if Rodriguez's work with ICE was sanctioned by the Juarez cartel, or if he was merely playing both ends against the middle. However, when one examines the reach, scope and sophistication of the Mexican cartels' intelligence efforts, it is clear that several of the cartels have demonstrated the ability to operate more like a foreign intelligence service than a traditional criminal organization. This means that it is highly possible that

Rodriguez was what we refer to in intelligence parlance as a double agent — someone who pretends to spy on an organization but is, in fact, loyal to that organization.

Whether Rodriguez was a double agent or just an out-of-control CI, this case provides a clear example of the problems encountered when law enforcement agencies handle CIs — problems that become even more pronounced when the informant is associated with a sophisticated and well-financed organization.

Choirboys Need Not Apply

While CIs can be incredibly valuable sources of information, running a CI is a delicate operation even under the best of circumstances and poses a wide array of problems and pitfalls. The first and most obvious issue is that most people who have access to the inner workings of a criminal organization, and therefore the most valuable intelligence, are themselves criminals. Upstanding, honest citizens simply do not normally have access to the plans of criminal gangs or understand their organizational hierarchy. This means that authorities need to recruit or flip lower-level criminals in order to work their way up the food chain and go after bigger targets. In the violent world of the Mexican drug cartels, sending an undercover agent to infiltrate a cartel is extremely dangerous. Therefore, using CIs is even more important in such investigations than it is while working against other types of criminals.

The fact that many CIs are criminals means that not only do they frequently come with a heavy load of psychopathic and sociopathic baggage, but in order to stay in good standing within their organization, they often need to continue to commit illegal acts while working for the government, though the type of criminal activity permitted is often carefully delineated by the government. Not infrequently, these illegal acts can come back to haunt the agency operating the CI, so maintaining control of the CI is very important.

CIs can also come with a host of motivations. While some informants are motivated by money, or promises to have charges dropped or reduced, other informants will provide information to the authorities out of revenge or in order to further their own criminal schemes by using law enforcement as a way to take out rival gangs or even a rival within their own organization. Because of these varying motivations, it can be very difficult to tell when CIs are fabricating information or when they are trying to manipulate the authorities. In fact, it is not at all uncommon for inexperienced or vulnerable handlers to lose control of a CI. In extreme cases, it is even possible for a smooth and sophisticated CI to end up controlling their handler. And this is not just confined to ICE or small-town police departments; there have been instances of FBI and U.S. Drug Enforcement Administration (DEA) agents being manipulated and controlled by their CIs.

Out-of-control CIs can do things like refuse to follow orders, shut off recorders or edit recordings, tape meetings and calls with handlers, or even commit murders and other serious crimes while working with authorities. There have also been cases of handlers getting involved in sexual relationships with CIs, providing drugs to CIs, and even committing crimes with CIs who were manipulating them.

At the high end of the threat scale, there is also the possibility that informants will be consciously sent to the authorities in order to serve as double agents, or that the criminal organization they work for will double them back once it is learned that they have decided to begin cooperating with the authorities. Many federal agencies polygraph sources, but polygraph operators can be fooled and polygraphs are of limited utility on people who have no moral compunction about lying. Therefore, while agencies take efforts to vet their CIs, such efforts are often ineffective.

Double agents are particularly useful for the criminal organization because they can intentionally feed very specific information to the authorities in order to manipulate enforcement activities. For example, in the case of the Juarez cartel, they could tip off authorities to a small shipment of narcotics in one part of the sector in order to draw attention away from a larger shipment moving through another part of the sector. Of course, the fact that the CI provided accurate information pertaining to the smaller shipment also serves to increase his value to the authorities. In the case of a double agent, almost everything he provides will usually be accurate — although this accurate information is pretty much calculated to be harmless to the criminal organization (though organizations have used double agents to pass on information to the authorities that will allow them to take action against rival criminal gangs). The outstanding accuracy of the intelligence reported will cause the double agent to be trusted more than most regular CIs, and this makes double agents particularly difficult to uncover.

Not Typical Criminals

When considering the Mexican drug cartels, it is very important to remember that they are not typical criminal gangs. The cartels are billion-dollar organizations that employ large groups of heavily armed enforcers, and many of the cartels have invested the time and resources necessary to develop highly sophisticated intelligence apparatuses.

Such intelligence apparatuses are perhaps best seen in the realm of public corruption. Some of the Mexican cartels have a long history of successfully corrupting public officials on both sides of the border. Groups like the Beltran Leyva Organization (BLO) have recruited scores of intelligence assets and agents of influence at the local, state and even federal levels of the Mexican government. They even have enjoyed significant success in recruiting agents in elite units such as the anti-organized crime unit of the Mexican attorney general's office. The BLO even allegedly recruited Mexico's former drug czar, Noe Ramirez Mandujano, who reportedly was receiving $450,000 per month from the organization. This recruitment also extends to all levels of government in the United States, where cartels have recruited local, state and federal officials. Many of the assassination operations the cartels have launched against one another and against senior Mexican officials have also demonstrated the advanced intelligence capabilities of the Mexican cartels.

With the money to buy foreign expertise and equipment, the Mexican cartels have been able to set up counterintelligence branches that can administer polygraph examinations, signals intelligence branches that can intercept the authorities' communications and even elaborate (and well-funded) units designed to identify and bribe vulnerable public officials. The Mexican cartels also assign people to infiltrate law-enforcement agencies by applying for jobs. According to a report released last week, in a 10-month period, four applicants for U.S. border law enforcement positions were found through background checks and polygraph examinations to be infiltrators from drug-trafficking organizations. It is important to remember that these four were only those who were caught, and not all agencies submit applicants to the same scrutiny, so the scope of the problem is likely much larger. In light of this history of cartel intelligence activity, it is not unreasonable to assume that the cartels possess the sophistication and skills to employ double agents.

Alphabet Soup

Running a CI against a Mexican cartel is also greatly complicated by the number of agencies involved in the struggle against them. Among local, state and federal entities there are scores of agencies in El Paso alone with some sort of jurisdiction working against the cartels. The agencies range from obvious ones such as the DEA, FBI, Texas Rangers, El Paso Police and Bureau of Alcohol, Tobacco, Firearms and Explosives to the less obvious such as the Internal Revenue Service, the Union Pacific Railroad Police and the U.S. Army's Criminal Investigation Command at Fort Bliss.

This jumble of jurisdictions creates a very difficult environment for working with CIs. Not only are agencies legitimately concerned about protecting the identities of their CIs due to the possibility of corruption in other agencies, but there is also the issue of competition. Agencies are afraid of other, better-funded agencies stealing their informants. If a local police detective has developed a very good dope source, the last thing in the world he wants is for ICE or the DEA to take control of his source, which would in all likelihood mean that he would lose all the information the CI was providing. Likewise, if an ICE agent has developed a good Mexican cartel source, the last thing he wants is for the DEA or FBI to take control of the source.

In the human intelligence world, there is a lot of jealousy and suspicion. This not only means that information is not fully shared across agencies but also that agencies are very reluctant to run checks on their CIs through other agencies for fear of divulging their identities. This insulation results in some CIs double- or even triple-dipping, that is, working with other agencies and providing the same information in exchange for additional payments. This fragmentation also results in the agency running the CI not being able to learn of critical information pertaining to the past (or even current) activities of their CI. It means, too, that the agency that recruits the CI in some cases is simply not in the best position to take full advantage of the information provided by the CI, or that agency competition and institutional rivalries prevent the CI from being turned over to a more capable agency. Certainly, on its face, ICE would not be the best, most logical agency to handle a source like Rodriguez, who was a lieutenant in the Juarez cartel tasked with conducting assassination operations.

The fear associated with the potential compromise of CI identities inside an agency or task force due to corruption can also affect the operational effectiveness of law enforcement operations. It is hard to get much of anything done when people are worried about who may be a mole on the cartel payroll.

Nowhere to Hide

One last thing to consider in the Gonzalez assassination is that it highlights the fact that even though targets will seek shelter inside the United States, Mexican drug cartels will follow them across the border in order to kill them, something we have discussed for several years now. Moreover, incidents like the Gonzalez hit will likely cause high-value cartel targets to move even deeper into the United

States to avoid attack — and their enemies' brazen and sophisticated assassins will likely follow.

Rodriguez's use of teenage assassins to kill Gonzalez is also in keeping with a trend we have seen in Laredo and elsewhere, that of the cartels recruiting young street-gang members and training them to be assassins. Young gunmen working for Los Zetas in Laredo, Houston, San Antonio and elsewhere have been given the nickname "Zetitas," or little Zetas. In is not surprising to see the Juarez cartel also employing young gunmen. Not only are the young gunmen easily influenced, fearless, and hungry for money and respect, but the cartels believe that the younger offenders are expendable if caught or killed, and will also do less time than an adult if they are arrested and convicted. These young killers are also not given much information about their employers in the event they are captured and interrogated by police.

In the final analysis, CIs are a necessary evil and can be a very effective weapon in the law enforcement arsenal. Like any weapon, however, CIs must be carefully managed, maintained and employed to make sure they are not used against the law enforcement agencies themselves.

43: Mexico: Emergence of an Unexpected Threat
Sept. 30, 2009

At approximately 2 a.m. on Sept. 25, a small improvised explosive device (IED) consisting of three or four butane canisters was used to attack a Banamex bank branch in the Milpa Alta delegation of Mexico City. The device damaged an ATM and shattered the bank's front windows. It was not an isolated event. The bombing was the seventh recorded IED attack in the Federal District — and the fifth such attack against a local bank branch — since the beginning of September.

The attack was claimed in a communiqué posted to a Spanish-language anarchist Web site by a group calling itself the Subversive Alliance for the Liberation of the Earth, Animals and Humans (ASLTAH). The note said, "Once again we have proven who our enemies are," indicating that the organization's "cells for the dissolution of civilization" were behind the other, similar attacks. The communiqué noted that the organization had attacked Banamex because it was a "business that promotes torture, destruction and slavery" and vowed that ASLTAH would not stop attacking "until we see your ashes." The group closed its communiqué by sending greetings to the Earth Liberation Front (ELF), the Animal Liberation Front (ALF) and the "eco-pyromaniacs for the liberation of the earth in this place." Communiqués have also claimed some of the other recent IED attacks in the name of ASLTAH.

On Sept. 22, authorities also discovered and disabled a small IED left outside of a MetLife insurance office in Guadalajara, Jalisco state. A message spray-painted on a wall near where the device was found read, "Novartis stop torturing animals," a reference to the multinational pharmaceutical company, which has an office near where the IED was found and which has been heavily targeted by the group Stop Huntingdon Animal Cruelty (SHAC). Novartis is a large customer of Huntingdon Life Sciences, the research company SHAC was formed to destroy because Huntingdon uses animals in its testing for harmful side effects of drugs, chemicals and consumer items. A second message spray-painted on a wall near where the device was found on Sept. 22 read, "Novartis break with HLS." Two other IEDs were detonated at banks in Mexico City on the same day.

These IED attacks are the most recent incidents in a wave of anarchist, animal rights, and eco-protest attacks that have swept across Mexico this year. Activists have conducted literally hundreds of incidents of vandalism, arson and, in more recent months, IED attacks in various locations across the country. The most active cells are in Mexico City and Guadalajara.

For a country in the midst of a bloody cartel war in which thousands of people are killed every year — and where serious crimes like kidnapping terrorize nearly every segment of society — direct-action attacks by militant activists are hardly the biggest threat faced by the Mexican government. However, the escalation of direct-action attacks in Mexico that has resulted in the more frequent use of IEDs shows no sign of abating, and these attacks are likely to grow more frequent, spectacular and deadly.

The Wave

Precisely quantifying the wave of direct-action attacks in Mexico is difficult for a number of reasons. One is that the reporting of such incidents is spotty and the police, the press and the activists themselves are often not consistent in what they report and how. Moreover, is often hard to separate direct-action vandalism from incidents of plain old non-political vandalism or tell the difference between an anarchist IED attack against a bank and an IED attack against a bank conducted by a Marxist group such as the Popular Revolutionary Army (EPR). Then there is the issue of counting. Should a series of five Molotov cocktail attacks against ATMs or the destruction of 20 Telmex phone booths in one night be counted as one attack or as separate incidents?

If we count conservatively — e.g., consider a series of like incidents as one — we can say there have been around 200 direct-action attacks to date in 2009. But if we count each incident separately, we can easily claim there have been more than 400 such attacks. For example, by our count, there have been more than 350 Telmex phone booths smashed, burned or otherwise vandalized so far this year. (Activists will do things like glue metal shavings into the calling-card and coin slots.) However, for the sake of this analysis we'll go with the conservative number of about 200 attacks.

Now, Telmex seems to be the most popular target so far for direct-action attacks. In addition to hitting phone booths, activists also have attacked Telmex vehicles and offices and have cut Telmex cables. From their statements, the activists appear to hold a special hatred for Carlos Slim, one of the richest men in the world and the chairman of Telmex and several other companies. In many ways, Slim — a patriarchal billionaire industrialist — is the personification of almost everything that the anarchistic activists hate. In addition to Telmex and banks, the activists also have attacked other targets such as restaurants (including McDonald's and KFC), meat shops, pet shops, fur and leather stores, luxury vehicles and construction equipment.

The activists' most common tactics tend to be on the lower end of the violence scale and include graffiti and paint (frequently red to symbolize the blood of animals) to vandalize a target. They also frequently release captive birds or animals as well as use superglue and pieces of metal to obstruct locks, pay phones and ATM card readers. Moving up the violence continuum, activists less frequently will break windows, burn buildings and vehicles, and make bomb threats — there have been at least 157 incidents involving arson or incendiary devices so far in 2009. To help put this into perspective, these activists have conducted more arson attacks in Mexico to date in 2009 than their American counterparts have conducted in the United States since 2001.

At the high end of the violence spectrum are the IED attacks, and this is where there has really been an increase in activity in recent weeks. In the first six months of 2009, there were several bomb threats and hoaxes and a few acid bombs, but only two real IEDs were used. In June, July and August there was one IED attack per month — and so far in September there have been seven IED attacks in Mexico City alone and one successful attack and one attempted attack in Guadalajara. Again, by way of comparison, these eight IED attacks by Mexican activists in September are more than American activists have conducted in the United States since 2001.

Proliferation of IEDs

There are several factors that can explain this trend toward the activists' increasing use of IEDs. The first is, quite simply, that IEDs generate more attention than graffiti, glue or even an arson attack — indeed, here we are devoting a weekly security report to activist IED

259

attacks in Mexico. In light of the overall level of violence in Mexico, most observers have ignored the past lower-level activity by these activist groups, and IEDs help cut through the noise and bring attention to the activists' causes. The scope and frequency of IED attacks this month ensured that they could not be overlooked.

The second factor is the learning curve of the cells' bombmakers. As a bombmaker becomes more proficient in his tradecraft, the devices he crafts tend to become both more reliable and more powerful. The improvement in tradecraft also means that the bombmaker is able to increase his operational tempo and deploy devices more frequently. It is quite possible that the few IEDs that were reported as hoaxes in March, April and May could have been IEDs that did not function properly — a common occurrence for new bombmakers who do not extensively test their devices.

The third factor is thrill and ego. In many past cases, militant activists have launched progressively larger attacks. One reason for this is that after a series of direct-action attacks, the activists get bored doing lower-level things like gluing locks or paint-stripping cars and they move to more destructive and spectacular attacks, such as those using timed incendiary devices. For many activists, there is a thrill associated with getting increased attention for the cause, in causing more damage to their targets and in getting away with increasingly brazen attacks.

Finally, in recent years, we have noted a shift among activist groups away from a strict concern for human life. Many activists are becoming convinced that less violent tactics have been ineffective, and if they really want to save the Earth and animals, they need to take more aggressive action. There is a small but growing fringe of hardcore activists who believe that, to paraphrase Lenin, you have to break eggs to make an omelet.

The Ruckus Society, a direct-action activist training organization, explains it this way in a training document: "There is a law against breaking into a house. However, if you break into a house as part of a greater good, such as rushing into the house to save a child from a fire, it is permissible to break that law. In fact, you can say that there is even a moral obligation to break that law. In the same way then, it is permissible to break minor laws to save the Earth." In general, activists do not condone violent action directed at humans, but neither do they always condemn it in very strong terms — they often explain that the anger that prompts such violence is "understandable" in light of what they perceive as ecological injustice and cruelty to animals.

In recent years there has been a polarization in the animal rights and environmental movements, with fringe activists becoming increasingly isolated and violent — and more likely to use potentially deadly tools like IEDs in their attacks.

Confluences

The very name of ASLTAH — the Subversive Alliance for the Liberation of the Earth, Animals and Humans — illustrates the interesting confluence of animal rights, ecological activism and anti-imperialism/anarchism that inhabit the radical fringe. It is not uncommon for one cell of independent activists to claim it carried out its attacks under the banner of "organizations" such as ELF, ALF or SHAC. In true anarchistic style, however, these organizations are amorphous and nonhierarchical — there is no single ELF, ALF or SHAC. Rather, the individual activists and cells who act on behalf of the organizations control their own activities while adhering to guidelines circulated in meetings and conferences, via the Internet, and in various magazines, newsletters and other publications. These individual activists and cells are driven only by their consciences, or by group decisions within the cell. This results in a level of operational security that can be hard for law enforcement and security officials to breach.

As noted above, these activists have been far more active in Mexico than they have in the United States. One reason for this is that the operating environment north of the border is markedly different than it is in Mexico. In the United States, the FBI and local and state police agencies have focused hard on these activists, and groups like

ELF and ALF have been branded as domestic terrorists. There have been several major investigations into these groups in recent years.

South of the border it is a different matter. Mexican authorities are plagued with problems ranging from drug cartels to Marxist terrorist/insurgent groups like the EPR to rampant police and government corruption. Simply put, there is a vacuum of law and order in Mexico and that vacuum is clearly reflected in statistics such as the number of kidnappings inside the country every year. The overall level of violence in Mexico and this vacuum of authority provide room for the activists to operate, and the host of other crime and violence issues plaguing the country work to ensure that the authorities are simply too busy to place much emphasis on investigating activist attacks and catching those responsible for them. Therefore, the activists operate boldly and with a sense of impunity that often leads to an increase in violence — especially within the context of a very violent place, which Mexico is at the present time.

This atmosphere means that the activist cells behind the increase in IED attacks will be able to continue their campaigns against assorted capitalist, animal and ecological targets with very little chance of being seriously pursued. Consequently, as the IED campaign continues, the attacks will likely become more frequent and more destructive. And given Mexico's densely populated cities and the activists' target sets, this escalation will ensure that the attacks will eventually turn deadly.

44: Company Cuts and Howling Protests
Oct. 16, 2009

Mexicans took to the streets in Mexico City on Oct. 15 in support of members of the Mexican Electricians Union (SME) who were laid off in a move by Mexican President Felipe Calderon to shut down state-owned electricity distribution company Luz y Fuerza del Centro (LyFC). Calderon's move was a response to the company's penchant for running at a net loss (costing approximately twice as much to run as its income, according to Calderon) and meant the lay-offs of more than 44,000 workers. The move also effectively crushed SME as a union and has brought howls of protest from across the country.

While the expected turnout for the Oct. 15 protest was somewhere around 30,000, official estimates put the final turnout at 150,000. Union leaders put the number even higher, at 350,000. The extremely high turnout reflects strong support for SME from Mexico's working classes.

Calderon's decision to close LyFC comes on the heels of a new economic policy under which he wants Mexico to do more with less. One of his priorities is to reduce the size of government in order to correct government finances after a damaging year of recession. This is a response to Mexico's dire economic situation, as the central bank projects a total decline of gross domestic product (GDP) of as much as 7.5 percent in 2009. Calderon must also face the fact that government oil revenues from Mexican state-owned energy company Petroleos Mexicanos have declined by 22 percent in 2009 alone. Total revenues are down 6.7 percent. As a result, the Mexican government, which has had a balanced budget for four years running, is expecting a deficit of at least 2 percent of GDP by the end of the year. Although the government is considering a bill that would raise value-added taxes by 2 percent on a wide range of goods, the fact remains that there are serious questions about the viability of the Mexican budget.

Strategically cutting companies that bleed revenues away from the government can certainly help Calderon face the economic challenges plaguing the Mexican state. However, such moves bring with them enormous political challenges. As a country with a politically active labor force, Mexico has a difficult time making structural changes that impact the stability of workers and unions, even in the name of efficiency. Calderon's move against SME is not only bold but also potentially dangerous — something that was seen clearly in this round of protests. There is a high level of dissatisfaction with the economy in Mexico, and even on a good day the potential for social unrest is high. But if Calderon is making a policy of shutting state-run companies and taking on the unions — no holds barred — Mexico can expect to see a great deal of unrest in the future.

The real question is whether the Mexican state has the resources to keep the peace in Mexico City while fighting a debilitating cartel war on the country's frontier. We do not underestimate Mexico's ability to face protests — they are a common occurrence in the Federal District, as well as throughout the country — but large-scale protests could very well continue. And should Calderon try to utilize his two-front strategy in a broader fashion, he must be prepared to handle significant unrest. Should that come to pass, Mexico may find itself strained to the limit.

45: La Familia North of the Border
Dec. 3, 2009

In an indictment handed down Nov. 20, the U.S. Federal District Court for the Northern District of Illinois accused 15 individuals of being involved in the trafficking of cocaine and other narcotics in the Chicago area. The 15 were arrested in a nationwide counter-narcotics operation led by the U.S. Drug Enforcement Administration (DEA) dubbed "Project Coronado," which was aimed at dismantling the drug trafficking network of La Familia Michoacana (LFM), a mid-sized and relatively new drug cartel based in Michoacan state in southwestern Mexico.

The U.S. investigation of LFM has revealed many details about the operation of the group in the United States and answered some important questions about the nature of Mexican drug trafficking and distribution north of the border.

LFM stands out among the various drug cartels that operate throughout Mexico for several reasons. Unlike other drug trafficking organizations (DTOs) that have always been focused on drug trafficking, LFM first arose in Michoacan several years ago as a vigilante response to kidnappers and drug gangs. Before long, however, LFM members were themselves accused of conducting the very crimes they had opposed, including kidnapping for ransom, cocaine and marijuana trafficking and, eventually, methamphetamine production. The group is now the largest and most powerful criminal organization in Michoacan — a largely rural state located on Mexico's southwestern Pacific coast — and maintains a significant presence in several surrounding states.

Beyond its vigilante origins, LFM has also set itself apart from other criminal groups in Mexico by its almost cult-like ideology. LFM leaders are known to distribute documents to the group's members that include codes of conduct and pseudo-religious quotations from Nazario Moreno Gonzalez, also known as "El Mas Loco" ("the craziest one"), who appears to serve as a sort of inspirational leader of the group.

Unanswered Questions

In April 2009, STRATFOR published a report on the dynamics of narcotics distribution in the United States. It laid out the differences between trafficking (transporting large quantities of drugs from the suppliers to the buyers over the most efficient routes possible) and distribution (the smaller scale, retail sale of small quantities of drugs over a broader geographic area) as well as the various gangs on the U.S. side that are involved in drug trafficking. The report outlined the differences in the resources and skills required to transport tons of narcotics hundreds of miles through Mexico versus picking up those loads at the border and managing the U.S. retail networks that distribute narcotics to the individual buyers on the street.

In our April analysis, we identified several intelligence gaps in the interface between the Mexican-based drug traffickers (such as the Sinaloa Cartel, the Beltran-Leyva Organization [BLO] and Los Zetas) and the U.S.-based drug distributors (such as MS-13, Barrio Azteca and the Mexican Mafia). One question we were left with was:

How deeply involved are the Mexican DTOs in the U.S. distribution network? While it appeared that narcotics changed hands at the border, it wasn't clear how or even whether the relationships between gangs and drug traffickers had an effect on the distribution of narcotics within the United States. Although we suspected it, there was little evidence that showed cartel involvement in the downstream or retail distribution of narcotics in the U.S. market.

Command and Control in Chicago

Now there is evidence. The indictment handed down Nov. 20 in Chicago clearly alleges that a criminal group in Chicago was directly conspiring with the drug trafficking organization LFM to distribute shipments of cocaine. The indictment specifically links the criminal group in Chicago to LFM and labels it a "command and control group" run by someone in Michoacan. While the indictment only referred to this person as "individual A," we suspect that the unidentified person was LFM operational manager Servando Gomez Martinez, the second in command of LFM. The manager of the Chicago command and control group, Jorge Luis Torres-Galvan, and the distribution supervisor, Jose Gonzalez-Zavala, were allegedly in regular contact with their manager in Mexico, updating him on accounting issues and relying on him to authorize which wholesale distributors the group could do business with in the United States.

These wholesale distributors also appear to have had close ties to the command and control group. According to the indictment, they were allowed to sell cocaine on consignment — they could wait to pay Zavala once the entire load was sold — an agreement that indicates a great deal of trust between the supplier and the retail distributor. It was likely a matter of the LFM commander in Mexico authorizing their involvement and probably was based on an existing business or extended-family relationship. Due to LFM's ideological basis, its members should be thought of more as adherents than employees. The group does not operate using the same business objectives as most other major DTOs, so we would expect personal relationships to be more valued than strictly business relationships among LFM members.

Another member of the group, Jorge Guadalupe Ayala-German, allegedly operated stash houses in the Chicago area where deliveries of narcotics would come in and shipments of cash would leave. The indictment says Ezequel Hernandez-Patino was responsible for physically delivering the shipments of cocaine to the wholesale distributors, and Ismail Flores with Oscar Bueno were responsible for transporting money south to Dallas, where they would deliver cash proceeds from the sale of cocaine and pick up more cocaine to sell. The indictment does not indicate that Flores or Bueno supplied any other markets between Dallas and Chicago, which suggests that the Chicago-based LFM members were fairly compartmentalized.

Project Coronado

The larger operation from which the Chicago indictment emerged, the DEA-led Project Coronado, was a joint operation with the FBI, the U.S. Bureau of Alcohol, Tobacco, Firearms and Explosives (ATF) and numerous other agencies. It followed several similar nationwide sweeps such as Operation Xcellerator, a multi-year effort to dismantle the Sinaloa cartel's connections in the United States, and Project Reckoning, which went after a Gulf cartel network in the United States that was trafficking cocaine to Italy. Under Project Coronado, the DEA, FBI and ATF, along with other federal, state and local law enforcement agencies, have made a total of almost 1,200 arrests, seized $32.8 million in U.S. currency and seized 11.7 tons of marijuana, methamphetamines, cocaine and heroin since the operation began in 2005. Dozens of other indictments and criminal complaints (in addition to the Chicago indictment) have been unsealed against associates of the group across the country since Oct. 22, the official culmination of Project Coronado.

The other cases revealed more details about LFM's operations in the United States: how it trafficked methamphetamines and cocaine from Mexico to Dallas, how a cell in Nashville was supplied by a

267

distribution hub in Atlanta, and how a group in New York had obtained automatic assault rifles, high-caliber pistols and ammunition with the intent to smuggle those weapons back to Mexico to supply LFM. LFM has been responsible for a substantial level of violence in southwestern Mexico, and former Mexican Attorney General Eduardo Morina Mora recently called it the most dangerous cartel in Mexico.

The Northern District of Texas had the most cases as a result of Project Coronado. It appears that Dallas was a major U.S. hub for LFM, where it managed drug shipments from Mexico to other regions (Chicago and Arkansas were specifically mentioned) and the collection of cash from those distributors before shipping the cash back to Mexico. Dallas is a logical hub for such activity because of its proximity to Mexico and its location along Interstate 35 and Interstate 20, which link Dallas to the rest of the United States as well as points to the south. In at least one case, an individual attempting to smuggle four kilograms of methamphetamines to Dallas passed through the McAllen, Texas, border crossing on a passenger bus but was interdicted by police.

Most indictments (including the one in Chicago) pointed out that LFM groups in the United States conducted countersurveillance while moving drug shipments. On one occasion, accused Dallas drug distributor Soto Cervantes changed the location of a meet-up point when he learned that the person he was meeting suspected that he was being followed. The change in location caused the police (who were indeed following the transporter) to call off the surveillance mission in order to not compromise their investigation. As a result, authorities relied primarily on electronic surveillance of the suspects' communications through wiretaps on home and cellular phones — of which the suspects had many and which they changed frequently.

There were other cases when police were unable to follow suspects due to such surveillance detection tactics, when targeted traffickers called off meetings and changed vehicles in an effort to confuse police. While seemingly simple, these tactics indicate a higher degree of tradecraft and professionalism among the suspects linked to LFM, who don't appear to be members of run-of-the-mill street gangs. It is unclear if these tactics have been institutionalized in the LFM network, but judging by the frequency that police encountered them in various U.S. cities during Project Coronado, they appear to be a standard practice for many if not all LFM members.

Implications

The details released in the Nov. 20 indictment provide solid evidence that drug trafficking organizations in Mexico (specifically LFM) have established command and control groups inside the United States that report to and receive orders from commanders in Mexico. And this shows that LFM has had an international presence far beyond what we originally suspected and is not just a small-time trafficking group in southwestern Mexico.

Whereas most drug distribution in the United States is carried out by individual gangs serving their own interests and operating on their own familiar turf, the criminal group in Chicago working for LFM was carrying out orders issued by a drug trafficking organization some 3,000 miles away. And based on the interaction the Chicago group had with its contact in Mexico, the use of such tactics as countersurveillance measures, the coordination among groups in different cities and reports from STRATFOR sources within U.S. counternarcotics agencies, it is likely that the individual in Mexico was managing several groups throughout the United States.

Most criminal enterprises avoid this kind of command and control structure for two reasons. First, distribution in a foreign country is not typically in a Mexican-based drug trafficker's area of expertise. Their interests tend to focus on their own territory, which they can control much more easily due to their familiarity with and proximity to it. Second, as seen in these latest arrests, U.S. law enforcement agencies are much more proficient at thwarting drug distribution operations than Mexican law enforcement agencies are. (LFM has recently proved very proficient indeed at challenging Mexican security forces.) By passing the drugs off to gangs in the United States, major cartels are also able to avoid a great deal of liability at the hands of U.S. law enforcement. In a way, LFM's efforts to move downstream, farther from the source of the cocaine, mirror those of other, larger Mexican DTOs that are expanding their control over the supply of cocaine in South America as they move upstream, closer to the source.

And this raises the question: Why would LFM want to expand its operations so deeply into the United States when other Mexican DTOs maintain a more superficial presence there? One possible answer is that LFM is much smaller than Sinaloa, Los Zetas and BLO, controls much less territory and gets a smaller share of the narcotics being trafficked through Mexico. By expanding business into the United States, LFM is able to leverage what little control it does have in order to gain access to the highly lucrative retail market. And then there is LFM's ideological bent, which makes it behave at times more like a cult than a purely pragmatic business.

Our answer to the above question is only conjecture. What is certain, at this point, is that there is now a precedent for Mexican DTOs to have a greater influence over their lower-level supply-chain operations in the United States. The details released in the Chicago indictment provide a better understanding of how Mexican-based drug traffickers impact the drug distribution network inside the United States and prove that at least one, "La Familia," is taking a very hands-on approach.

4397011

Made in the USA
Charleston, SC
13 January 2010